JN293486

Civil Liability for Defects
in Information in Electronic Form

Civil Liability for Defects in Information in Electronic Form

NORIKO KAWAWA

Shinzansha International

Shinzansha International
6-2-9-102 Hongo, Bunkyo-ku Tokyo, Japan
Tel +81 (0)3-3818-1019   Fax +81 (0)3-3818-0344
henshu@shinzansha.co.jp
© 2002, Noriko Kawawa, 川和功子 printed in Japan
ISBN4-7972-3103-3 C3332

All rights reserved. No part of this publication may be reproduced, stored in a retrieval system, or transmitted, in any form or by any means, electronic, mechanical, photocopying, recording or otherwise, without the prior permission of Shinzansha International.

Whilst every effort has been made to ensure that the information contained in this book is correct neither the author nor Shinzansha International can accept any responsibility for any errors or omissions or for any consequences resulting therefrom.

Preface

Transactions involving information in electronic form have become an essential part of business and social life in modern society. A defect in information held in electronic form may cause serious economic and personal damage. However, the present legal system is not adequately equipped in analysing liabilities concerning defects in information in electronic form.

In this book, I first I conducted a comparative analysis of tort law relating to liability for injury caused by information in traditional form and information in electronic form. This is to examine whether the authorities pertaining to information in traditional form are likely to have a significant impact upon liability for publication or dissemination in electronic form, particularly computer programs and human-readable information in electronic form on the internet, or in an online database.

Second, I explored contractual liability for information in electronic form. Contractual liabilities relating to information in electronic form may differ in accordance with the classification of a given transaction. In accordance with the classification, as sale of goods, supply of services or, possibly, transactions for information, there are rules providing for the creation, disclaimer of express or implied obligations, limiting or excluding remedies available, and other rules controlling the contract terms.

In this book, the feasibility of having legal classifications such as those between information in electronic and in traditional form, contract and tort liabilities, economic and physical losses, act and statement, products and information, and sale of goods and supply of services is examined by way of comparative studies between authorities in England and in the United States. The legal issues surrounding information in electronic form typify the way

Preface

in which such classifications are undermined, as such information may cause economic and physical losses and supply of such information may contain elements of act and statement, products and information, and sale of goods and supply of services.

Contract and tort liabilities with respect to information in electronic form should be considered, by taking into account distinctive characteristics of such transactions, particularly, expertise involved in creating such information, disparities in expertise between suppliers and customers, customers' reliance on the expertise, and representations made regarding standard of performance, along with special consideration for consumer and standard form contracts.

I would like to express my gratitude to Professor Zentaro Kitagawa, Professor Tsuneo Matsumoto and Professor Miyoko Motozawa for their kind encouragement and support.

I would like to thank my husband Alexis D'Hautcourt, for his patience and support in finalising the formatting of this book.

I would like to thank my parents, Yoko and Takaho Kawawa, and this book is dedicated to my mother, Yoko Kawawa, who will be missed by her families and friends.

I have been fortunate to receive Grant-in-Aid for Scientific Research (Grant-in-Aid for Publication of Scientific Research Resufts), for which I am grateful.

January 2002

Noriko Kawawa
Associate Professor, Osaka Prefecture University
(LL.B, LL.M, Attorney at Law: New York State)

Contents

Outline Table of Contents i

Table of Contents iii

Table of Cases xiv

Table of Statutes and Statutory Instruments xxii

Bibliography xxxvi

Outline Table of Contents

Chapter 1 Introduction 1

  § 1.01 The Value of Information in the Era of Information Technology 2

  § 1.02 Meaning Defined 7

  § 1.03 Different Types of Information 9

Chapter 2 The Law of Tort Relating to Liability for Injury Caused by Information in Traditional and in Electronic Form ... 15

  § 2.01 Purpose 16

  § 2.02 Form of Injuries 20

§ 2.03 Theories Relevant to Imposing Liability 25

§ 2.04 Liability in the Chain of Distribution 145

§ 2.05 Issues Regarding Tort and Contract 152

§ 2.06 Imposition of Liability with Respect to Information 161

Chapter 3 The Law of Contract Relating to Liability for Injury Caused by Information in Electronic Form 165

§ 3.01 Introduction 166

§ 3.02 Classification of Contracts 167

§ 3.03 Express Terms or Warranties 229

§ 3.04 Implied Terms or Warranties 252

§ 3.05 Remedies and Standard of Performance 271

§ 3.06 Limitation or Exclusion of Remedies 273

§ 3.07 Construction and Statutory Controls on Contractual Terms ... 285

§ 3.08 Contractual Liability on Information in Electronic Form ... 307

Chapter 4 Conclusion 311

§ 4.01 Civil Liability for Information in Electronic Form 312

Table of Contents

Chapter 1 Introduction ·· 1

§1.01 The Value of Information in the Era of Information Technology
·· 2
  [1] Value of Information ·· 2
  [2] Defects in Information ·· 2
  [3] The Scope of Information in Electronic Form Discussed in this Book ·· 3
  [4] Transactions Involving Information in Electronic Form ············ 3
  [5] Contents of the Following Chapters ·································· 4
    [a] The Law of Tort Relating to Liability for Injury Caused by Information in Traditional and in Electronic Form ············ 4
    [b] The Law of Contract Relating to Liability for Injury Caused by Information in Electronic Form ·································· 5
  [6] Nature of Information in Electronic Form and Legal Consequences
·· 5

§1.02 Meaning Defined ·· 7
  [1] Dictionary Meaning ·· 7
  [2] Meaning in Relation to Modern Technology ·························· 8
  [3] Use of Information in Electronic Form in Statutes ·················· 8

§1.03 Different Types of Information·· 9
  [1] The Difference between Information and Data ······················ 9
  [2] The Difference between Protected Information and Unprotected Information ·· 10
  [3] The Difference between Machine-Readable Information and Human-Readable Information ·································· 12
  [4] The Difference between Statements and Acts ······················ 12
  [5] The Difference between Core and Peripheral Information ······ 13

Table of Contents

    [6] The Difference between Information and Instructions 13
    [7] The Difference between Active Information and Passive
        Information (with Respect to Intended Use) 14

Chapter 2   The Law of Tort Relating to Liability for Injury Caused by Information in Traditional and in Electronic Form 15

§ 2.01 Purpose 16
    [1] Introduction 16
       [a] Contents of the Chapter 16
       [b] Liabilities for Information in Electronic Form and in
          Traditional Form 16
       [c] Role of Information 17
    [2] Mental State of Defendants and Tort Theory of Liability 17
    [3] Chain of Distribution 18
    [4] Concurrent Liability 19
    [5] Form of Injuries 19

§ 2.02 Form of Injuries 20
    [1] Three Scenarios 20
    [2] First Scenario -Direct Injury 20
    [3] Second Scenario -Indirect Injury 22
    [4] Third Scenario 23

§ 2.03 Theories Relevant to Imposing Liability 25
    [1] Overview 25
    [2] Fraud 26
       [a] Reasons for Bringing Fraud Claims 26
       [b] England 27
          [i] Information in Traditional Form 30
          [iii] Information in Electronic Form 31
             [A] General 31
             [B] In the Context of Professional Liability - Disparity
                 of Expertise 33
       [c] United States 34

[i] Requisites, Information in Traditional Form 34
[ii] Information in Electronic Form 35
    [A] Minnesota Law 35
    [B] New York Law 36
    [C] In the Context of Professional Liability - Disparity of Expertise 40
[d] Comparison 41
[3] Negligence 43
  [a] Introduction 43
  [b] England 44
    [i] Physical and Economic Injury 44
    [ii] Defective Articles, Compensation for Lack of Quality ... 47
    [iii] Rendering Services 51
    [iv] Implication of Restrictions on Contractual Terms 53
    [v] Omission of Act 55
    [vi] Transactions Involving Special Skills 56
    [vii] Professional Liability of Computer Programmers 58
  [c] United States 60
    [i] Claims based on Negligence and Strict Liability 60
    [ii] Physical Injury -Inherently Dangerous Articles 60
    [iii] Defective Articles, Compensation for Lack of Quality ... 62
    [iv] Actions Based on Warranties 68
    [v] Liability Based on Expertise 70
    [vi] Omission of Act 72
      [A] Physical Damage 72
      [B] Economic Loss 74
    [vii] Professional Liability of Computer Programmers 77
      [A] Exercising Professional Standard of Care 77
      [B] Exercising Ordinary Standard of Care 78
      [C] Standard of Care for Professionals Supplying Information 78
      [D] Difference between a Profession and a Business 79
      [E] Overlapping Professional Duties -Computer Consultants and Accountants 80

[F] Requisites for Allowing Professional Liability 83
[d] Comparison 84
[4] Negligent Misrepresentation 86
   [a] Negligent Misrepresentation and Information in Electronic Form 86
   [b] England 87
      [i] Physical Injury 87
      [ii] Economic Loss 88
         [A] Special Relationship 88
         [B] Special Relationship -Scope of the Class of Plaintiffs and the Defendants 90
         [C] Liability of Accountants and Auditors 94
         [D] Representations in Traditional Form with Respect to Information in Electronic Form 96
   [c] United States 98
      [i] Physical Injury 98
      [ii] Economic Loss 99
         [A] Special Relationship -Liability of Auditors 99
         [B] Representations in Information in Traditional Form with Respect to Information in Electronic Form -Distinction Between Negligent Misrepresentation and Fraud in Inducement 106
         [C] Information in Electronic Form -Negligent Referral ... 108
         [D] Content of Information in Electronic Form 109
   [d] Defences for Negligence 111
   [e] Comparison 113
[5] Strict Products Liability 116
   [a] Overview of Statutes in England and in the United States ... 116
      [i] England 116
      [ii] United States 119
   [b] Generic Policy Issues 120
      [i] Products 120
      [ii] Policy Reasons 121
      [iii] Core Information 125

xii

Table of Contents

        [iv] Different Types of Defects ·································· 126
     [c] Reasons for Applying Strict Liability or Negligence for
         Information in Traditional Form and in Electronic Form ······ 127
        [i] Similarity to Physical Products ······························· 127
        [ii] Mass Distribution ··· 130
        [iii] Intended Use ··· 132
    [d] England ··· 135
    [e] United States ·· 136
    [f] Defences for Products Liability Law ····························· 139
        [i] The Development Risk ·· 139
         [A] England ··· 139
         [B] United States ·· 141
        [ii] Defence for Manufacturers of Components ··············· 143
         [A] England ··· 143
         [B] United States ·· 143
    [g] Comparison ··· 144

§ 2.04 Liability in the Chain of Distribution ···························· 145
   [1] Information in Traditional Form ····································· 145
     [a] Negligence ··· 145
        [i] Authors, Publishers and Sellers of Books ·················· 145
        [ii] Defamation ·· 147
         [A] England ··· 147
         [B] United States ·· 147
     [b] Products Liability Law ··· 148
   [2] Information in Electronic Form ···································· 150
     [a] Negligence ··· 150
     [b] Products Liability ·· 151
   [3] Some Issues with Respect to the Liability in the Chain of
      Distribution ·· 152

§ 2.05 Issues Regarding Tort and Contract ···························· 152
   [1] Overview ·· 152
   [2] England ··· 153
     [a] Information in Traditional Form ······························ 153

xiii

Table of Contents

        [b] Information in Electronic Form 154
    [3] United States 155
        [a] Information in Traditional Form 155
        [b] Information in Electronic Form 158
    [4] Comparison 160

§ 2.06 Imposition of Liability with Respect to Information 161

Chapter 3 The Law of Contract Relating to Liability for Injury Caused by Information in Electronic Form 165

§ 3.01 **Introduction** 166

§ 3.02 **Classification of Contracts** 167
    [1] Classification of Contracts 167
        [a] The Structure of the Classification 167
        [b] Contracts for Goods 167
        [c] Contracts for Services 168
        [d] Contracts for Information 169
    [2] The Effect of Classification 178
        [a] The General Purpose 178
        [b] Evidence 178
        [c] Limitation Period 178
        [d] Implied Obligation 179
        [e] Comparison 181
    [3] Uncertain Nature of the Criteria in Classification -Examples of Actions by Suppliers to Recover Payment for the Work Done in Cases Where Customers Refuse to Accept 182
        [a] General Factors Considered in Classification 182
        [b] Delivery of a Chattel 183
        [c] Substance of the Contract 184
        [d] Analysis of the Different Approach and the Statute of Fraud Defence 185
        [e] Different Factors of Consideration and Contracts Relating to Information in Electronic Form 185

Table of Contents

[4] Nature of Licensing Agreements -Relationship With Intellectual Property 187
[5] England 189
    [a] Effect of Classification -Samuels v. Davis 189
    [b] Classification and Application of Statute 190
    [c] Obligation Specific to Contracts Involving Computer Programs 193
    [d] Physical Medium and Intangibles 194
    [e] Breach of Express Duties 197
    [f] Professional Liability 198
    [g] Classification and Implied Terms and Express Terms 198
    [h] Contracts for Information 199
[6] United States 200
    [a] Different Tests for Classification 200
    [b] Predominant Test, Contract for the Sale of Goods 202
        [i] Turn-Key Computer System 202
        [ii] Customised (Bespoke) Software 205
    [c] Predominant Purpose Test, Supply of Services 206
    [d] Gravamen of the Action Test, Contract for the Supply of Services 210
    [e] Factors Considered in the Classification 213
        [i] Important Factors 213
        [ii] Physical Configuration 213
        [iii] Process of Performance 215
        [iv] Method of Distribution 216
        [v] Remuneration 217
        [vi] Comparison with Traditional Subject Matters 218
    [f] Contracts for Information 218
[7] The Effect of the Enactment of the U.C.I.T.A. -Basic Concepts ... 221
    [a] Basic Terms 221
    [b] Three Different Legal Traditions 224
[8] Classification of Contracts with Respect to Information in Electronic Form 226

§ 3.03 Express Terms or Warranties ········· 229
[1] Express Obligations ········· 229
[2] England ········· 230
[a] Type of Express Terms and Remedies ········· 230
[i] Result-Oriented Terms and Process-Oriented Terms ······ 230
[ii] Collateral Contract ········· 231
[iii] Result-Oriented Terms ········· 232
[iv] Process-Oriented Terms ········· 233
[b] Exclusion of Express Terms ········· 236
[i] Statutes ········· 236
[ii] Disclaimer ········· 237
[iii] Integration Clauses ········· 238
[3] United States ········· 238
[a] Types of Express Warranties and Remedies ········· 238
[i] Statutes ········· 238
[ii] Express Warranties and Advertising or Demonstration-Result- Oriented Terms ········· 239
[iii] Express Warranties Concerning Important Functions-Result- Oriented Terms ········· 241
[b] Exclusion of Express Warranties ········· 241
[i] Statutes ········· 241
[ii] Inconsistent Disclaimer ········· 242
[iii] Integration Clauses ········· 243
[A] Examination of all the Documents ········· 243
[B] Application of Parol Evidence Rule ········· 246
[4] The U.C.I.T.A. ········· 249
[5] Comparison ········· 251

§ 3.04 Implied Terms or Warranties ········· 252
[1] England ········· 252
[a] Statutory Control Over Implied Terms ········· 252
[b] Implied Terms: Contract for the Supply of Services ········· 252
[c] Implied Terms: From Merchantable Quality to Satisfactory Quality ········· 253

[d] Implied Terms: Fitness for Intended Purpose 254
[e] Exclusion of Implied Terms 255
   [i] Statutes 255
   [ii] Inconsistent Terms 256
[f] Contract to Transfer Information 257
[2] United States 257
  [a] Implied Warranties of Merchantability 257
  [b] Implied Warranty of Fitness for Particular Purpose 258
  [c] Exclusion of Implied Warranties 259
   [i] Statutes 259
   [ii] Sufficient Language in Disclaiming Implied Warranty ... 259
   [iii] Conspicuousness of the Warranty Exclusion 261
   [iv] Integration Clauses, Unconscionability 262
  [d] Contract for Information 262
[3] The U.C.I.T.A. 262
  [a] Implied Warranties 262
  [b] Disclaimer or Modification of Warranty 269
[4] Comparison 270

§ 3.05 Remedies and Standard of Performance 271

§ 3.06 Limitation or Exclusion of Remedies 273
[1] Different Methods of Limiting or Excluding Remedies 273
  [a] England 274
   [i] Restricting Obligations Incurred, Damage for which
      Compensation is Payable 274
   [ii] Restricting the Cure to Which the Victim is Entitled, Damage
      for which Compensation is Payable, and Money Payable
      on Breach 274
   [iii] Consequential Damages 280
  [b] United States 280
   [i] The Cure to which the Victim is Entitled 280
   [ii] The Damage for which Compensation is Payable 283
[2] Comparison 284

§ 3.07 Construction and Statutory Controls on Contractual Terms ··· 285
    [1] England ·· 285
    [2] United States ·· 286
    [3] Reasonableness Test and Unconscionability ························ 287
        [a] Reasonableness Test ·· 287
        [b] Unconscionability ·· 288
    [4] Standard Form Contracts and Consumers ···························· 291
        [a] Necessity of Statutory Control over Standard Form Contract
            and Consumer Contracts ·· 291
        [b] England ··· 292
            [i] Unfair Contract Terms Act 1977 ····························· 292
            [ii] The Unfair Terms in Consumer Contracts Regulations
                1999 ·· 294
        [c] United States ··· 296
        [d] Shrink-Wrap Licences ··· 298
        [e] The U.C.I.T.A. ·· 301
            [i] Consumer Contracts ·· 301
            [ii] Mass-Market Transactions ······································ 301
        [f] Comparison ·· 306
§ 3.08 Contractual Liability on Information in Electronic Form ··· 307

Chapter 4   Conclusion ·· 311

§ 4.01 Civil Liability for Information in Electronic Form ············· 312
    [1] Transactions Involving Information in Electronic Form ········· 312
    [2] Tort Law Relating to Liability for Injury Caused by Information
        In Traditional Form and in Electronic Form ·························· 314
        [a] Economic Loss and Special Relationship ······················· 314
        [b] Products Liability ·· 318
        [c] Chain of Distribution ··· 319
        [d] Concurrent Liability ·· 319
    [3] Contract Law Relating to Liability for Injury Caused by
        Information in Electronic Form ··· 320
        [a] Special Law for Information in Electronic Form ············· 320

    [b] Liabilities for Representations ································· 321
    [c] Implied Obligations ·· 322
    [d] Limiting or Excluding Remedies ······························· 323

Table of Cases ·· 327
    ENGLISH CASES (327)
    UNITED STATES CASES (331)
    OTHER CASES (339)

Bibliography ··· 349
    [BOOKS] (349)
    [ARTICLES] (349)

Table of Statutes and Statutory Instruments ························· 340
    ENGLISH STATUTES AND STATUTORY INSTRUMENTS (340)
    UNITED STATES STATUTES (343)
    INTERNATIONAL STATUTES (347)

Chapter 1 Introduction

§1.01 The Value of Information in the Era of Information Technology

[1] Value of Information

The economic value of information has increased dramatically due to the development of technology. Information is now a commodity in itself, independently of goods or services. Despite its independent commercial value and the ability to cause physical or economic loss, the law has not adequately incorporated information in electronic form within its scope.

Information is manufactured, packaged, and sold in the mass—market. Those with more information, knowledge and intelligence may accumulate more wealth than those without such resources.

[2] Defects in Information

Certain forms of information, such as computer programs and databases, play essential roles in modern society. For instance, computer programs control traffic signals and even fly airplanes and space shuttles. Computer databases may supply important financial information, which can lead to on-line transactions on a large scale. Transactions involving information in electronic form have become an essential part of business and social life in modern society. A defect in information in electronic form may cause substantial damage.[1] Furthermore, even non-defective information may become defective during processes that involve electronic transmission, manipulation, storage, or display.

Such defects may cause serious economic loss and personal injury. Because of the increasing number of transactions involving information in electronic form and the impending disputes arising from such transactions, analysis of the liabilities concerning defects in information in electronic form is essential in the era of information technology law. Analysis of such issues may help in

---

[1] I. LLOYD, INFORMATION TECHNOLOGY LAW 408 (2d ed. 1997).

establishing the standard of quality in supplying information in electronic form.

   [3] The Scope of Information in Electronic Form Discussed in this Book

The ultimate objective of this book is to determine the tortious and contractual liabilities arising from defects in information in electronic form. For the purpose of the book, information is largely divided into information in traditional form and information in electronic form.

Information in traditional form contains human-readable information in a traditional, non-electronic medium. Information in electronic form includes both human-readable information on the Internet or online databases and machine-readable computer programs such as software and hardware. Of course, computer programs, with the aid of peripherals such as keyboard and screen, can also be viewed in human-readable form. I am dealing with both human-readable information in electronic form and machine-readable computer programs in this book, as both types of information may cause physical or economic injury.

   [4] Transactions Involving Information in Electronic Form

The present legal system has failed to provide comprehensive laws to determine liabilities concerning defects in new subject matter, such as information in electronic form. There are no set rules to determine liability for injury caused by information in electronic form.

If the present legal system is not equipped to deal with specific issues with the present legal framework, new legal frameworks should be considered. For instance, in the field of tort law, even though physical injuries are attributed to computer programs, computer programs are not considered per se products. In the area of contract law, transactions pertaining to information in electronic form have mainly been classified into sale of goods and supply of services. Such classification was considered inadequate in the United States and this concern led to the adoption of the Uniform Computer Information Transactions Act (hereinafter, "U.C.I.T.A.").[2] One of the important issues is evaluation of this new law specifically designed for computer information, and comparison of the present application of law in England and the pre-U.C.I.T.A. law of the United States.

Information in electronic form may have a variety of characteristics which are not shared with traditional subject matters. For instance, information in electronic form has the characteristics of both acts and statements. A computer program is machine-readable information which may cause direct physical effects with the aid of peripheral devices such as computer hardware or other types of machine. On the other hand, software such as Lotus 1-2-3, with the aid of hardware and screen, is meant to be operated by human beings to produce certain results. These results or this output may be relied on by the readers. Likewise, information in electronic form on the Internet, in an online database or in an encyclopaedia in CD-Rom may be relied on by human beings and cause damage.

[5] Contents of the Following Chapters
   [a] The Law of Tort Relating to Liability for Injury Caused by Information in Traditional and in Electronic Form

By analysing contractual and tortious liabilities relating to defects with respect to various types of information, I intend to explore the meaning and impact of information on legal disciplines relating to modern technology. I will first attempt to conduct comparative analysis of tort law relating to liability for injury caused by information in traditional form and information

---

[2] Uniform Computer Information Transaction Act (last modified August 23, 2001), available at http://www.law.upenn.edu/bll/ulc/ucita/ucita01.htm.

Chapter 1

in electronic form. This is to examine whether the authorities pertaining to information in traditional form are likely to have a significant impact upon liability for publication or dissemination in electronic form, particularly computer programs and human-readable information in electronic form on the Internet, or in an online database.

Comparative analysis of works such as architectural plans and structures, maps or sculptures will be of particular importance in providing the basis for comparative analysis with information in electronic form.

[b] The Law of Contract Relating to Liability for Injury Caused by Information in Electronic Form

Second, I intend to explore contractual liability for information in electronic form. I am not conducting a comparative analysis between information in traditional form and information in electronic form in this chapter. Contractual terms between the parties primarily define the parties, the content and extent of their obligations and what types of remedies are available for breach. In the absence of detailed agreements between the parties or where the application of their contractual terms is not appropriate, then the law will supplement the terms of the contract. Contractual liabilities relating to information in electronic form may differ in accordance with the classification of a given transaction. In accordance with the classification, as sale of goods, supply of services or, possibly, transactions for information, there are rules providing for the creation, disclaimer of express or implied obligations, limiting or excluding remedies available, and other rules controlling the contract terms.

[6] Nature of Information in Electronic Form and Legal Consequences

Prior to examining liabilities for defects in information, I will attempt to determine the precise nature of information in electronic form.

To achieve the goals stated above, it is useful first to define and classify information. The objectives of this chapter are to analyse the meaning of information in general, as well as the meaning of information in modern technology, and examine the significance of information in a legal context.

I will start by identifying the dictionary meanings of information and related terms as well as identifying the meaning of information in modern technology. I will then identify different types of information, listed below, as such differences may be important in terms of legal consequences in subsequent chapters.
1) the difference between information and data;
2) the difference between protected information and unprotected information;
3) the difference between "commodity" information and "non-commodity" information;
4) the difference between statements and acts;
5) the difference between active information and passive information (with respect to intended use); and
6) the difference between information and instructions.

In chapter 2 and 3 of this book, I am examining contractual and tortious liability only, even though there are many other areas of law that have been altered or revised in order to incorporate the development in computer technology. I am dividing those issues with respect to contractual and tortious liability into two separate chapters even though there are a number of issues that involve both areas of law. In this book, the feasibility of having legal classifications such as those between information in electronic and in traditional form, contractual and tortious liabilities, economic and physical losses, act and statement, products and information, and sale of goods and supply of services is examined by way of comparative studies between authorities in England and in the United States. This will show that the development of computer technology has been undermining the existing classifications which may be no longer viable to incorporate such development.

§1.02 Meaning Defined

[1] Dictionary Meaning

According to the second edition of the Oxford English Dictionary [2.1](hereinafter "OED"), the term 'information' has various meanings:

(1) The action of informing ; formation or moulding of the mind or character, training, instruction, teaching; communication of instructive knowledge.

(2) The action of informing ; communication of the knowledge or 'news' of some fact or occurrence; the action of telling or fact of being told of something.

(3) Knowledge communicated concerning some particular fact, subject, or event; that of which one is apprised or told; intelligence, news. *spec.* contrasted with *data*.

(4) with *an* and *pl.* An item of information or intelligence; a fact or circumstance of which one is told. In earlier use, an account, relation, narrative (*of* something). *Obs.*

(5) Separated from, or without the implication of, reference to a person informed: that which inheres in one of two or more alternative sequences, arrangements, etc., that produce different responses in something, and which is capable of being stored in, transferred by, and communicated to inanimate things.

Most of the meanings of information are closely associated with communication of specific knowledge, news, and events. In this sense, all information is knowledge.

[2.1] OXFORD ENGLISH DICTIONARY(2d ed.1989).

[2] Meaning in Relation to Modern Technology

The meaning of the word information and its significance have been changed dramatically by modern technology. The term information technology typifies the meaning of information in this sense. Information technology as defined in the OED is "the branch of technology concerned with the dissemination, processing, and storage of information, esp. by means of computers."

With respect to sending information, the term "information superhighway" in the interlinked computer networks called "cyberspace", has become an important slogan for future economic growth of the United States; the term "information superhighway" is defined in the Concise Oxford Dictionary of Current English[3] as "an extensive electronic network such as the Internet, used for the rapid transfer of information in digital form".

The definitions of information, data, databases and data processing indicate that the computer program is essential to information technology. With computer technology, dissemination, processing and storage of information is available on a large scale.

[3] Use of Information in Electronic Form in Statutes

The development of technology has prompted information in electronic form to be incorporated into various statutory provisions. The Local Government Finance Act 1992,[4] section 14(1)(b) of the schedule 4, provides for admissibility of a document of record produced by computer. In the Civil Evidence Act 1995[5] section 13, " 'document' means anything in which information of any description is recorded, and 'copy', in relation to a document, means anything onto which information recorded in the document has been copied, by whatever means and whether directly or indirectly."

---

[3] CONCISE OXFORD DICTINARY OF CURRENT ENGLISH 698 (10th ed. 1999).
[4] c. 14.
[5] c. 38.

§1.03 Different Types of Information

[1] The Difference between Information and Data

The meanings of information described above can be contrasted with the meaning of datum, which is defined in the OED as "A thing given or granted; something known or assumed as fact, and made the basis of reasoning or calculation; an assumption or premiss from which inferences are drawn." In its plural form, defined as "The quantities, characters, or symbols on which operations are performed by computers and other automatic equipment, and which may be stored or transmitted in the form of electrical signals, records on magnetic tape or punched cards, etc." and "Facts, esp. numerical facts, collected together for reference or information."

In relation to the meaning of information described above in [1] Dictionary Meaning (3), it has been said that "In administrative data processing, a distinction is sometimes made between data and information by calling raw facts in great quantity 'data', and using the word 'information' for highly concentrated and improved data derived from the raw facts."[6]

Legislatures of various countries have recognised the importance of personal data in modern technology. Personal data relating to all aspects of everyday life are constantly stored on computers, enabling various types of entities or people to gain access through the network system.

The Data Protection Act 1998 provides for the regulation of the processing of information relating to individuals, including the obtaining, holding, use or disclosure of such information.[7]

Under Section 1(1) of the Data Protection Act 1998, "data" means information which--- "(a) is being processed by means of equipment operating automatically in response to instructions

---

[6] OED, *supra* note 2.1.
[7] Data Protection Act 1998 (c. 29).

given for that purpose, (b) is recorded with the intention that it should be processed by means of such equipment, (c) is recorded as part of a relevant filing system or with the intention that it should form part of a relevant filing system, or (d) does not fall within paragraph (a), (b) or (c) but forms part of an accessible record as defined by section 68."

Under Section 1(1), "'personal data' means data which relate to a living individual who can be identified- (a) from those data, or (b) from those data and other information which is in the possession of, or is likely to come into the possession of, the data controller; and includes any expression of opinion about the individual and any indication of the intentions of the data controller or any other person in respect of the individual."

Therefore, data may generally mean information in more concentrated or organised form which can be processed by the aid of equipment. Misuse of such data may cause damage and may be regulated by statutes.

[2] The Difference between Protected Information and Unprotected Information

Intellectual property law protects ideas and information. Protection of intellectual property has become an important issue in many countries as the development of nations depends largely upon exploitation of information and knowledge. Nevertheless, to qualify for legal protection, information has to fall within the categories of intellectual property to which it is claimed that the information belongs.

Whether the subject matter of transaction is protected by intellectual property law or not, is not directly relevant as to the quality of performance and in terms of liability issues. The fact that the subject matter of transaction is protected by intellectual property law does not weaken the responsibility for promised obligations of the licensor of the intellectual property. Information in electronic form discussed for the purpose of this book does not

Chapter 1

need to be protected by intellectual property law, though suppliers' lack of ownership of intellectual property right incorporated in the subject matter is relevant to the issue of implied obligations.[8]

If information in electronic form is protected by intellectual property law, some policy considerations come into play with respect to fair dealings, development of technology or dissemination of ideas. An attempt unduly to restrict the use of intellectual property or monopolise such information may be regulated.[9] Under the United Kingdom copyright law,[10] limitations to exclusive right include fair dealing,[11] making of back-up copies and decompilation of computer programs,[12] incidental inclusion of copyright material,[13] educational use,[14] and use for libraries and archives. The Council Directive on the Legal Protection of Computer Programs,[15] permits "decompilation" or reverse engineering, for the sole purpose of achieving interoperability under certain conditions.[16]

---

[8] U.C.I.T.A. § 401 (2001); see § 3.02 Classification of Contracts [4] Nature of Licensing Agreements -Relationship With Intellectual Property.

[9] The Council Directive (EEC) 91/250 on the Legal Protection of Computer Programs, preamble (stating that states within its territory are "fully committed to the promotion of international standardisation"); U.C.I.T.A. § 105(a) (2001); U.S. v. Microsoft Corp., 253 F.3d 34 (D.C. Cir. 2001), cert. denied, 122 S. Ct. 350 (2001).

[10] Copyright, Design and Patent Act (C.D.P.A.) 1988 as amended (c. 48), s. 30.

[11] Id.

[12] Id. s. 50A, 50B; and 50 C for other acts permitted to lawful users.

[13] Id. s. 31.

[14] Id. ss. 32-36.

[15] The Council Directive (EEC) 91/250 on the Legal Protection of Computer Programs.

[16] Id. art. 6.

11

[3] The Difference between Machine-Readable Information and Human-Readable Information

There may be a distinction between information that was created for the purpose of communicating with other machines or for communicating with human-beings. For human-readable information, the principle of free speech may be of importance. For machine-readable information, such concern does not exist. Such a distinction is important in terms of imposition of liability for defective computer programs, as opposed to defective human-readable information discussed in § 2.03 Theories Relevant To Imposing Liability [5] Strict Products Liability.

[4] The Difference between Statements and Acts

Acts are traditionally considered to provoke more direct injury than are statements. However, such a difference can be minimised in accordance with different circumstances. Certain types of statement can be associated with direct actions. For instance, Lord Oliver in *Caparo Industries plc. v. Dickman*[17] indicated that the mislabelling of a dangerous medicine or negligent telephonic advice about the treatment of a sick child should be treated in the same manner as in cases where negligent acts cause physical injury.[18] As giving professional advice can also mean giving instructions to act, it is often not possible to distinguish whether a certain professional service was rendered in the form of acts or statements.[19]

Applying this in the context of computer technology, computer programs may consist partly of medical diagnostic devices, which directly interact with patients. A computer program is a set of

---

[17] [1990] 2 A.C. 605 (H.L.).
[18] *Id.* at 636; *see infra* § 2.03 Theories Relevant To Imposing Liability [4] Negligent Misrepresentation [c] United States [i] Physical Injury.
[19] *See infra* § 2.03 Theories Relevant To Imposing Liability [3] Negligence [b] England [iii] Rendering Services.

statements but, with the aid of hardware, it acts to bring about a physical result.[20]

[5] The Difference between Core and Peripheral Information

In the context of the products liability law, inadequacy of the information regarding products such as warnings or directions may provide grounds for liability even though the product itself is not defective. Products can be supplemented by instructions and warnings. In the context of information, there may be a difference between core information and peripheral information; for instance, a navigational chart can be core information and the instruction to use the chart can be peripheral information. There could be layers of information surrounding "core" information. In the same context, with respect to information in electronic form, there can be core information (computer programs) and peripheral information, such as instructions or hardware.[21]

[6] The Difference between Information and Instructions

Instructions are a sub-set of information. They are statements that answer the question 'how'. Instructions can also be associated with more direct actions than mere information. As discussed above, inadequacy of the information may provide gro-unds for liability.

Glidewell J. in *St. Albans City & District Council v. International Computers Ltd.*[22] took the position *obiter* that instruction manuals were "goods" under the Sales of Goods Act 1979[23] and

---

[20] *See infra* § 2.03 Theories Relevant To Imposing Liability [4] Negligent Misrepresen-tation [b] England [i] Physical Injury.
[21] *See infra* § 2.03 Theories Relevant To Imposing Liability [5] Strict Products Liability [b] Generic Policy Issues.
[22] [1996] 4 All E. R. 481.
[23] c. 54.

that if manuals including instructions on the maintenance and repair of a particular make of a car were wrong in important respects, they were likely to cause serious damage to the engine of the car.[24] Such a decision would be likely to have a great impact on any judgement determining whether or not certain information such as instruction manuals or computer programs are "products."[25]

[7] The Difference between Active Information and Passive Information (with Respect to Intended Use)

Information can be used actively or passively. Information such as instructions and repair manuals for commodities, may be intended to be used actively. Fictional novels may not be intended to be used actively, but passively and to convey information contained in the novels. There may be more of a possibility of causing injuries when relying on such information. In this context, the purpose of computer programs is to execute certain tasks. Computer programs are intended to be used "actively" to bring about certain results.[26]

---

[24] [1996] 4 All E. R. 481, 493.

[25] *See infra* § 2.03 Theories Relevant To Imposing Liability[5] Strict Products Liability [c] Reasons for Applying Strict Liability or Negligence for Information in Traditional Form and in Electronic Form [i] Similarity to Physical Products.

[26] *See infra* § 2.03 Theories Relevant To Imposing Liability[5] Strict Products Liability [c] Reasons for Applying Strict Liability or Negligence for Information in Traditional Form and in Electronic Form [iii] Intended Use.

Chapter 2 **The Law of Tort Relating to Liability for Injury Caused by Information in Traditional and in Electronic Form**

§ 2.01 Purpose

[1] Introduction

[a] Contents of the Chapter

This chapter describes tortious liability for injury caused by information in traditional form as compared to information in electronic form, and discusses whether the authorities pertaining to information in traditional form are likely to have a significant impact upon liability for publication or dissemination in electronic form.

In order to clarify the law relating to information in traditional form and in electronic form, I shall begin by classifying the form of injury in accordance with *human actions or interventions* during the process leading to the injury. Then, I will discuss *three scenarios*, which involve injuring parties, intermediate parties and victims. The purpose is to examine the process leading to injury and the type of involvement of the victim. I will specifically attempt to identify types of defect in information in traditional and in electronic form, and potential scenarios in cases where defects in such information cause injuries.

Subsequently, I will discuss relevant tortious theories and authorities regarding economic loss and physical injury for information in traditional and in electronic forms. In subsequent sections, I will first address some of the issues arising out of chains of liabilities and discuss concurrent liabilities.

[b] Liabilities for Information in Electronic Form and in Traditional Form

The analysis of liabilities for published information can be compared to and may clarify the analysis of the liabilities relating to information in electronic form. It is based on the presumption that there are similarities as well as dissimilarities between information in traditional and electronic form with respect to liability issues.

[c] Role of Information

In principle, information presented both in electronic and in traditional form communicates something, which may produce certain effects. However, computer programs may not directly convey information that is readily understandable by human beings even though they execute certain tasks, creating certain direct and physical effects.

A computer program has been defined by the United States Copyright Act as "a set of statements or instructions to be used directly or indirectly in a computer in order to bring about a certain result"[27] A computer program, therefore, has been regarded as information which conveys certain instructions. These instructions execute the tasks directly with the aid of peripheral devices such as computer hardware or other types of machinery.

On the other hand, information in the traditional form conveys information, which is readily understandable by human beings. In any case, because of the common function, that of communicating, one may draw upon the present law regarding information in traditional form when discussing liabilities relating to information in electronic form. Within the type of information in traditional form, I will focus on information that directly or indirectly causes economic loss or physical injury. Such information includes published audit reports, advertising, science books, mushroom encyclopedias and navigational charts. I will then consider whether the rationale for imposing liability for such information in traditional form can also be applied to information in electronic form.

[2] Mental State of Defendants and Tort Theory of Liability

Different types of tortious liability for published information can be imposed in accordance with the mental state of defendants.

---

[27] 17 U.S.C. §101 (2001).

Defendants can act intentionally, recklessly, or negligently in publishing certain information. On the other hand, strict tort liability can be imposed irrespective of the defendant's mental state. Tort law provides different causes of action corresponding to the existence or the non-existence of such different mental states. These include intentional misrepresentation, deceit or fraud, negligence and strict products liability. The conditions for these causes of actions vary in different jurisdictions.

[3] Chain of Distribution

When considering liability in tort, the type of involvement of various parties in the chain of distribution is very important. Those parties in the chain of distribution include parties who are involved in creating, implementing, distributing and using the information; and any other victims who are affected by the information.

Parties who may be involved in creating the information may include manufacturers, authors, designers, architects, accountants or computer programmers. Parties who may be involved in implementing the information may include manufacturers of the product in accordance with a specification provided by the product designer, or programmers responsible for coding into machine languages. Parties who are involved in distributing the information may include distributors, sellers and publishers.

Such a complicated structure of distribution means that end users and the original authors, designers, architects or programmers, those who exercise special skills, may not be in direct contractual relationship. Therefore, the only recourse for such end users is found in tort law.

With regard to computer technology, most computer programs are developed in different stages: starting from a description of the task to be accomplished; writing a program converting the flowchart into machine-readable language; debugging; preparing the documentation to explain the functioning of the program.

[4] Concurrent Liability

One of the important issues regarding a tortious claim with respect to information in electronic form is whether a tortious claim is allowed when there is a contractual relationship between the parties. The reasons for plaintiffs to bring claims in tort are mainly to evade application of 1) contractual terms which disclaim warranties, limit or exclude remedies available to the users, and 2) contractual periods of limitation which may differ from those in tort.

Although this issue will be dealt with when discussing the tort cases in the previous sections. I will examine the general requirements in bringing claims in tort prior to discussing contractual liability.

[5] Form of Injuries

Parties involved at different stages in the chain may be liable for all or part of the loss caused by the injury. The type of liability imposed on those parties may depend upon the existence or non-existence of particular mental states, depending on the cause of action in tort. However, before the stage of identifying possible defendants and investigating any issues regarding their liability, injury or a serious threat of some injury must have occurred to a victim. Therefore, I will discuss the form of injury before discussing liabilities in each cause of action. By "form" I do not here mean the type of injury such as physical, emotional, financial, loss of reputation etc. I mean to try to depict the chain of events and actions involved in the occurrence of the injury. The form of liability may differ according to whether there were human actions or interventions by the injuring party or the victim and how such injuries were caused during the process leading to the injury. The analysis concerning these types of actions or interventions is directly related to the allocation of damages in terms of joint liability or contributory negligence.

§ 2.02 Form of Injuries

[1] Three Scenarios

Scenarios leading to injury caused by published information, whether accurate or inaccurate, may be separated into three categories in terms of the involvement of the victim subsequent to the supply of the information.

The first scenario is where the injuring party supplies information which directly injures the victim who is completely passive; the second scenario is where the victim acts upon the information causing damage to himself; and the third scenario is where an intermediate party or parties act upon the information causing damage to a third-party victim.

This distinction emphasises the difference between the type of information in terms of the action and reaction of the victim. One type of information directly causes injury, whereas another type of information indirectly causes injury; it needs to be acted upon to cause injury.

[2] First Scenario -Direct Injury

The first scenario involves the supply of information by the creator of information and the victim who is directly affected thereby. If there is no action or intervention involved, then the information directly injures the victim - that is, when the victim is affected by, but does not act on, the information. If there is an action or an intervention by the victim himself or herself, then the information indirectly injures the victim.

The most simple and straightforward case of information in traditional form, the first scenario case, which involves direct injury to the victim, is illustrated in *Wilkinson v. Downton*.[28] There, the statement to a wife of an injury to her husband, deliberately

---

[28] Wilkinson v. Downton [1897] 2 Q.B. 57.

and falsely made by the defendant as a joke, caused serious illness to the wife. Direct effect, in the sense that the information reached the victim without alteration by the victim, caused nervous shock and physical injury. In this sense, the information directly causes its natural result, which is injury. There is no human action or an intervention by the victim. She does not act, she is affected, her nervous system reacts and she suffers injury; thus the second type does not apply in this case. The information directly reacted to cause injury to the victim.

In *Wilkinson v. Downton*, the wife was injured as the direct result of such a statement. However, the falsity of the information was not a factual cause of the injury. The wife would have been injured anyway had it been true. Nevertheless, liability would not have been imposed if the statement were true. It was the falsity of the information that made the defendant liable.

It should be noted that, in different circumstances, liability could have been, in rare circumstance, imposed even if the statement were true. A person can maliciously try to hurt the wife, knowing that she is weak and vulnerable, by telling her the information in the most upsetting way, causing mental distress. The existence of liability depends on the circumstances in which the information is put to use.

As previously described, information in electronic form, particularly computer programs, may comprise instructions which purport to execute certain tasks. If there is a defect, such information could directly, without any intervening act by the victim, cause an effect with the aid of peripheral devices such as hardware. For instance, a computer-operated space shuttle may explode due to faults in a computer system.

I include cases relating to computer hardware because the decision as to whether to embody certain functional aspects into hardware or software may be an arbitrary decision made by manufacturers. Furthermore, even injury apparently caused by hardware defects may be attributed to software defects; for instance, the cause of RSI, repetitive strain injury, may be attributed to software, which could have been, but was not, designed to minimise keystrokes.

[3] Second Scenario -Indirect Injury

The second scenario involves the creator of the information and the victim who acts on the information supplied. In this sense, the information may indirectly cause the injury. This means that between receipt of information and the injury, there is an action or an intervention by the victim. The action of the recipient depends on the degree of reliance by the recipient, and reliance may vary in accordance with the circumstances of supply of the information. The recipient would be likely to rely on information if the same kind of information were not available from other sources. Information would be likely to be relied on when the creator of the information has employed expertise in creating such information. Such reliance is most obvious and most clearly justified when there is disparity in expertise between creator and the victim and the victim, has directly paid an expert for the information.

For instance, the navigational chart described in *Aetna Casualty & Surety Co. v. Jeppesen & Co.*,[29] was the kind of information which was designed to be heavily relied on. Jeppesen designed and published instrument approach charts to aid pilots in making instrument approaches to airports. The pilots had to fly the airplane by referring to the charts. An act of the pilot is involved before damage can occur. The court determined that the navigational chart was to be deemed a defective product under product liability theory.[30] The court concluded that the purpose of the chart was to translate the information or mere data to an instantly understandable graphic representation and this constituted

---

[29] 642 F.2d 339 (9th Cir. 1981).
[30] *Id.* at 342.

the usefulness of the chart, which invited reliance by Jeppesen.[31]

Similar types of information, which contain charts, maps or diagrams, can also be represented in electronic format. Such information may be relied upon and acted upon to create certain indirect results. Computer programs such as Excel are meant for human beings to operate to produce certain results. Defects in such software may produce wrong results, which may be relied on. Information in electronic form may also contain or incorporate by reference, human readable computer-processed data, a database or information contained on the Internet.

[4] Third Scenario

The third scenario involves a creator of information, an intermediate party and a third-party victim injured by action or intervention by the intermediate party. For example, when traffic lights give the wrong signals, the intermediate party driver may act on such information and injure a third-party victim.

The creator of information may produce defective or non-defective information; and the intermediate party may act on or incorporate the information to cause injury to the third party-victim.

When determining the liability here, one has to take into consideration the liability of the creator of information and of the intermediate party, and to what extent she or he has contributed to the injury caused to the victim. This type of scenario is open-ended, and can include any number of intermediaries interacting with each other.

As described in [2] First Scenario -Direct Injury, even if the information itself is correct as produced, the circumstances where information is put to use may determine the imposition of liability. There may be cases where even if the computer program itself were perfect, as in the case when the information was true, it

---

[31] *Id.* at 342.

may nevertheless be considered as "ineffective" or "defective," simply because the computer program is used in an inappropriate environment when assembled or combined together with other programs. A typical example of a "perfect program" in an inappropriate environment is incompatibility between different computer programs, which are required to work together.[32] Some computer programs are meant to be used together with other computer programs, for instance, with specific operating systems.[33]

Suppliers of such programs may be held responsible when these programs do not work together properly. If a program is not meant to be used with another program, users may still attempt to use the programs together due to the failure of the manufacturer to warn that they are not supposed to be used together. On the other hand, there are programs that are highly specialised and are not amenable to a variety of usages.

For instance, in *Sparacino v. Andover Controls Corp.*,[34] the plaintiff, a chemistry teacher, was injured because he could not activate the exhaust fan to draw out noxious chlorine gas to be used in a class room experiment at 6:15 a.m. This was due to the fact that a computerised energy management system (EMS), which was manufactured by one company and incorporated by another company into a heating, ventilating, air conditioning (HVAC) system, was scheduled to be inoperative until 6:30 a.m.[35]

With respect to the third scenario, evaluation of the types of involvement of an intermediate party is essential in determining liability of the parties. For instance, the manufacturer of a hoist (the

---

[32] *See* Dunn Appraisal Co. v. Honeywell Info. Sys., Inc., 687 F.2d 877 (6th Cir. 1982).

[33] An operating system such as Microsoft Windows is widely distributed and has become the standard operating system in the market.

[34] 592 N.E.2d 431(Ill. App. Dist. 1992).

[35] *Id.* at 433.

intermediate party) may assemble the machine using the operating system of another company to manufacture a computer-operated hoist.[36] In another example, IBM (the intermediate party) may refer a third party to one of its distributors to sell customised software and IBM hardware to the third party.[37] A computer database provider (intermediate party) may enable Dow Jones News to be online to be accessed by the readers.

The level of involvement of intermediate parties and their respective duties in each transaction varies. These intermediate parties may include manufacturers, sellers, publishers or providers of Internet services.[38] The role of such intermediate parties and their different levels of liability will be discussed more fully in § 2.04 Liability in the Chain of Distribution.

§ 2.03 Theories Relevant to Imposing Liability

[1] Overview

Recovery of damage in tort is essential for parties who are not in a contractual relationship or for parties whose contractual claim is barred by statutes of limitation or clauses limiting the remedies for a plaintiff.

Computer systems can comprise various parts, from different manufacturers; therefore, the ultimate users may not be in privity of contract with the manufacturer of the defective parts. Likewise, an architect or a manufacturer of carpets may not have any direct contractual relationship with the owners of a house. In such cases, unless specifically provided otherwise, the only available remedy, for the plaintiff is one in tort. It should be noted that, even if there is a contract between the parties, the statutes of limitation

---

[36] Columbus McKinnon v. China Semiconductor Co., Ltd., 867 F. Supp. 1173 (W.D.N.Y. 1994).
[37] Pied Piper, Inc. v. Datanational Corp., 901 F. Supp. 212 (S.D.W.Va 1995).
[38] See infra § 2.04 Liability in the Chain of Distribution.

relating to the contract may run while relatively unskilled users of the computer systems are unable to discover defects.

I shall conduct some comparative analysis of tort law relating to liability for injury caused by information in traditional and in electronic form. This considers whether the authorities pertaining to liabilities on information in traditional form have an impact for liabilities on information in electronic form, particularly computer programs and human-readable information in electronic form such as information on the Internet or in online databases. Analysis of works such as architectural plans and structures, maps or books containing factual information, and works with utilitarian characteristics will be of particular importance in providing the basis for the comparative analysis with information in electronic form.

This analysis of the case law shows that the distinctions between statements and acts; between physical and economic injuries; and the strict rule which has differentiated between the circumstances in which plaintiffs may bring causes of actions either in tort or in contract are of diminishing importance, in circumstances especially where the special skill of defendants and a limited class of plaintiffs are involved. Many transactions involving information in electronic form are of such a kind.

[2] Fraud

[a] Reasons for Bringing Fraud Claims

This section concerns transactions involving computer programs and services related to supply of computer programs. Computer suppliers generally make representations as to the capabilities of the system or other collateral services to attract clients. The end users may not necessarily acquire the computer programs from the manufacturers. However, in many cases, it must be noted that the manufacturers attempt to establish a direct contractual relationship with the end-users by licensing the computer programs. The claim of fraud in inducement is advantageous to plaintiffs in several important respects.

When there is a contract between the parties, one of the reasons for claiming fraud is to circumvent contractual restrictions and provisions.[39] It takes the transaction out of the scope of the contracts between the parties, of clauses limiting liability. The claimants may be able to extend a limitation period[40] or introduce evidence that contradicts contractual provisions despite the parol evidence rule.[41]

The distinction between fraud and misrepresentation normally depends upon whether a representation was made knowingly or recklessly; however, in some jurisdictions, the destinction is not as clear. Plaintiffs' decisions to bring fraud or misrepresentation may depend on the courts' acceptance of such claims in different circumstances.

[b] England

In England, a plaintiff may bring an action in deceit when 1) a false representation of an existing fact is made knowingly or recklessly, 2) with the intention that it shall be acted upon, and 3) the plaintiff acts upon the representation and suffers damage.[42]

Therefore, a statement of present intention as to future conduct or promise, when not fulfilled, may not be considered as deceit unless the statement of fact involved in the promise was not true or there was no intention to fulfil the promises made. Mere puff is considered inadequate for bringing an action for deceit. The determination as to whether a statement is considered mere puff

---

[39] R. T. NIMMER, THE LAW OF COMPUTER TECHNOLOGY ¶ 10.04, 10-7(1992); C.TAPPER, COMPUTER LAW 239-40 (1986).
[40] AccuSystems, Inc. v. Honeywell Info. Sys., Inc., 580 F. Supp. 474, 482 (S.D.N.Y.1984).
[41] APLications Inc. v. Hewlett-Packard Co., 501 F. Supp. 129 (S.D.N.Y. 1980).
[42] Pasley v. Freeman (1789) 3 T.R. 51; Derry v. Peek (1889) 14 App. Cas. 337 (H.L.(E.)); Bradford Building Society v. Borders [1941] 2 All E.R. 205, 211, (H.L.) (Viscount Maugham).

may depend on the circumstances of the transaction.[43]

Where there is a contract between the parties, the Misrepresentation Act 1967 may apply. Section 2(1) of the Misrepresentation Act 1967 provides that a person may be held liable for damages for making a misrepresentation, notwithstanding that the misrepresentation is not made fraudulently.[44] If there is no contract between the parties, under *Hedley Byrne & Co. Ltd. v. Heller & Partners Ltd.*,[45] careless statements recklessly but honestly made would not be actionable in fraud but actionable in negligence if there are circumstances to disclose a duty to be careful.[46] Therefore, "the tort of deceit is needed for those cases where a fraudulent statement has induced a person to act to his detriment otherwise than by entering into a contract."[47]

Therefore, a plaintiff who incurred damage due to fraud may assert remedies under the Misrepresentation Act 1967, common law rules pertaining to fraud, and common law rules pertaining to innocent misrepresentation, should that ever be appropriate. If a plaintiff can satisfy the heavy burden of proof to establish fraud, the defendant is liable for all damages directly flowing from the misstatement, liability is not limited to foreseeable damage.

It should be noted that in England, the law regarding innocent

---

[43] Andrews v. Hopkinson [1957] 1 Q.B. 229.

[44] c. 7 ("Where a person has entered into a contract after a misrepresentation has been made to him by another party thereto and as a result thereof he has suffered loss, then, if the person making the misrepresentation would be liable to damages in respect thereof had the misrepresentation been made fraudulently, that person shall be so liable notwithstanding that the misrepresentation is not made fraudulently, unless he proves that he had reasonable ground to believe and *did* believe up to the time the contract was made that the facts represented were true.").

[45] [1964] A.C. 465 (H.L.(E.)).

[46] *Id.* at 508 (Lord Hodson).

[47] 10th Report of the Law Report Committee (Innocent Misrepresentation), cmmd. 1782. para. 22 at 11 (1962).

Chapter 2

misrepresentation is designed to restrict freedom of contract in cases "where one party is in a much weaker position to the other, either through lack of expert knowledge or absence of professional advice, or because he is presented with a standard form of contract to which no alteration is permitted."[48]

In England, the Unfair Contract Terms Act 1977, and possibly the Unfair Terms in Consumer Contracts Regulations 1999 provide comprehensive rules, including rules for consumer transactions to restrict unfair contractual terms. Such rules may be used against the representors and the suppliers of the contractual terms to restrict contractual terms excluding or limiting express or implied terms.[49]

Therefore, in England, if there is a contract between the parties, the strict statutory control over contractual terms provided by the Misrepresentation Act 1967, the Unfair Contract Terms Act 1977, and the Unfair Terms in Consumer Contracts Regulations 1999 makes it unnecessary to invoke fraud for the plaintiffs to seek remedies.[50]

Whereas in the United States, in order to avoid contractual restrictions the buyer may be required to bring a suit in tort for deceit.[51] The law regarding negligent misrepresentation is not designed actively to control contractual terms in the United States. The freedom to decide contractual terms is emphasised

---

[48] *Id.* para. 23 at 12.
[49] *See infra* § 2.03 Theories Relevant To Imposing Liability [3] Negligence [iv] Implication of Restrictions on Contractual Terms.
[50] *See supra*, for the Unfair Contract Terms Act 1977 (c. 50) and the Unfair Terms in Consumer Contracts Regulations 1999; *see infra* § 2.03 Theories Relevant To Imposing Liability [3] Negligence [b] England [iv] Implication of Restrictions on Contractual Terms and § 3.07 Construction and Statutory Controls on Contractual Terms [4] Standard Form Contracts and Consumers [b] England.
[51] *See infra* § 2.03 Theories Relevant To Imposing Liability [2] Fraud [c] United States.

and all the contractual terms are supposedly valid if such terms are in accordance with the required language and format unless fraudulent misrepresentation is involved.[52]

[i] Information in Traditional Form

In *Langridge v. Levy*,[53] it was held that the son of the purchaser of a gun could recover compensation for the injury he sustained under the theory of fraud from the defendant who knowingly made a false representation that the gun was safe. The court stated that "The warranty between these parties has not the effect of a contract; it is no more than a representation; but it is no less."[54]

In *Andrews v. Hopkinson*,[55] based on a representation by a dealer in second-hand cars, the plaintiff hire-purchased the car from the finance company which purchased the car from the seller. The defendant stated that "It's a good little bus; I would stake my life on it; you will have no trouble with it."[56] The plaintiff was injured because the drag-link joint of the steering mechanism had failed owing to the badly worn condition of the socket and the ball. It was held that that such statement was a warranty that the car was in good condition and reasonably safe and fit for use on a highway.[57] The court held that the plaintiff entered into the hire-purchase agreement on the basis of the warranty and could enforce the warranty against the dealer.[58]

As in *Langridge v. Levy*, and *Andrews v. Hopkinson*, the direct contractual relationship between the parties may not be present in many cases, nevertheless, certain express representations may be considered warranties.

---

[52] *See* U.C.C. § 2-316 (1998).
[53] (1837) 2 M. & W. 519.
[54] *Id.* at 532.
[55] [1957] 1 Q.B. 229.
[56] *Id.* at 230.
[57] *Id.* at 232.
[58] *Id.* at 235.

[ii] Information in Electronic Form
[A] General

The users of computer programs do not necessarily have a direct contractual relationship with the creator of computer programs, as users may acquire the computer programs from the retailers, or through a leasing transaction. The users in such transactions would be likely to be obtaining the computer programs based on representations regarding specifications of computer programs. If there are express representations, as in *Langridge v. Levy*, and *Andrews v. Hopkinson* they may be regarded as warranties.

If a buyer buys a computer system from a distributor, relying on the misstatement of the original supplier of the computer system that the system is fit for providing efficient book-keeping, the original supplier may be held liable. In such a case, there can be, between the buyer and the original supplier, a contract collateral to the main contract.[59] In a collateral contract, representations and promises can be considered warranties outside the main contract.

However, it may be noted that in a number of cases, manufacturers of computer programs attempt to establish a direct contractual relationship by licensing agreements with users, despite the existence of intermediaries. Such licensing agreements or sales agreements often contain clauses restricting the use of the computer program in a certain way as well as limiting or excluding remedies available to the users.

In *Mackenzie Patten & Co. v. British Olivetti Ltd.* (B.O.L.),[60] the defendants supplied to the plaintiffs an office computer for book-keeping through a lease transaction involving a third party. Prior to the acquisition of the computer system, the defendant told the plaintiff that the machine would provide an efficient book-keeping service and that the defendants would assemble,

---

[59] Wells v. Buckland Sand [1965] 2 Q.B. 170.
[60] 11 January 1984 (Q.B.) (unreported) LEXIS; 1 C. L. & P. 92 (1984); 48 M.L.R. 344 (1985).

set up and train the plaintiffs' staff. The firm sued the computer supplier for breach of warranty, misrepresentation under section 2 of the Misrepresentation Act 1967 and negligence. In this case, the statement made to induce the plaintiff to enter into a leasing contract was held to constitute collateral, contractual warranties, and such warranties were considered breached by the defendants.

The court found that there was a sales contract between the parties but the plaintiffs were not in the position to pay outright. Nevertheless, the court did examine the content of the "sales contract", Clause 10 stated: "B.O.L.'s liabilities hereunder shall be limited to death or direct physical injury caused by the negligence of B.O.L. or its employees and B.O.L. shall not be liable for any other direct or indirect loss or loss of profits howsoever caused and of whatsoever nature save any losses which cannot lawfully be excluded". Clause 11stated: "This agreement is in lieu of and to the exclusion of all liabilities, obligations and warranties and conditions statutory or otherwise implied or expressed and including those (if any) contained in an order submitted by the user save for any which cannot lawfully be excluded."

In considering this issue, the court asked the question as to "whether it is fair or reasonable to allow reliance on a contract excluding or limiting liability for a breach of contract can only arise after the breach. The nature of the breach and the circumstances in which it occurred cannot possibly be excluded from 'all the circumstances of the case' to which regard must be had".[61] The court held that these clauses did not satisfy the provision of the Unfair Contract Terms Act 1977 in terms of reasonableness.

Davis J. did not embark on the misrepresentation or negligence claims, as the breach of warranty theory had provided adequate remedies to the plaintiffs; however, he noted that this could be examined if the plaintiffs sought to uphold their alternative bases

---

[61] *Id.*; George Mitchell (Chester hall) Ltd. v. Finney Lock *See*ds Ltd. [1983] Q.B. 284, 301-302 (Lord Denning M.R.).

if the decision were challenged.

Mackenzie Pattern & Co. v. British Olivetti Ltd. illustrates typical transactions for acquiring computer systems by leasing where an action based on breach of warranty and the application of the Misrepresentation Act 1967 was possible.

[B] In the Context of Professional Liability - Disparity of Expertise

The gap of knowledge between the parties creates the strong presumption that the representations made by the defendants are to be relied on.

In *Mackenzie Patten & Co. v. British Olivetti Ltd.*,[62] the plaintiffs conveyed their specific needs to the defendants, and the defendants orally gave assurances as to the suitability of the computer system, both in terms of the purpose of the plaintiffs and in terms of operation by the plaintiffs' employees. The defendants had special knowledge and expertise in the field, whereas the plaintiffs were entirely ignorant in the field. The statements of the defendants were made with the intention of inducing the plaintiffs to enter into a transaction with the defendants and were in fact relied on by the plaintiffs.

[c] United States
[i] Requisites, Information in Traditional Form

In the United States, the definition of fraud is different depending on the state laws applicable to each case. If fraud is proved, punitive damages can be awarded.[63] For instance, in Ohio, the elements of fraud are as follows: (1) There must be an actual or implied representation or concealment of a matter of fact (2) which relates to the present or past, (3) which is material to the transactions and, (4) which is false when made. (5) The statement must be made with knowledge of its falsity, or with reckless

---

[62] 11 January 1984 (Q.B.) (unreported) LEXIS; 1 C. L. & P. 92 (1984); 48 M.L.R. 344 (1985).

[63] *See* Glovatorium, Inc. v. NCR Corp., 648 F.2d 658, 663 (9th Cir. 1982).

disregard for whether it is true or not and, (6) with the intent to mislead the other party into relying upon it. (7) The other party must be ignorant of the fact averred, causing (8) justifiable reliance and (9) injury resulting as a consequence of such reliance.[64]

Fraudulent statements may be used to induce plaintiffs to enter into contracts. Fraud in the inducement in *JoAnn Homes at Bellmore, Inc. v. Dworetz*,[65] under the law of New York State required that there was a representation of fact, which was either untrue and known to be untrue or recklessly made, and which was offered to deceive the other party and to induce it to act upon it, causing injury.[66] In *JoAnn Homes at Bellmore, Inc. v. Dworetz*, the seller represented that the property would be "156 legal building plots"; however, the land contained insufficient fill and the shoreline was not properly sloped, not meeting the required standard set by the ordinances of the town of Hemstead. There was evidence that the defendants had known that there was not enough fill to complete the job, as reported by engineers. Despite this, the defendants continuously made assurance as to the suitability of the property.[67] The court held that the purchase of "156 legal building plots", in light of the nature of the property conveyed and in view of the negotiations that preceded the contract, this statement was intended to guarantee the sufficiency of the fill and the existence of proper shorelines.[68] As in this case of property, plaintiffs often do not have the expertise to make intelligent decisions about the characteristics of the subject matter of the transactions. This may also be true in transactions involving information in electronic form, such as computer programs.

---

[64] Block v. Block, 135 N.E. 2d 857, 858 (Ohio 1956); *see also* RESTATEMENT (SECOND) OF TORTS § 525-26 (1979).
[65] 250 N.E.2d 214 (N.Y. 1969).
[66] *Id.* at 119.
[67] *Id.*
[68] *Id.* at 120.

When it is alleged that the contract was obtained fraudulently, the action of fraud may be preferred over the action based on contract, in which remedies available are controlled by written agreement. If the claim based on fraud is allowed, restriction of remedies under contractual terms may be avoided and the obligation outside the contract may be created as a result.

[ii] Information in Electronic Form

In this section, I am considering examples of cases in Minnesota and New York states to show the diversity of law with regard to fraud.

[A] Minnesota Law

In *Clements Auto Co. v. Service Bureau Corp.*,[69] under Minnesota law, the plaintiff was engaged in the business of electronic data processing. The defendant agreed to furnish data processing services to the plaintiff. The defendant stated that the proposed data processing system would be capable of supplying to the company sufficient information, when fully implemented, and would be effective for inventory control. The defendant also stated that there were error-control features in the system, and made specific representations about the suitability and capability of the input device used in the data processing system.

The trial court enumerated the elements of a fraud in Minnesota as follows: 1) there must be a representation; 2) that representation must be false; 3) it must have to do with a past or present fact; 4) that fact must be material; 5) it must be susceptible of knowledge 6) the representor must know it to be false or, alternatively, must assert it as his own knowledge without knowing whether it is true or false; 7) the representor must intend to have the other person induced to act, or to justify acting upon it; 8) that person must be so induced to act or to justify acting; 9) that person's action must be in reliance upon the representation; 10)

---

[69] 444 F.2d 169 (8th Cir. 1971).

that person must suffer damage; and, 11) that damage must be attributable to the misrepresentation - i.e., the statement must be the proximate cause of the injury.[70]

In Minnesota, the element of scienter, or intent to deceive, or even recklessness is not necessary to bring an action for fraud.[71] There is a right of recovery when loss results from reliance upon false statements. An action for misrepresentation could be maintained, even when the contract disclaims all warranties.[72]

In this case, the court determined that merger and disclaimer provisions in the contract negated reliance on the representations. However, the inequality of knowledge between the parties in the computer field was considered and it was found that the reliance on the representation was justified.[73] The plaintiffs were awarded the sum paid to the defendants for data - processing services, increased expenses including the cost of maintenance, clerical personnel, office supplies, and salary to executives. The court imposed the liability on the defendants until that time when the plaintiffs realised that there was no utility in continuing the transaction, explaining that continued reliance of the plaintiffs after that time was not justifiable.[74]

This case shows that contractual terms restricting liability can be considered in the light of the inequality of knowledge between the parties. Such inequality may exist in most of the transactions involving computer programs.

[B] New York Law

In *AccuSystems, Inc.* (AccuSystems) *v. Honeywell Information*

---

[70] *Id.* at 175; *see also* ; Hanson v. Ford Motor Co., 278 F. 2d 586, 591 (8th Cir. 1960).

[71] *Clements,* 444 F. 2d at 176; *see* Swanson v. Domning, 86 N.W. 2d 716, 720-21 (Minn. 1957).

[72] *Clements*, 444 F. 2d at 181.

[73] *Id.* at 184.

[74] *Id.* at 186.

Systems., Inc. (Honeywell),[75] AccuSystems, Inc (AccuSystems) a New York corporation, and its sole shareholder, Selden, sought to establish payroll-processing operations to supply payroll services to clients through the use of Honeywell Information Systems (Honeywell) computers and related software. Honeywell recommended the purchase of hardware known as Level 6 and its related software, the TL-6 operating system. Honeywell represented that the Level 6 and the TL-6 operating system would support 32 terminals on line but advised that the number be kept down to around 20 to achieve faster response time. Honeywell issued a document that provided that the TL operating system had been extensively tested, had been installed in a number of other locations where it was functioning well, and that it was capable of multitasking.[76]

The plaintiff and Honeywell signed three contracts. "OEM Agreement for Computer Equipment, Services and Software Products between Honeywell Information Systems Inc. and AccuSystems Inc." warranted that the equipment sold by Honeywell would be free from defects in workmanship or materials under normal use and service for 30 days and limited Honeywell's liability in contract, tort, or otherwise to the repair or exchange of parts returned to Honeywell as being defective. "OEM Software Product License Supplement" limited Honeywell's liability to AccuSystems in contract, tort or otherwise for any software product licensed to AccuSystems to 10% of the charges paid by AccuSystems to Honeywell for each applicable software product, or $5,000, whichever was less. "Maintenance Service Agreement for Data Processing Equipment between Honeywell Information Systems Inc. and AccuSystems Inc." limited Honeywell's liability in contract, tort, or otherwise to the repair or exchange of

---

[75] 580 F. Supp. 474 (S.D.N.Y. 1984).
[76] *Id.* at 476-77.

parts returned to Honeywell as being defective, and provided that Honeywell would not be liable for any indirect, special or consequential damages. It also provided for the two-year statute of limitation.[77]

After all the contracts were signed on January 17, 1978, the plaintiff having numerous difficulties with Honeywell Level 6 and TL-6, instituted a suit against the defendant on October 8, 1980. The trial testimony established that the TL-6 operating system failed when more than three terminals were in operation; that the TL-6 operating system could only process simple programs; that AccuSystems was the first installation site for the TL-6 operating system; and that no recorded tests of the TL-6 were conducted by Honeywell until more than a year after the sale to AccuSystems. Therefore, Honeywell intentionally made false representations regarding the present status of the system.[78]

Fraud in the inducement under the law of New York State requires a representation of fact, which was known by a presenter to be untrue or recklessly made, offered to deceive plaintiffs and to induce them to act upon the representation, causing injury. It is for the plaintiffs to produce clear and convincing evidence of the fraud.[79]

The court concluded that the representations of the existing capabilities made by Honeywell to the plaintiff prior to the agreement were known to be false or were made recklessly, without knowing whether they were true or false, in order to induce the plaintiffs to enter into an agreement; therefore Honeywell acted with scienter.[80] The court also stated that due to the dynamic growth of the industry, "Selden's reliance on

---

[77] *Id.* at 477.
[78] *Id.* at 481-82.
[79] JoAnn Homes at Bellmore, Inc. v. Dworetz, 250 N.E.2d 214 (N.Y. 1969).
[80] *AccuSystems,* 580 F. Supp. at 482.

Honeywell's representations with respect to the TL-6 operating system was reasonable." Therefore, the two-year limitation period contained in the agreement did not time-bar the plaintiff's claim for fraud in the inducement.[81] The plaintiffs were entitled to damages for their actual pecuniary loss but not for loss of profits.[82]

In *Phoenix Technologies, Inc. v. Quotron Systems, Inc. (Quotron).*,[83] the defendant provided real-time financial market data through a nationwide computer network and the plaintiff purchased the defendant's maintenance and technical support service department. In connection with the purchase, the parties agreed that the plaintiff would provide support services to the defendant's customers who were using the defendant's proprietary hardware, designed for the defendant and its customers. The parties agreed that the defendant or the third party would operate a "Call-In Center" which would receive customer telephone calls and forward requests for technical assistance to the plaintiff; and the plaintiff would provide support service to the defendant's customers, the cost to be paid by the defendant.[84] The plaintiffs alleged that they were fraudulently induced to enter into the service agreement because the defendant concealed the contract transferring the operation of the Call-In Center to IBM, which provided preliminary technical advice over the telephone, reducing return from on-site services provided by the plaintiffs.[85] The court ruled that the special relationship required for a cause of action in fraud could be based on the duty to disclose when one party has superior knowledge not readily available to the plaintiff and knows

---

[81] *Id.*
[82] *See also* APLications Inc. v. Hewlett-Packard Co., 501 F. Supp. 129 (S.D.N.Y. 1980) (applying California law, regarding fraudulent misrepresentation of the response time of the computer system).
[83] 1997 WL 220285 (E.D.Pa 1997), *aff'd*, 135 F.3d 766 (7th Cir. 1997).
[84] *Id.* at *9.
[85] *Id.* at *35.

that the plaintiff is acting and reasonably relying on the basis of mistaken knowledge.[86]

The plaintiffs alleged that the defendant concealed the contract transferring the operations of the Call-In Center to IBM in order to induce the plaintiffs to enter the service agreement. As this claim was considered separate from the breach of contractual claim, an independent claim based on fraud in inducement was duly presented. However, the court found that the defendant did not make a material false representation as the plaintiffs knew that the defendant had entered into an agreement with IBM before signing the service agreement. The plaintiffs failed to prove that the defendant had a duty to disclose as the plaintiffs did not have superior knowledge of the likely effect on plaintiffs if IBM ran the Call-In Center more efficiently, thus reducing the dispatches of plaintiffs' customer engineers.[87] In this case, the court considered that the agreement was between two companies who were knowledgeable and the main issue of the dispute was on the business arrangement and not about defects in computer systems.

[C] In the Context of Professional Liability - Disparity of Expertise

In *Clements Auto Company v. Service Bureau Corporation*,[88] in allowing the claim for fraud, the court emphasised the inequality of knowledge between the parties in justifying the reliance on the representations made by the defendants. Fundamental defects were solely within the defendant's field of expertise, even though, the plaintiff's lack of knowledge of its own operations attributed to its loss.[89]

---

[86] *Id.* at *36.
[87] *Id.* at *37.
[88] 444 F.2d 169 (8th Cir.1971).
[89] *Id.* at 184.

In *AccuSystems, Inc. v. Honeywell Information Systems Inc.*[90], the court rejected Honeywell's contention that it was not reasonable for the plaintiff to rely on the system since Selden had prior computer experience. In reaching this conclusion, the court noted that the TL-6 operating system was different from the other systems that Selden had been familiar with.[91]

The court may have considered that Selden, a sole shareholder of AccuSystems, was in the computer business for a number of years. He was employed by International Business Machines between 1954 and 1964, where he participated in software product development and taught computer science. However, if users of the computer systems are not familiar with the computer technology, it may be more justified for the users to continue to rely on the assurances to repair made by the suppliers of the computer systems.

In *Phoenix Technologies, Inc. v. Quotron Systems, Inc.*[92], the court stated that there was a duty to disclose when one party has superior knowledge not readily available to the other and knows that the other is acting on the basis of mistaken knowledge.[93]

[d] Comparison

The theory of fraud in inducement provides a remedy for those parties who are induced to make a contract. The theory allows them to avoid contractual clauses limiting available remedies and the statutes of limitations.

The essential requisites in all of the cases are as follows: 1) defendants' specific representations and assurances regarding the systems; 2) defendants had special knowledge and skills, (i.e. the gap of knowledge); 3) plaintiffs were induced into contracting with the defendants relying on the specific representations made by the

---

[90] *Accusystems*, 580 F.Supp. 474 (S.D.N.Y. 1984).
[91] *Id.* at 482.
[92] 1997 WL 220285 (E.D.Pa 1997), *aff'd*, 135 F.3d 766 (7th.Cir. 1997).
[93] *Id.* at *35.

defendants; 4) defendants either knew or should have known that the systems would not have worked.

Compared to the cases involving traditional subject matter, it is more likely that in transactions involving computer programs, there will be disparity of expertise between the parties. Courts are willing to find that plaintiffs' reliance is justified and impose a duty on suppliers to perform in accordance with the representations made.

Furthermore, representations regarding present capabilities of a computer system can often be interpreted as representations about the future performance of the systems. Unless specifically warned, unsophisticated users may simply assume that the system will work. The disparity in expertise contributes to users' reliance on such representations.

In the United States, as the defendant's intent to defraud or even recklessness are not essential in some states, claims based on fraud can reasonably be asserted in most cases where plaintiffs incur injury because of false statements. Therefore, the plaintiffs may assert both fraud and negligent misrepresentations for injuries caused by the same statements.[94]

As described above and to be discussed later in the section on negligent misrepresentation, in England, the tort of deceit and negligent misrepresentation may be needed only for those cases where there is no contract between the parties. In such cases, warranty or collateral contract theories also help to impose liability based on representations regarding the quality of articles obtained. If there is a contract between the parties, the plaintiffs may be able to obtain sufficient remedies without invoking a claim based on fraud because of the strict statutory control over contractual terms provided by the Misrepresentation Act 1967, the Unfair Contract Terms Act 1977 and the Unfair Terms in Consumer Contracts

---

[94] Clements Auto Co. v. Serv. Bureau Corp., 444 F.2d 169 (8th Cir.1971).

Regulations 1999.

In the United States, in order to set aside the restrictions in contractual terms, plaintiffs may be required to bring a cause of action based on fraud in inducement. The law regarding negligent misrepresentation is not designed actively to control contractual terms in the United States. As will be described, the cause of action based on negligent misrepresentation may not be allowed unless there is a special relationship between the parties.

[3] Negligence
[a] Introduction
I will discuss negligence in terms of both physical injuries and economic loss in this section. In transactions involving information in electronic form, damage tends to be economic; however, information in electronic form, such as a computer program, may be incorporated in electronic appliances such as medical diagnostic devices or cars, and cause direct physical injury. Therefore, examination of physical injury is needed as well as examination of economic loss.

Physical loss includes injuries to person and property. Economic loss is defined as financial or pecuniary loss that is not produced by or has no connection to personal or physical harm suffered by the plaintiff.[95] Historically, recovery for economic loss has been restricted by concerns with respect to "floodgates" of liability on defendants and a boundary between tort and contract regarding financial interests.[96]

Such a distinction poses difficulties when physical injury is limited to negligently made products themselves. Purchasers of negligently made defective products, in the absence of personal

---

[95] B.S. MARKESINIS & S.F. DEAKIN, TORT LAW 88, 211 (4th ed. 1998).
[96] *See* Spartan Steel & Alloys Ltd. v. Martin & Co. Ltd. [1973] 1 Q.B. 27 (C.A.); E. River S.S. Corp. v. Transamerica Delaval, Inc., 476 U.S. 858 (1986).

injury or property damage other than the defective products themselves, have difficulties in recovering for compensation. Such purchasers tend to resort to fraud in inducement or breach of warranty to seek remedies.[97]

When discussing issues of recovery of economic loss, in England the courts tend to distinguish negligence theory and strict liability theory, whereas in the United States, courts tend not to distinguish in most cases. In England, a number of cases deal with the issue of negligent acts causing economic injuries, whereas there has not been much discussion concerning solely negligent acts causing economic injury in the United States. Courts in the United States tend to emphasise the fact that economic loss is, as a matter of principle, not recoverable under tort theory, without distinguishing strict liability and negligence theory.[98] Therefore, much of the discussion concerning "tort" recovery for economic loss is here presented in the strict liability section.

[b] England
[i] Physical and Economic Injury

Donoghue v. Stevenson[99] provides English and Scottish law's general principle in negligence with respect to physical injury to a person who is not in privity with a defendant or to the property of such a person other than the product itself. A manufacturer of ginger-beer was liable to the ultimate purchaser or consumer of the product for personal injury. This case established the scope of legal duties upon which legal liability is based, without a specific contractual relationship between the parties; as demonstrated in a statement by Lord Atkin of the relationship as comprising, "persons who are so closely and directly affected by my act that I ought

---

[97] *See infra* § 2.03 Theories Relevant To Imposing Liability [3] Negligence [c] United States.

[98] *See E. River*, 476 U.S. at 859, 865, 876; D. B. Gaebler, *Negligence, Economic Loss, and the U.C.C.*, 61 IND. L. J.593, 594 (1986).

[99] [1932] A.C. 562. (H.L. (Sc.)).

Chapter 2

reasonably to have them in contemplation as being so affected when I am directing my mind to the acts or omissions which are called in question."[100] This "neighbour principle" remains valid with respect to physical injury cases.

By contrast, as mentioned above, the courts have generally restricted recovery of pure economic loss with respect to negligent acts, unless arising directly from physical harm. [101] The recovery of economic loss, such as repairing or replacing cost or lost profits, presents problems under tort law.

The basic rule regarding the distinctions of recovery of physical and economic damages is explained in *Spartan Steel & Alloys Ltd. v. Martin & Co. Ltd.*[102] The court held that the physical damage to one melt and the loss of the profit of that melt while being processed when the electricity was cut off was recoverable; such profit was considered consequential economic loss originating from the physical damage to the melt, but not the loss of profit on the other work which would have been done but for the interruption of the supply. Such loss was considered purely economic.[103]

Lord Denning gave reasons as to why the plaintiffs were not able to recover in this particular case. The first consideration was that allowing recovery for the loss of the profit on the work would expose the electricity board to liability for damages to the inhabitants en masse. Parliament did not intend to expose the electricity board to such liability. The second consideration was that the nature of the hazard was of a type ordinarily expected without

---

[100] *Id.* at 580.
[101] *See* Spartan Steel & Alloys Ltd. v. Martin & Co. Ltd. [1973] 1 Q.B. 27 (C.A.); Muirhead v. Indus. Tank Specialities Ltd. [1986] 1 Q.B. 507. (C.A.) (holding the supplier of a defective pump liable to the builder of a tank for the plaintiff's lobsters).
[102] [1973] 1 Q.B. 27 (C.A.).
[103] *Id.* at 39.

seeking compensation from anyone. The third consideration was that there would be no end to claims for economic loss. The loss of profit here would be foreseeable but could be extended to an indeterminate class of plaintiffs and to an indeterminate amount of damage for the electricity board to bear. The fourth consideration was that for such a hazard, the risk of economic loss should be shared by the whole community. The fifth consideration was that "the law provides for deserving cases." Physical injury can be recovered if the defendant was negligent in cutting off the electricity supply causing actual physical damage to person or property. Recovery for actual physical damage to person or property is adequate.[104]

However, some of the reasons why the electricity board should not be held liable may not be applicable to the other cases with private defendants, a determinate class of plaintiffs, and a determinate amount of losses. It should also be taken into account that the electricity board has a public function to supply electricity.

Economic loss may be caused in circumstances where a determinate class of plaintiffs and a determinate amount of damages are involved. Pure economic loss, such as repairing or replacing cost or lost profits, is normally recoverable based on the expectation measure under the contract theory rather than the reliance measure under the tort theory.[105] Even though it is reasonable, generally, to give greater protection to personal health and safety, value in tangible property has become an important interest worthy of protection under the tort principle.[106]

Recent tort cases confirm that the recovery of economic loss caused by negligent statement or act is allowed, despite the absence

---

[104] *Id.* at 37-39.
[105] [1986] 1 Q.B. 507, 562 (C.A.).
[106] *See* MARKESINIS & DEAKIN, *supra* note 95 at 88-89.

of privity, where damages are determinable in amount, plaintiffs identifiable, and where the defendant, with special skills, has undertaken the task and consciously assumed the responsibility.[107]

[ii] Defective Articles, Compensation for Lack of Quality

Murphy v. Brentwood D.C.,[108] is said to establish the rule that tortious liability is not to be imposed in cases where defects in quality have not caused injury to the occupier or another property. In this case, the recovery of economic loss, namely, the diminution in the value of the house, was denied against the local authority that passed the plans for construction in reliance on negligent advice from an independent contractor. According to this holding, the preventive cost (the cost incurred to prevent such known imminent danger) is considered economic in nature and thus is not recoverable in the absence of a sufficiently proximate relationship.[109] Such preventive cost is awarded only if such defects remain a potential source of injury to persons or property on neighbouring land or the highway.[110] Therefore, according to Lord Bridge, the occupier plaintiff can recover only where there is an injury, whereas the neighbours can be protected from injury. This would lead to the conclusion that the buyers of goods in general may not be entitled directly to pursue tortious responsibility to remote sellers for lack of quality. A friend of a purchaser of ginger beer,

---

[107] *See* White v. Jones [1995] 2 A.C. 207 (H.L.(E.)); Henderson v. Merrett Syndicates Ltd. [1995] 2 A.C. 145 (H.L.(E.)); MARKESINIS & DEAKIN, *supra* note 95 at 88 (4th ed.1998); J. Stapleton, *Duty of Care and Economic Loss: A Wider Agenda*, 107 L.Q.R. 249, 295-96 (1991); J. Stapleton, *The Normal Expectancies Measure in Tort Damages*, 113 L.Q.R. 257, 260-61 (1997) (stating that normal expectancy is awarded when "the law re-positions the plaintiff to the position he would have reached by the date of trial ...had the defendant not acted tortiously").

[108] [1991] 1 A.C. 398. (H.L.(E)).

[109] *Id.* at 475(Lord Bridge).

[110] *Id.*

such as in *Donoghue v. Stevenson*,[111] would not have recovered for the purchase price of the drink from the manufacturer had she discove-red the defects in the drink before consuming it.[112]

This court denied recovery for fear of creating liability in an indeterminate amount for an indeterminate time to an indeterminate class[113] and exposing the manufacturer to obligations of an indefinitely transmissible warranty of quality.[114] The court upheld the distinctions between contract and tort law and parties' freedom to define their liabilities. Furthermore, it was considered more appropriate to deal with the responsibility of a local authority by the enactment of special laws.[115]

Murphy v. Brentwood D.C.,[116] limited the circumstances when tortious liability is allowed. Those circumstances include, where there is a contractual or a special relationship of proximity[117] or where there exist dangerous characteristics of products to the health or safety of any person, or risk of damage to any other property belonging to the plaintiff in negligence.[118] The *Murphy* case regarded the earlier case, *Junior Books Ltd. v. Veitchi Co.*

---

[111] [1932] A.C. 562. (H.L. (Sc.)).

[112] [1991] 1 A.C. 398, 475 (H.L.(E.).

[113] Ultramares Corp. v. Touche, 174 N.E. 441, 444 (N.Y. 1931).

[114] Murphy v. Brentwood D.C. [1991] 1 A.C. 398, 480-81 (H.L.(E.)).

[115] *Id.* at 481(Lord Bridge) ("It would be remarkable to find that similar obligations in the nature of a transmissible warranty of quality, applicable to buildings of every kind and subject to no such limitations or exclusions as are imposed by the Act of 1972, could be derived from the builder's common law duty of care."); Defective Premises Act 1972 (c.35), s. 1; W.V.H. ROGERS, WINFIELD & JOLOWICZ ON TORT 321-22 (15th ed.1998). *But see* Invercargill City Council v. Hamlin [1996] A.C. 624 (accepting that, in the Privy Council, in the absence of such special laws, courts in other countries may decline to follow Murphy v. Brentwood D.C.).

[116] [1991] 1 A.C. 398(H.L.(E.)).

[117] *Id.* at 475, 480 (H.L.(E.)).

[118] *Id.* at 466.

Ltd.,[119] to be within the situations where "the tortious liability arose out of a contractual relationship with professional people, the duty extended to take reasonable care not to cause economic loss to the client by the advice given."[120]

Junior Books Ltd. v. Veitchi Co. Ltd.[121] challenged such bars to the recovery of economic loss in tort and held that, in some cases, there may exist sufficient proximity for imposition of liability. Even though the holding of this case has been weakened by subsequent decisions, the essence of the holding of this case may have a significant implication for cases when applied to transactions with regard to the supply of information in electronic form.

In the *Junior Books* case, the defendant was sub-contracted by a building company to lay flooring for the plaintiff. It was held that the plaintiff was able to recover from the sub-contractor, the cost of repairing the floor and compensation for the less profitable operation of the business due to the heavy cost of maintenance of the floor. It was explained that the "floodgates" argument against the recovery of economic loss was overcome by the fact that the defendants certainly knew or had the means of knowing the identity of the plaintiff (*determinable, known or identifiable plaintiffs*). The injury to the plaintiff was considered a direct and foreseeable result of negligence by the appellants *(foreseeability, known specific plaintiffs)*. The fact that the defendant was nominated as "a specialist sub-contractor" by the plaintiff was considered an

---

[119] [1983] 1 A.C. 520 (H.L.(Sc.)).

[120] [1991] 1 A.C. 398, 466, 481 (H.L.(E.)(stating, "There may of course, be situations where, even in the absence of contract, there is a special relationship of proximity between builder and building owner which is sufficiently akin to contract to introduce the element of reliance so that the scope of the duty of care owed by the builder to the owner is wi*de* enough to embrace purely economic loss. The decision in *Junior Books Ltd. v. Veitchi Co. Ltd.* [1983] 1 A.C. 520 can, I believe, only be understood on this basis.").

[121] [1983] 1 A.C. 520. (H.L.(Sc.)).

indication that the defendant assumed the responsibility and the plaintiff had relied upon their skill and knowledge (*assumption of responsibility and skill and knowledge relied on*).[122] It was probably crucial to the plaintiff's victory in the *Junior Books* case that, on the facts, the plaintiff had relied upon the defendant's skill and knowledge and there was only one possible plaintiff and one type of damage and both were known to, and not just foreseeable by, the defendant. The fact that there was an expressed representation regarding quality must have worked in favour of the plaintiff. The problem of an indefinitely transmissible warranty of quality may be avoided by the fact that there are known specific plaintiffs.

In the *Junior Books* case, Lord Fraser cited the holding in *Voli v. Inglewood Shire Council*,[123] Australian case, that if an architect undertakes "to design a stage to bear only some specified weight, he would not be liable for the consequences of someone thereafter negligently permitting a greater weight to be put upon it."[124]

Conversely, if the stage could not bear the weight contrary to an expressed presentation regarding specified weight or other qualities, liability based on the expressed specification might be imposed in respect to the quality, as such express representation may induce plaintiffs to purchase the goods. The cases with respect to the liability of an architect or an engineer offer helpful guidance in considering the liability of a computer consultant.

It is easier to place the *Junior Books* case, because of the special skills possessed by the defendants which were relied upon, as an extension of a well established case regarding negligent misstatement, namely, *Hedley Byrne & Co. Ltd. v. Heller & Partners Ltd.*[125] In the Hedley Byrne case, liability was imposed

---

[122] *Id.* at 546.
[123] (1963) 110 C.L.R 74, 85 (Windeyer J.).
[124] *Junior*, [1983] A.C. at 533-34.
[125] [1964] A.C. 465 (H.L.(E.)).

in circumstances where there was a special relationship between the parties such that the representor was deemed voluntarily to assume or undertake the responsibility, and that the representor should know that another person was relying on his or her special skill.[126]

It has to be noted that section 1 the Contracts (Rights of Third Parties) Act 1999[127] provides that a third party to a contract may in his or her own right enforce a term of the contract if the contract expressly provides that he or she may, or the term purports to confer a benefit to the said party and the said party is expressly identified in the contract.

[iii] Rendering Services

The opinion expressed regarding pure economic damage based on the principle of assumption of responsibility in *Hedley Byrne & Co. Ltd. v. Heller & Partners Ltd.*[128] has been reinforced by recent decisions. In *Henderson v. Merrett Syndicates Ltd.*,[129] it was held that if someone has special knowledge which he undertakes to apply for the assistance of another, and that other person relies upon such skill, the *Hedley Byrne* principle should extend beyond the provision of information and advice to include performance of other services.[130]

In the *Henderson* case, the plaintiffs, underwriting members or "Names" at Lloyds, alleged that defendant managing agents were negligent in their conduct of the plaintiff's underwriting affairs, and in breach of their legal obligations. Those "Names" were either directly in contractual relationship with the managing

---

[126] *Id.* at 503 (H.L.(E.)) (Lord Morris).
[127] c. 31.
[128] [1983] 1 A.C. 520 (H.L.(Sc.)).
[129] [1995] 2 A.C. 145 (H.L.(E)).
[130] *But see id.* at 196 (The House of Lords carefully avoided discussion of the *Junior Books* case and refused to approve it in *Henderson v. Merrett Syndicates Ltd.*).

agent (direct Name) or indirectly connected with the managing agent by becoming a member of a syndicate which was managed by another managing agent(indirect Name). In the latter case, the Name's underwriting agent entered into a sub-agency agreement appointing the managing agent as sub-agent to act in relation to the Name.[131]

In the *Henderson* case, the court held that for both types of Names, the managing agents had assumed a direct responsibility. Liability could be imposed if the relationship between the parties was based upon the defendant's special skill or knowledge, and if there was reliance by the plaintiff. There also has to be an assumption of responsibility by the defendant in holding himself or herself up as possessing special expertise to advise on the suitability of risks to be underwritten.[132] Lord Goff stated that if a person assumes responsibility to another, in respect of certain services, there is no reason why she or he should not be liable to damages to the other, in respect of economic loss that flows from the negligent performance of those services.[133]

Therefore, the imposition of liability might be based on a professional or quasi-professional relationship not only for giving negligent advice but also for acting as an advisor, requiring the exercise of reasonable care and skill.[134]

Extension of the *Hedley Byrne* principle liability to acts in the form of negligent services seems appropriate, as giving or not giving professional advice can also mean giving or not giving instructions to act: it is often not possible to distinguish whether a certain professional service was rendered in the form of acts or statements.

---

[131] *Id.* at 170.
[132] *Id.* at 182.
[133] *Id.* at 181.
[134] *Id.* at 180-81.

Furthermore, Lord Goff stated that irrespective of whether there is a contractual relationship between the parties:

> [A]n assumption of responsibility coupled with the concomitant reliance may give rise to a tortious duty of care, and in consequence, unless his contract precludes him from doing so, the plaintiff, who has available to him concurrent remedies in contract and tort, may choose that remedy which appears to him to be the most advantageous.[135]

This principle laid out by Lord Goff is helpful in holding remote computer manufacturers responsible for their negligent acts, i.e., supplying defective computer parts, if there is a relationship between the parties based upon special skill or knowledge in the field of computer technology.

The *Junior Books* and the *Henderson* case both dealt with professional or special skills, and identifiable plaintiffs claiming a determinate amount of damages. These cases have significant implications regarding transactions involving bespoke computer programs.

[iv] Implication of Restrictions on Contractual Terms

When manufacturers of goods are not in privity with end users as the goods are distributed through different distributors and to retailers, the final purchasers may need to reach the manufacturer through a series of contractual indemnifications. Therefore, statutory restrictions on contractual terms have an impact on the remedies to which the end users are finally entitled.

On the contrary, if there are contracts between the parties, plaintiffs may resort to tortious remedies in order to avoid

---

[135] *Id.* at 194.

contractual terms limiting or excluding available remedies. However, if statutory control over contractual terms limiting or excluding the remedies is stricter, there is less need to resort to different theories in tort for recovery.

Furthermore, recently, there have been more attempts to illuminate the difference between tortious and contractual remedies, as discussed above in the *Henderson*[136] case in certain limited circumstances.

In England, such statutory control over contractual terms is stricter than in the United States, especially with respect to consumer or standard form transactions.

For instance, the Unfair Contract Terms Act 1977 imposes a requirement of reasonableness in excluding liabilities. Section 3 imposes a requirement of reasonableness on contractual terms excluding or restricting any liability for breach of contract between contracting parties where one of them deals as consumer or on the other's written standard terms of business. Section 2(2) of the Unfair Contract Terms Act 1977 imposes a requirement of reasonableness on contractual terms excluding or restricting liability for negligence.

For transactions involving sale of goods, implied terms that the goods supplied under the contract are of satisfactory quality[137] and implied terms that goods supplied under the contract are reasonably fit for that purpose[138] are subject to the test of reasonableness.[139] For consumer transactions involving the sale of goods, such implied terms for quality cannot be excluded.[140]

For transactions involving the supply of services, exclusion of

---

[136] *Id.*
[137] Sale of Goods Act 1979 as amended in 1994 (c. 54), s. 14(2).
[138] *Id.* at s.14(3).
[139] Unfair Contract Terms Act 1977 (c. 50), ss. 2 and 3.
[140] *Id.* at s. 6(2).

implied terms as to reasonable care and skill[141] is subject to the test of reasonableness.[142]

The restriction of liabilities for the express obligation of the original supplier would be severely restricted in the light of the reasonableness test and common law principle.

[v] Omission of Act

It has been argued that failure to utilise computer technology may amount to negligence. Such duties include adopting, using and operating appropriately certain technology.[143] The duty required may vary depending on the injury caused and the type of defendants.

The courts have to determine whether to impose a duty to be equipped with the technology in accordance with the industry standard or some higher duty considered necessary by the courts. It may technically be possible to implement the latest systems available; yet, it may not be feasible to implement it due to the fast development in computer technology.[144] However, a number of cases concerning physical damage requires not only the duty to adopt certain devices but also knowledge of the specific danger involved.

The Lady Gwendolen[145] held a shipowner responsible for ensuring that the shipmaster would be competent to use radar and for preventing the shipmaster from activities which might endanger the safety of life at sea.[146] In this case, the shipowner had knowledge that the shipmaster tended to speed excessively.

---

[141] Supply of Goods and Services Act 1982 (c. 29), s. 13.
[142] Unfair Contract Terms Act 1977 (c. 50), ss. 2 and 3.
[143] *See* TAPPER, *supra* note 39, at 246-50.
[144] *See infra* § 2.03 Theories Relevant To Imposing Liability [4] Negligent Misrepresen-tation [d] Defences for Negligence.
[145] *The Lady Gwendolen* [1965] 2 All E.R. 283.
[146] *Id.* at 302.

In *Grand Champion Tankers v. Norpipe A/S (The Marion)*,[147] the court imposed a duty to use current navigational charts, destroy or segregate from the current chart the obsolete or superseded charts, and keep them up-to-date at all times,[148] by refusing to allow shipowners to limit their liability under the Merchant Shipping Act 1894,[149] as amended by the Merchant Shipping (Liability of Shipowners and Others) Act 1958.[150]

The duty of the defendants may be different in accordance with the kind of potential injuries and with their skills. When potential danger is high, industry custom may be found totally inadequate as in *Henderson v. Henry E. Jenkins & Sons*.[151] Furthermore, once the essential system is adopted, keeping such system up to date is also important. In transactions with respect to computer technology, omission of practice accepted as standard in industry may be considered negligent. However, it may be difficult to determine the standard in a rapidly developing industry. It may also be difficult for courts to determine when such a standard in industry is not adequate.[152]

[vi] Transactions Involving Special Skills

The supply of computer technology can involve a supply of tangibles and/or a supply of services. In many transactions involving customised computers, as opposed to mass-marketed computers, the subcontractors or suppliers may hold themselves out to possess considerable skill and knowledge, which may be

---

[147] [1984] A.C. 563 (H.L.(E.)).
[148] *Grand Chanpion*, [1984] A.C. at 573.
[149] c. 60.
[150] c. 62; *Grand Chanpion* [1984] at 571.
[151] [1970] A.C. 282. (H.L.(E.)) (holding the defendant liable for the knowledge of special facts which could render their system defective even though they had no knowledge of the defects).
[152] For further discussion, *see infra* § 2.03 Theories Relevant To Imposing Liability [3] Negligence [c] United States [vi] Omission of Act; *see also, see* I. J. LLOYD, *supra* note 1, at 435-36 (enumerating various indusyry sandards).

relied on by the ultimate user. As there can be various financial reasons for avoiding direct contracts, it is possible that there is no contract between the parties even if there is direct negotiation between them. In such cases, the same reasoning for imposing liability under the *Henderson*[153] case, can also be applicable.

In transactions involving computer programs, users often tend to buy articles containing computer programs while relying on the expertise of suppliers, and the user may have no direct contractual relationship with the supplier. User's reliance on specification or advertisement may be justified because these are express representations of the quality of the programs and there is disparity in expertise. In accordance with the *Henderson*,[154] case, the user of such programs may be able to sue the manufacturer directly. However, it may be noted that a number of computer programs are meant to be licensed directly to their users. Such licensing agreements arguably create privity between the users and manufacturers. The contractual terms in such licensing agreements, if found valid, are controlled by the Unfair Contract Terms Act 1977, the Unfair Terms in Consumer Contracts Regulations 1999, and the Misrepresentation Act 1967.

The recent expansion of tortious liability may be criticised for awarding damages based on a contractual expectation measure. Under tort theory, an injured party should be placed in the same position that he would have been in had the tort not been committed. However, Dr. Stapleton proposes using the term "normal expectancy measure," that includes improvements in a victim's position that a person in a defendant's position would normally achieve. She argues that once the defendant has undertaken the task or has chosen to act despite the absence of privity relationship, the law of tort assesses damages according

---

[153] [1995] 2 A.C. 145 (H.L.(E)).
[154] *Id.*

to what could have happened had the defendant used care, and the measure of damages which the plaintiff in tort receives are normal expectancies.[155] Therefore, the holding in *Junior Books Ltd. v. Veitchi Co. Ltd.* or *White v. Jones*[156] awarded no more than the ordinary tortious measure of normal expectancies: neither case recognised an obligation on the defendants to achieve improvements in the plaintiff's normal expectancies. As stated in the holding of *White v. Jones*, the law of tort should be able to offer an effective remedy when the law of contract is unable to provide the remedy.[157]

[vii] Professional Liability of Computer Programmers

Professional liabilities of lawyers, accountants, or doctors have been well recognised by the courts. Imposition of professional liability on computer consultants could have posed difficult problems since they are not within the scope of the recognised categories of professions upon which the courts have imposed professional liability. Nevertheless, English courts seem to accept the idea that computer consultants have special skills to design and to implement computer programs, and disparity in expertise supports the fact that the plaintiff is justified in relying on the special skills of the defendants. It is reasonable for clients to rely on a computer supplier's representation as to the function of the computer programs based on the supplier's knowledge and skills in the field of computer technology, especially in cases where the supply of a customised computer system is involved.

Recognition of the transactions involving special skills and assumption of duties served as a sufficient basis for Judge Hicks to determine that a computer consultant was liable for negligence in

---

[155] *See*, Stapleton, *Normal Expectancies, supra* note 107, at 278-80.
[156] [1995] 2 A.C. 207 (H.L.(E)).
[157] *Id.* at 262.

Stephenson Blake (Holdings) Ltd. v. Streets Heaver Ltd.[158]

In the *Stephenson Blake* case, the plaintiff, Stephenson Blake (Holdings) was a manufacturing and trading company and the defendant was in the business of providing specialised computerised information systems and a business planning consultancy. The defendant acted as consultant to the plaintiff in connection with the acquisition by the plaintiff of a computerised accounting system. The plaintiff purchased the system recommended by the defendant from the third party. The plaintiff was dissatisfied with it and replaced the whole system and sued the defendant for negligence and breach of contract. The court held that the defendant had a duty to use due care and skill to ensure that the recommended system conformed to the description of the system specification and, if it were impossible to recommend such a system, to warn the plaintiff in plain terms of that fact and its likely consequences. There was also a general duty to use care and skill to ensure that the suppliers were competent and used sound methods, and that the recommended system would carry out efficiently the functions for which the plaintiff required it and would have an acceptable minimum of operational faults or bugs or, if no supplier was capable of meeting these criteria, then to advise the plaintiff to that effect. The court found that the plaintiff would not have purchased the system recommended but for the breach by the defendant. As the plaintiffs were described as "computer illiterate", they were entitled to rely on the expertise of the defendants.

Judge Hicks, listed some specific duties of computer consultants, such duties include: the use of due care and skill to ensure that the system meets the client's stated requirements; advising on whether the budgetary constraints are compatible with operational or other requirements; advising on the competence of key members

---

[158] Stephenson Blake (Holdings) Ltd. v. Streets Heaver Ltd. Q.B.D. (O.R.) H.H.J.Hicks Q.C., March 2, 1994 (unreported).

of the client's staff; and, the use of due care and skill to ensure that the recommended hardware would perform in conjunction with the recommended software in such a way that the intended computer operations could be carried out with reasonable speed. These duties as listed by Judge Hicks, are instructive in determining the specific duties of computer consultants under tort theory.

[c] United States
[i] Claims based on Negligence and Strict Liability

As discussed previously, the United States courts often do not distinguish causes of action based on negligence and strict liability with regard to economic loss. Therefore, most of the discussions involving negligently made products causing property and physical damage discussed here overlap with the content of the strict liability section. As a result, there has not been much discussion in the United States concerning solely negligent acts causing economic injury. The courts were concerned with the fear of fraudulent claims, mass litigation, and limitless liability, or liability out of proportion to the defendant's faults.[159] As a number of courts in the United States tend to emphasise the fact that economic loss is, as a matter of principle, not recoverable under tort theory, much of the discussion regarding economic loss under strict liability appears here.[160]

[ii] Physical Injury -Inherently Dangerous Articles

With regard to compensation for physical injury to property, a number of cases hold that the recovery of compensation for damage to the property is allowed if the manufactured article, if negligently made, is inherently dangerous causing catastrophic occurrences.

---

[159] People Exp. Airlines v. Consol. Rail, 495 A.2d 107, 110 (N.J. 1985).

[160] *See* E. River S. S. Corp. v. Transamerica Delaval, Inc., 476 U.S. 858 (1986); Utah Int'l, Inc. v. Caterpillar Tractor Co., 775 P.2d 741 (N.M. Ct. App. 1986); Gaebler, *supra* note 98, at 594.

In *MacPherson v. Buick Motor Co.*,[161] Cardozo J. stated that:

> If the nature of a thing is such that it is reasonably certain to place life and limb in peril when negligently made, it is then a thing of danger. Its nature gives warning of the consequences to be expected. If to the element of danger there is added knowledge that the thing will be used by persons other than the purchaser, and used without new tests, then irrespective of contract, the manufacturer of this thing of danger is under a duty to make it carefully.[162]

In this case, the plaintiff was injured while driving a defective car. The scope of the recovery was later extended to include physical harm to properties.

In *Seely v. White Motor Co.*,[163] it was held that, in order to preserve a proper role for the law of warranty, imposition of tortious liability should be precluded when defective products cause purely monetary harm, not accompanied by bodily harm or property damage other than to the defective property itself.[164]

The plaintiff entered into a conditional sales contract with the retailer for an automobile manufactured by the defendant. The truck overturned and was damaged due to brake failure. The court awarded lost profits and refund of the purchase price based on the warranty created by the defendants. There was an express warranty to the plaintiff in the purchase order that each new motor vehicle sold by the manufacturer be free from defects in materials and workmanship, therefore, no privity of contract was required.[165]

---

[161] 111 N.E. 1050 (N.Y. 1916).
[162] *Id.* at 1053.
[163] 403 P.2d 145 (Cal. 1965).
[164] *Id.* at 158.
[165] *Id.* at 148.

In the *Seely* case, a manufacturer was held liable for physical injuries caused by defects requiring the manufacturer's goods to match a standard of safety defined in terms of conditions that create an unreasonable risk of harm. The court stated that if manufacturers are held liable for some of the business losses that are caused by the failure to meet the unknown specific needs of the users and if liability cannot be disclaimed by contracts, they would be liable for damages of unknown and unlimited scope. On the other hand, the law of warranty should be preserved and the defendant should be entitled to define their liability in accordance with the U.C.C.[166]

It should be noted that under the holding of this case, the warranty required does not have to be in the form of contractual agreement as long as express representations exist. The court did not hesitate to impose liability based on an express representation made.[167]

[iii] Defective Articles, Compensation for Lack of Quality

A minority of courts uphold the liability of the manufacturer for lack of quality without any violent accident. In *Santor v. A & M Karagheusian, Inc.*,[168] an ultimate purchaser of defective carpeting was able to sue a carpeting manufacturer for recovery of its cost.[169] The manufacturer of carpets sold carpets through its wholly owned subsidiary distributor, which sold the carpeting to the retailer. The plaintiff bought the carpets from the retailer. The manufacurer advertised nationwide as a supplier of "Guilistan" carpets. The

---

[166] *See* N. Power & Engineering Corp. v. Caterpillar Tractor Co., 623 P.2d 324, 326-27 (Alaska 1981).

[167] *See infra* § 2.03 Theories Relevant To Imposing Liability [4] Negligent Misrepresentation [c] United States [ii] Economic Loss [iv] Actions Based on Warranties.

[168] 207 A.2d. 305 (N.J. 1965).

[169] *Id.* at 306.

purchaser was able to maintain an action for breach of implied warranty of reasonable fitness, despite the absence of privity of contract. In this case, the retailer, a wholly owned subsidiary of the manufacturers had moved to another state. The court argued that there is no justifiable reason to distinguish between personal injury claims and loss of bargain claims. If consumers are not allowed to sue the manufacturer regardless of privity of contract, the manufacturer may finally be obliged to compensate only after " an expensive, time consuming and wasteful process, and it may be interrupted by insolvency, lack of jurisdiction, disclaimers, or the statute of limitations."[170] The court stated that:

> [T]he manufacturer is the father of transaction. He makes the article and puts it in the channels of trade for sale to the public. No one questions the justice of a rule which holds him liable for defects arising out of the design or manufacturer, or other causes while the product is under his control..... The dealer is simply the way station, a conduit on its trip from manufacturer to consumer..... From the standpoint of principle, we perceive no sound reason why the implication of reasonable fitness should

---

[170] *Id.* at 310; *see* W.L. Prosser, *The Assault Upon the Citadel (Strict Liability to the Consumer)*, 69 YALE L.J. 1099, 1122-24 (1960)(stating, "the arguments which have proved convincing to the courts which have accepted the strict liability are three: 1. The public interest in human life, health and safety demands the maximum possible protection that the law can give against dangerous defects in products which consumers must buy...2. The supplier, by placing the goods upon the market, represents to the public that they are suitable and safe for use; and by packaging, advertising or otherwise, he does everything that he can to induce that belief...3. It is already possible to enforce strict liability by resort to a series of actions, in which the retailer is first held liable on a warranty to his purchaser and indemnity on a warranty is then sought successively from other suppliers, until the manufacturer finally pays the damages, with the added cost of repeated litigation" *Id.*).

be attached to the transaction and be actionable against the manufacturer where the defectively-made product has caused personal injury, and not actionable when inadequate manufacture has put a worthless article in the hands of an innocent purchaser who has paid the required price for it.[171]

The court held that the manufacturer should be responsible for strict liability in tort because of the mere presence of the product on the market, by applying the principles of implied warranty of reasonable suitability of the article manufactured for the use for which it was reasonably intended to be sold.[172] As the general public has neither adequate knowledge nor sufficient opportunity to determine if articles bought or used are defective, they rely upon the skill, care and reputation of the maker. Therefore, when the manufacturer presents his goods to the public for sale, he accompanies them with a representation that they are suitable and safe for the intended use.[173] It was explained that this strict liability in tort was not conditioned upon advertising to promote sales but arose from the mere presence of their product on the market, an enterprise liability; as the manufacturers who put the products in the channels of trade, rather than by the injured or damaged persons who are ordinarily powerless to protect themselves, should bear the cost of injuries or damages.[174] Such an outcome ensures the imposition of liability on the manufacturer who is in the best position to spread the cost of the risks and avoids a chain of litigation.

---

[171] *Santor*, 207 A.2d. at 309.
[172] *Id.* at 312.
[173] *Id.* at 311.
[174] *Id.* at 312; *see also* Greenman v. Yuba Power Prod. Inc., 377 P.2d 897, 901 (Cal. 1962).

Chapter 2

Such a holding was not supported in the Supreme Court decision in *East River S.S. Corp. v. Transamerica Delaval Inc.*,[175] which held that manufacturers had no duty under negligence or strict liability theory to prevent a product from damaging itself, causing purely economic loss.[176] The court upheld the position taken in the *Seely* case and held that a manufacturer in a commercial relationship had no duty under either a negligence or strict products-liability theory to prevent the product from injuring itself.

The *East River* court rejected the "intermediate approach" taken by *Pennsylvania Glass Sand Corp. v. Caterpillar Tractor Co.*[177] This approach permits a products-liability action when a product injures only itself by drawing "a distinction between the type of injury to a defective product that constitutes mere economic loss, and the type of injury that amounts to the sort of physical harm traditionally compensable in tort" and allowing only the latter to be sued upon in tort.[178]

In the *Pennsylvania Glass* case, the plaintiff was able to recover damages, including the amount spent on repair and replacement incurred as a result of fire in a defectively made front-end loader. The court considered that such damage caused by hazardous conditions constituted physical damage. Therefore, recovery in tort should be allowed.[179]

The *East River* court found such distinctions "which essentially turn on the degree of risk, are too indeterminate to enable manufacturers easily to structure their business behavior."[180] Nor did the court find "persuasive a distinction that rests on the

---

[175] 476 U.S. 858 (1986).
[176] *Id.* at 871.
[177] *Id.* at 870; 652 F.2d 1165 (1981).
[178] *Pennsylvania Glass*, 652 F.2d at 1173 (1981).
[179] *Id.* at 1175.
[180] *E. River*, 476 U.S. at 870.

manner in which the product is injured"[181] The court rejected the Santor holding because of the need to keep products liability and contract law in separate spheres and to maintain a realistic limitation on damages. The harm to the product itself is considered as the failure of the purchaser to receive the benefit for its bargain, which was traditionally the core concern of contract law.[182] It should be noted that the *Santor* case was also criticised by the *Seely v. White Motor Co.*[183] court in that it is acceptable to base liability on the representation of quality of the manufacturers, but not on the fact that the manufacturer was the source. Manufacturers might be held liable for the quality of a rug as first grade, and the court would have been justified in holding that the rug was defective.[184]

The *East River* court also argued that when a person is injured, the cost of injury is so overwhelming that a normal person is not in a position to meet the cost.[185] On the contrary, when a product injures itself, the commercial user can stand to lose the value of the product and such losses could be insured. Furthermore, it argued that the maintenance of product value and quality is precisely the purpose of express and implied warranties, precluding the application of a warranty theory. The court concluded that the increased cost to the public that would result from holding a manufacturer liable in tort for injury to the product itself is not justified.[186]

It is true that personal health is of prime importance. However, it is not always true that the cost of personal injury is so overwhelming as compared to property damage. Economic losses

---

[181] *Id.*
[182] *Id.* at 870-71.
[183] 403 P.2d 145 (Cal. 1965).
[184] *Id.* at 151.
[185] E. *River*, 476 U.S. at 871.
[186] *Id.*

may become overwhelming as well.

With regard to unsafe and hazardous products, the imposition of the liability should not depend on the outcome of the damage, as purchasers are equally exposed to the risks regardless of the outcome.[187]

It may be true that commercial entities may be able to insure against commercial losses. However, ordinary consumers may not be prepared to bear the cost of the loss in value. Consumers do not have the bargaining power to negotiate the terms of recovery. As products become increasingly sophisticated with special skills in manufacturing them, it is possible that only their manufacturers can repair defects in the quality of the product. Manufacturers are primarily responsible for controlling the quality of the products. The manufacturer may be the only party available to answer the claims regarding the systems made by consumers.

With respect to economic loss, not connected to dangerous materials, an adoption of an enterprise strict liability under the *Santor* case, may seem over-broad. However, the effect of express representations such as advertising and special or specific skills involved should be taken into account in determining the liability as in England. The United States courts may be able to explore the imposition of liability under negligence theory, distinguished from strict liability theory.

The factual situation in the *Santor* case is similar to the English case of *Junior Books Ltd. v. Veitchi Co. Ltd.*,[188] except that in the *Junior Books* case, the connection between the manufacturer and the end user was closer. In the *Junior Books* case, the defendant was nominated as "a specialist sub-contractor" by the plaintiff, which was considered as an indication that the defendant assumed the responsibility and the plaintiff had relied upon their skill and

---

[187] *See* Cloud v. Kit Mfg. Co., 563 P.2d 248, 250-51 (Alaska 1977).
[188] [1983] 1 A.C. 520 (H. L. (Sc.)).

knowledge.[189] It was probably crucial to the plaintiff's victory in the *Junior Books* case that, on the facts, the plaintiff had relied upon the defendant's skill and knowledge and there was only one possible plaintiff and one type of damage and both were known to, and not just foreseeable by the defendant.

For sophisticated products such as computer systems, specifications or manuals as to the capability of the system are attached when such a system is transferred. These specifications or manuals can be considered as warranting the quality of the system. Consumers often purchase PCs manufactured by a specific company because of its reputation for technical competence. Considering these factors, it is understandable that PCs normally come with the manufacturer's warranties.

[iv] Actions Based on Warranties

There are a number of cases that hold that an express or implied warranty relating to products is adequate to hold the third-party manufacturer liable. Many such cases involve consequential damages resulting from utilising the defective products.

In *Seely v. White Motor Co.*,[190] it was held that a remote manufacturer can be held liable for economic damages including lost profits and the purchase price of a truck, the liability being based on an express warranty regarding the quality of the motor vehicle.[191] The manufacturer warranted each new motor vehicle sold by it to be "free from defects in material and workmanship under normal use and services, its obligation under the warranty being limited to making good at its factory any parts thereof."[192] The court stated that:

---

[189] *Junior*, [1983] 1 A.C. at 531.
[190] 403 P.2d 145 (Cal. 1965).
[191] *Id.* at 148.
[192] *Id.*

The reliance on the warranty, and the warranty itself were manifested by plaintiff's continued efforts to have the truck repaired, and by defendant's acceptance of the responsibility to correct the galloping.[193]

Limitation of the defendant's obligation to repair and replace was found not valid as the defendant repeatedly failed to correct the defects as promised. The defendant was liable under the warranty theory for the commercial loss suffered by the plaintiff, the lost profits, and refund of the money paid for the truck.[194] The court stated that the distinction between tortious recovery for physical injuries and warranty recovery for economic loss rests on an understanding of the nature of the responsibility a manufacturer must undertake in distributing products.[195]

As discussed previously, the *Seely* court criticised *Santor v. A & M Karagheusian, Inc.*,[196] in that, contrary to the *Santor* case, the imposition of the liability was appropriate solely because of the representations of the quality made by the manufacturer. The rug was marketed as "Grade # 1". If the rug had been sold "as is," then there would have been no basis for imposing strict liability in tort, unless someone had been injured because the rug was unsafe.[197]

It has to be noted that courts may find some articles warranted, and impose liability based on such warranties. Typical articles the courts find warranted include cars, seeds or chemicals.[198] In

---

[193] *Id.*
[194] *Id.* at 148.
[195] *Id.* at 151.
[196] 207 A.2d. 305 (N.J. 1965).
[197] *Seely*, 403 P.2d at 151.
[198] *See* Klein v. Asgrow Seed Co., 54 Cal Rptr. 609 (Cal. Dist. Ct. App. 1966) (dealing with seeds); Posey v. Ford Motor Co., 128 So. 2d 149 (Fla. Dist. Ct. App. 1961) (dealing with cars); Randy Knitwear, Inc. v. Am. Cyanamid Co., 181 N.E.2d 399, (N.Y. 1962) (dealing with chemicals).

Graham v. John R. Watts & Son,,[199] the court imposed liability based on false representation on a defendant, a remote supplier who mislabelled seed purchased and planted by the plaintiff. The court considered that the defendant made continuing false representations intending to influence the final consumers, who were a class of farmers to which the plaintiff belonged.[200] The plaintiff relied on the representations made by the defendant and the plaintiff might not have purchased the sack of seed had it not been for the representation contained in the label. Such mislabelling was also in violation of a labelling statute.[201]

It seems appropriate and fair, to impose liability based on express representations made by a manufacturer. This is so especially if the kinds of articles are ones which require expertise or special skills in creating the article and evaluating their quality. For ordinary consumers, defects in cars, chemicals, seeds or computer programs may not be apparent at the time of purchase.

[v] Liability Based on Expertise

Courts generally uphold the recovery of purely economic loss when a "special relationship" exists. In *A.E. Investment Corp. v. Link Builders, Inc.,*[202] the defendant architect firm was found liable for negligently failing to adequately supervise the construction by the building company.[203] The court stated that:

---

[199] 36 S.W.2d 859 (Ky. 1931).

[200] *Id.* at 862.

[201] *Id.* at 861.

[202] 214 N.W.2d 764 (Wis. 1974).

[203] *Id.* at 767 (stating, "We believe that the narrow concept of duty relied on by the defendant architect has long been discarded in Wisconsin law.....A defendant's duty is established when it can be said that it was foreseeable that his act or omission to act may cause harm to someone. A party is negligent when he commits an act when some harm to someone is foreseeable....Where, as here, it is alleged that the architect knew the purpose for which the building was being constructed, it was clearly foreseeable that a future tenant of the building was within the ambit of the harm. Hence, the harm to the particular plaintiff was

Under Wisconsin negligence law, architects may be liable to third parties with whom they are not in privity of contract. The lack of privity does not constitute a policy reason for not imposing liability where negligence is shown to be a substantial factor in occasioning the harm....The very essence of a profession is that the services are rendered with the understanding that the duties of the profession cannot be undertaken on behalf of a client without an awareness and a responsibility to the public welfare.[204]

The court thereby emphasised the responsibility of professionals who have assumed the tasks, to the public welfare.

Courts have also allowed recovery for the beneficiaries against attorneys who negligently prepared wills, as evidenced in *Lucas v. Hamm*.[205]

In the *Lucas* case, the court stated that the determination as to whether the defendant would be liable to a third person not in privity is a matter of policy and requires the balancing of the following factors: 1) the extent to which the transaction was intended to affect the plaintiff; 2) the foreseeability of harm to the plaintiff; 3) the degree of certainty that the plaintiff suffered injury; 4) the closeness of the connection between the defendant's conduct and the injury suffered; 5) the moral blame attached to the defendant's conduct; and, 6) the policy of preventing future harm, such as whether the recognition of liability to beneficiaries of wills negligently drawn by attorneys would impose an undue burden on the profession.[206]

---

foreseeable, although under the methodology of this court, it is not necessary that either the person harmed or the type of harm that would result be foreseeable. The act or omission in the face of foreseeable harm was negligence.").
[204] *Id.* at 769.
[205] 364 P.2d 685 (Cal. 1961), *cert. denied,* 368 U.S. 987 (1962).

The court held that the lack of privity between plaintiffs and defendant did not preclude plaintiffs from maintaining an action in tort against the defendant. In this case, the plaintiffs had no other recourse, the policy of preventing future harm would be impaired if the plaintiffs were not able to maintain an action, and the extension of an attorneys' liability to beneficiaries injured by a negligently drawn will does not place an undue burden on the profession.[207]

The court also mentioned that an attorney, by accepting employment to give legal advice or to render other legal services, impliedly agrees to use such skill, prudence, and diligence as lawyers of ordinary skill and capacity commonly possess and exercise in the performance of the tasks which they undertake.[208] Therefore, as in *White v. Jones*,[209] the United States courts impose liability based on the assumption of tasks with special skills. However, the scope of such "special skills" seems to be limited to recognised professionals.[210] Most of the United States' courts are not ready to accept the idea that computer programmers are professionals.

[vi] Omission of Act
[A] Physical Damage

There is the possibility that negligence would be found when not utilising the computer technology. The *T.J. Hooper*[211] case held that coastal tugs which towed barges should have been equipped with working receiving sets. Two barges sank in a storm. If the tugs

---

[206] *Id.* at 687-88; *see also* Biakanja v. Irving, 320 P.2d 16, 19 (Cal. 1958).
[207] *Lucas*, 364 P.2d at 688.
[208] *Id.* at 689.
[209] [1995] 2.A.C. 207 (H.L.(E.)); Henderson v. Merrett Syndicates Ltd. [1995] 2 A.C. 145, 181 (H.L.(E.)).
[210] *See* Hosp. Computer Sys., Inc. v. Staten Island Hosp., 788 F. Supp. 1351 (D.N. J. 1992).
[211] 60 F.2d 737 (2d Cir. 1932).

which towed the barges had been equipped with working receiving sets, it would have been possible to receive a storm warning. The court held that the tugs should have been equipped with working receiving sets, reasoning that such a set would act as the ears of the tug to catch every spoken word, just as the master's binoculars were her eyes to see a storm signal ashore.[212] The court determined that even though receiving sets were not general or customary in the industry, there were precautions so imperative that even universal disregard of them would not excuse their omission. People who had not thought such a device necessary were considered too slack and in breach of their duty of care. [213]

The court imposed a duty of care higher than was customary in the industry. The court may exercise flexible judgement when the non-use of such a system is too "slack" despite the industry's custom. It should be noted that there was evidence that adequate receiving could have been obtained at small cost and was reasonably reliable if properly maintained.[214] Imposition of liability may be more justified if the cost of implementing the system is not too high.

Likewise, in *Torres v. North American Van Lines*,[215] the moving company was found negligent in monitoring a driver's working hours to avoid fatigue. The company had a sophisticated data processing system and could have implemented the system to control the driver's time.[216] Such a system would have cautioned the driver not to drive excessive hours. The company had the personnel and equipment to design and implement such a system. Even though the company had information regarding accidents

---

[212] *Id.* at 739-40.
[213] *Id.* at 740.
[214] *Id.* at 739.
[215] 658 P.2d 835 (Ariz. Ct. App. 1982).
[216] *Id.* at 838.

involving its drivers, such information had never been analysed to improve safety measures and reduce accidents. [217]

[B] Economic Loss

There are many cases where the negligence of banks is at issue. Only economic loss is concerned in such cases. Due to the development of the computer and the increase in numbers of computers in recent years, omission to use computer technology that is readily available or ordinarily accepted by other members of the industry may be considered negligent.

In *Broad Street Bank v. National Bank of Goldsboro*,[218] the court held that a bank was not negligent in failing to use processes and devices for writing cheques on special paper and designing the amount by a protectograph to prevent forgery. Such precautions were the usual custom and ordinarily adopted by other banks.[219] The court mentioned that such precautions do not offer complete protection and "it is well known that, day by day, the agents of these patent devices, enterprising and insistent, offer their wares claiming that they have the very latest and only efficient protection."[220] The court correctly referred to the difficulties in keeping up with the latest technologies.

However, the dissenting opinion stated that:

> [B]usiness methods have changed with the increased volume of business, with the multiplication of methods to falsify and forge such papers, and with the ready means of protection now at hand, by the use of the protectograph and special paper, such as the defendant itself was in the habit of using. The failure to do this on this occasion is alleged to be the proximate cause of the

---

[217] *Id.*
[218] 112 S.E. 11 (N.C. 1922).
[219] *Id.* at 18.
[220] *Id.* at 16.

forgery in this case, and that it is directly traceable to this negligence of the defendant.[221]

In a more recent case, *Sun Bank/Miami, N.A. v. First Nat'l Bank*,[222] the banks' duty to use technology readily available to them was affirmed. The court held that the bank was negligent for not checking with the computer databases reporting on stolen securities, before accepting the stolen securities. Even though such a system was available and the system could be operated without difficulty, it was not the bank's policy to use the system and its employees had not been trained to use it.[223]

On the contrary, in *Port City State Bank v. American National Bank*,[224] the court held that the bank was justified in delaying the commencement of emergency operations for the computer bookkeeping operation, resulting in failure to notify any dishonour prior to the deadline.[225] The bank had just implemented a computer bookkeeping operation to replace a manual system. Prior to transferring to the new system, the bank paralleled its manual system with computer operation for approximately two weeks. Subsequently, manual bookkeeping equipment was removed from the bank. The bank did not commence emergency operations because of American National Bank's own experience with computers and the industry history, and also because the bank believed the statement from the computer manufacturer who did not foresee the serious nature of the repairs.[226] Therefore, the bank was justified in believing its computer would be back in service soon and the bank was considered as not negligent. In this case, the fact that the

---

[221] *Id.* at 20.
[222] 698 F. Supp 1298 (Md.1988).
[223] *Id.* at 1305.
[224] 486 F.2d 196 (10th Cir.1973).
[225] *Id.* at 200.
[226] *Id.*

bank did not have the readily available expertise and relied on the computer company's assurance worked in favour of the bank.

Due to the development of the computer and the increase in numbers of computers in recent years, not using computer database (such as Lexis) may be considered negligent. In *United Nuclear Corp. v. Cannon*,[227] holding that attorneys could recover costs incurred in doing computerized legal research, the court stated "Lexis is an essential tool of a modern, efficient law office. As such, it saves lawyers' time by increasing the efficacy of legal research. Denial of reimbursement for Lexis charges in a proper case would be an open invitation to law firms to use high-priced attorney time to perform routine research tasks that can be accomplished quicker and more economically with Lexis."[228]

However, in the later case of *People v. Barnes*,[229] it was held that non-use of computer legal research was understandable "as the use of a computer database "may be unavailable to many attorneys who do not enjoy the luxury of computer-assisted research"[230] It was difficult to find the relevant case without the use of computer-assisted research because it was mainly about a different issue from that being litigated in *People v. Barnes* and there was an oversight of the editors at West Publishing Co. in indexing the case. Furthermore, even the District Attorneys of New York and Bronx counties had not yet "heard" about the case at issue.[231] With respect to the omission of the use of the legal computer databases, the court may take into account the resources of law firms, and the cost of using such databases. As it should technically be possible to use other sources to check the law, the court may not impose liability for failing to find cases that are discoverable only using

---

[227] 564 F. Supp. 581(D.R.I. 1983).
[228] *Id.* at 591-92.
[229] 499 N.Y.S.2d 343 (Sup. Ct. 1986).
[230] *Id.* at 346.
[231] *Id.* at 346.

computer databases. However, by now, courts may not consider that computer-assisted research is luxurious.

[vii] Professional Liability of Computer Programmers

As discussed previously, courts generally uphold the recovery of purely economic loss where there is a "special relationship". Whether the plaintiff may bring the cause of action based on negligence or negligent representation depends on the existence of the special relationship. To date, in the United States, most courts are reluctant to extend the doctrine of professional malpractice to include independent computer consultants. Those cases that recognise the special relationship base their opinions on different theories. In this section, I deal with both negligent acts and negligent misrepresentations, as they are difficult to distinguish when the rendering of special or professional skills is involved.

[A] Exercising Professional Standard of Care

Data Processing Services, Inc. v. L.H. Smith Oil Corp.,[232] applying Indiana law, was one of the few cases in which the court imposed professional liability and held that those who hold themselves out to the world as possessing skill and qualifications in their respective trades or professions impliedly represent that they possess that skill and that they will exhibit the diligence ordinarily possessed by well - informed members of that trade or profession.[233] The defendant was retained to design, develop and implement an electronic-data processing system to meet the plaintiff's specific needs. The court held such a transaction was not merely a sale of goods.

---

[232] 492 N.E.2d 314 (Ind. Ct. App. 1986).
[233] *Id.* at 318-19.

[B] Exercising Ordinary Standard of Care

In the cases of *Invacare Corp. v. Sperry Corp.*,[234] applying Ohio law, and *United States Welding, Inc. v. Burroughs Corp.*[235] applying Colorado law, both courts recognised the misrepresentation claim based on Restatement of Torts.

In the *Invacare* case, the plaintiff's allegation that the defendant was negligent in recommending the computer system and its augmentation, when the defendant knew or should have known in the exercise of ordinary care, that the system was totally inadequate to meet the plaintiff's needs, was found to be a valid claim.[236] The court's ruling was based on Restatement (Second) of Torts section 299A (1965), which imposes the *ordinary standard of care* on any person who undertakes to render services to another in the practice of a profession or a skilled trade. This type of "ordinary standard of care" applies not only to physicians or surgeons, but also to airplane pilots, precision mechanists, electricians, carpenters and blacksmiths. Therefore, the court did not create a new tort of computer malpractice; rather, it focused on the ordinary standard of care of a person who undertakes to render services to others in the practice of a skilled trade. The court stated that Invacare could claim that Sperry failed to perform at a level of ordinary care.[237] However, the level of *ordinary standard care* as compared to professional standard of care is not clear. It may not be easy for plaintiffs to prove that such ordinary standard of care is breached unless there is a serious misconduct on the part of defendants.

[C] Standard of Care for Professionals Supplying Information

In *United States Welding, Inc. v. Burroughs Corp.*,[238] a plaintiff

---

[234] 612 F. Supp. 448 (N.D. Ohio 1984).
[235] 587 F. Supp. 49 (D.Colo. 1984), *rev'd on other grounds*, 640 F. Supp, 350 (D. Colo. 1985).
[236] *Invacare,* 612 F. Supp. at 453.
[237] *Id.*

was able to assert negligent representation based on Restatement (Second) of Torts section 552 (1976),[239] which provides the liability for professionals for supplying false information for the guidance of others.

The defendant argued that the tort of negligent misrepresentation would not provide a remedy in cases where the loss was economic and where the transaction was governed by the provisions of Article 2 of the Uniform Commercial Code. However, the court determined, based on Colorado law, that section 552 recognises pecuniary loss and claims which allege no physical harm, and that such claims are not precluded by contemporaneous claims sounding in contract.[240]

[D] Difference between a Profession and a Business

On the contrary, in *Hospital Computer Systems, Inc. v. Staten Island Hospital*,[241] a computer malpractice cause of action was not recognised. The plaintiff had an arrangement to pay a monthly

---

[238] 587 F. Supp. 49 (D.Colo. 1984), *rev'd on other grounds*, 640 F. Supp, 350 (D. Colo. 1985).

[239] RESTATEMENT (SECOND) OF TORTS § 552 (1976)

((1) One who, in the course of his business, profession or employment, or in any other transaction in which he has a pecuniary interest, supplies false information for the guidance of others in their business transactions, is subject to liability for pecuniary loss caused to them by their justifiable reliance upon the information, if he fails to exercise reasonable care or competence in obtaining or communicating the information.

(2) Except as stated in Subsection (3), the liability stated in Subsection (1) is limited to loss suffered

(a) by the person or one of a limited group of persons for whose benefit and guidance he intends to supply the information or knows that the recipient intends to supply it; and

(b) through reliance upon it a transaction that he intends the information to influence or knows that the recipient so intends or in a substantially similar transaction.)

[240] *United States Welding*, 587 F. Supp. at 51.

[241] 788 F. Supp. 1351 (D.N.J. 1992).

"management fee" in consideration for the defendant's service to develop and implement a computerised patient accounting and billing system.[242] The system had many problems and the plaintiffs eventually replaced it. The court stated, by citing another holding of the New York Court of Appeals:[243]

> A profession is not a business. It is distinguished by the requirements of extensive formal training and learning, admis-sion to practice by a qualifying licensure, a code of ethics imposing standards qualitatively and extensively beyond those that prevail or are tolerated in the marketplace, a system for discipline of its members for violation of the code of ethics, a duty to subordinate financial reward to social responsibility, and, notably, an obligation on its members, even in non professional matters, to conduct themselves as members of a learned, disciplined, and honorable occupation.

The court then determined that no such duty applied to computer consultants.[244] The court distinguished this case from *Diversified Graphics, Ltd. v. Groves,*[245] where the accountant firm, Ernst & Whinney, acted as a consultant during the purchase and implementation of an in-house data-processing system.[246]

[E] Overlapping Professional Duties -Computer Consultants and Accountants

In *Diversified Graphics, Ltd. v. Groves,* the accounting firm's duty to act reasonably in accordance with its superior

---

[242] *Id.* at 1355.
[243] *Id.* at 1361, citing In re Estate of Freeman (Lincoln Rochester Trust Co. v. Freeman), 311 N.E.2d 480, 483(N.Y. 1974).
[244] *Hosp. Computer Sys.,* 788 F. Supp. at 1361.
[245] 868 F.2d 293 (8th Cir. 1989).
[246] *Hosp. Computer Sys.,* 788 F. Supp. at 1361.

knowledge was affirmed. The plaintiff, a screen printer and apparel manufacturer, hired the defendant accountant firm, Ernst & Whinney (hereinafter, E&W), as a consultant during the purchase and implementation of an in-house data processing system. The defendant recommended Richer Management Services, Inc., as a vendor of computer software and hardware.[247] The plaintiff requested a "turn-key" computer system, a self-sufficient system where the purchaser needs only to "turn the key" to commence operation. With the "turn-key" system, clients do not need to hire programmers or train employees to operate the system.[248]

The court found that the defendant accounting firm failed to act reasonably in accordance with its superior knowledge and expertise in the area of computer systems, as it did not take great care to detail the business's needs and properly to develop the specification for the computer system.[249] The court cited E & W's Guideline to Practice, which required that "due professional care" be exercised in providing management advisory services.[250]

The evidence showed that this type of customised and fully operational system requires great care to detail a business's needs and to develop appropriate specifications for the computer system.[251] The court found that there was sufficient evidence from which the jury could find that the defendant did not meet the standard for modifications, employee training, and additional staffing and consultation. This case was considered as a specific case against accountants, "who are universally recognized as professionals."

However, the court was reluctant to find liability on another case involving an accounting firm in New York.

---

[247] *Diversified*, 868 F.2d 293 at 294.
[248] *Id.* at 297.
[249] *Id.*
[250] *Id.*
[251] *Id.*

In *RKB Enterprises, Inc. v. Ernst & Young*,[252] the New York court held that there is no cause of action for professional malpractice in the field of computer consulting, and that the mere fact that a company holds itself out as a computer consultant does not re-establish a sufficient basis for tortious claims premised in malpractice allegations. [252.1]

In this case, the plaintiff entered into a contract with the defendant, Ernst & Young, formally, Ernst & Whinney (hereinafter E &W) to perform computer - consulting services for the plaintiff's new data -processing system. After analysing the plaintiff's needs, E &W recommended the proposal submitted by another defendant, System Software Associated (hereinafter SSA). The plaintiffs entered into a series of contracts with SSA for the purchase of computer hardware, the licensing of a computer software program, and the adaptation of the software to meet the plaintiff's specific needs. The plaintiff also entered into a contract with E&W in which the defendant agreed to help oversee and assist in the implementation of the new data system.

After experiencing extensive cost increases and delays resulting from difficulties adapting the computer program and system to its business, the plaintiff commenced an action alleging breach of contract and negligent and reckless rendition of professional computer-consulting services against the defendant. The court declined to create a new tort applicable to the computer industry, considering the fact that the computers were relatively new equipment of a complex technical nature. The court stated that a conventional business relationship did not create a fiduciary relationship in the absence of additional factors.[252.2] The court also mentioned that the allegations of negligence in the complaint

---

[252] 582 N.Y.S.2d 814 (App. Div. 1992).
[252.1] *Id.* at 816.
[252.2] *Id.* at 816.

merely paralleled the breach of contract claim; therefore, such an allegation is precluded. However, the court ruled that the allegation of fraud in the inducement could be sustained.[252.3] It must be noted that, even if claims based on negligence cannot be sustained, there is a possibility that claims based on fraud may be recognised.

[F] Requisites for Allowing Professional Liability

The fact that accounting firms are hired for the specific purpose of providing computer consultancy did not guarantee the courts' application of professional liability. However, contrary to *Hospital Computer Systems v. Staten Island Hospital*,[253] extensive formal training and learning may be required for computer programmers as well. Some countries impose national examinations to insure a standard of performance. Some of the ethical rules for professionals, such as those of lawyers', exist because of the nature of their work. Lawyers may have access to their clients' personal or intimate information and their action may have direct effects on the clients' legal rights as well as their financial status. The personal conduct of lawyers may have serious implications on the status of their clients.

Computer consultants may not share exactly the same work ethics of lawyers. However, they can be required to keep their clients' important data and other business information confidential. Computer consultants are hired to achieve certain tasks that cannot be achieved by the clients, and are expected to use their expertise in achieving such tasks. Therefore, they should also be held to the duties to exercise their expertise within the scope of their represented capabilities.

Some courts which do not recognise a special relationship in transactions involving the supply of computer programs and emphasise private autonomy in commerce between the parties. On

---

[252.3] *Id.* at 816-17.
[253] 788 F. Supp. 1351 (D.N.J. 1992).

the other hand, some courts recognise the existence of a special relationship based on ordinary or special skills. However, it should be noted that in the United States even if a cause of action based on negligent misrepresentation is not allowed, a cause of action based on fraud may be allowed.

If computer consultants, whether acting within the scope of recognised professional duties or not, were requested to customise computer systems to match clients' specific needs, and clients chose computer consultants based on consultants' special knowledge and skills, there is no reason why professional negligence claims should not be allowed. Professional negligence claims may be justified especially if there is a large gap in knowledge between the clients and the computer consultants, for instance, in cases where a customised "turn-key" computer system is requested by unskilled users, and the computer consultant takes responsibility for the customisation. The plaintiffs should not be forced to resort to claims in fraud. Negligent misrepresentation may be more appropriate than fraud in inducement claims for the courts to assess appropriate standards of duties and performance in accordance with each case.

[d] Comparison

As discussed previously, when considering recovery of economic loss, in England, the courts tend to distinguish between negligence theory and strict liability theory, whereas in the United States, courts tend not to distinguish between these theories and speak in terms of "recovery in tort" in most cases.

Therefore, in England there are more authorities regarding recovery of economic loss caused by negligent acts than in the United States. In England, if someone is exercising special or specific skills and assuming the responsibility, and such expertise is relied upon by plaintiffs, recovery of economic loss, caused by negligent statement or act is allowed under *Henderson v. Merrett Syndicates Ltd.*[254] The fact that the loss was caused by negligent statement or negligent acts is not essential in those

Chapter 2

cases involving special skills. As such, professional liability is not restricted to being imposed on specific professionals as special skills or knowledge are the essential factors in allowing recovery. This is reflected in the recognition of professional liability in *Stephenson Blake (Holdings) Ltd. v. Streets Heaver Ltd.*[255]

In the United States, recovery of economic loss under tort law is generally restricted under the *East River* case.[256] However, as stated in the *Seely* case[257] courts are willing to impose liability for warranty, or an express representation, as such a representation is considered an undertaking of responsibility by the manufacturers.[258] In the majority of courts in the United States, claims based on professional liability may be possible only for recognised professions. However, in the United States, courts tend to distinguish negligent acts and negligent statements when determining whether recovery is allowed, and some cases discussed above,[259] show that it may be possible for recovery to be based on negligent misrepresentation rather than general negligence.

Not using computer technology that is readily available and customarily used in industry would be likely to be considered negligent. Such duties tend to be elevated in cases where physical injury is involved. Courts may also find negligence if it is considered too "slack" not to use certain technology. The court may not impose negligent liability if such technology was not readily available to defendants in terms of cost or expertise.

---

[254] [1995] 2 A.C. 145 (H.L.(E)).
[255] Q.B.D. (O.R.) H.H.J.Hicks Q.C., March 2, 1994 (unreported).
[256] 476 U.S. 858 (1986).
[257] 403 P.2d 145 (Cal. 1965).
[258] *See infra* § 2.03 Theories Relevant To Imposing Liability [4] Negligent Misrepresentation [c] United States [iv] Actions Based on Warranties.
[259] *See supra* § 2.03 Theories Relevant To Imposing Liability [3] Negligence [c] United States [vii] Professional Liability of Computer Programmers.

[4] Negligent Misrepresentation
   [a] Negligent Misrepresentation and Information in Electronic Form

Liability under negligent misrepresentation theory may become an important issue in three main scenarios; 1) Transactions in information in electronic form may involve representations made by manufacturers, and users may rely on their statements to purchase computer programs or hardware and other related services. The end users suffer damage from acquiring such defective systems, relying on the statements. 2) Computer programs, such as Exel and Lotus 1-2-3, produce outputs that are relied upon. When a computer program, such as an accounting system or an ordering system, malfunctions and an individual relies on the wrong output information and acts on such information, this information may cause economic or physical injuries. 3) Human-readable information on the Internet or in on-line databases may be relied upon and cause damage.

These cases normally fit into the second injury scenario, where the injured party acts on the information supplied. It must be noted, as described previously, that the supply of professional service or services with special skills often involves both acts and statements.

With regard to 3), there is no fundamental difference between human-readable (as opposed to machine-readable) information distributed in the form of books and human-readable information on the Internet or online database. However, some significant differences are worth noting. On-line databases can be viewed only with the aid of the computer screen. It may not be as easy to read the documents on the screen as reading the documents on paper. The scope of materials available for viewing may be smaller on screens. When reading books or other information on paper, more information is available for viewing and for peripheral vision. When viewing computer screens, some people experience a flickering sensation.[260] Occasionally, the main text and footnotes are not on the same screen to be viewed simultaneously with the text.

People tend to assume that an on-line database is relatively accurate and kept up to date. As people may specifically retrieve the documents they are looking for, for instance, in cases of a medical database or a database listing hotels in England, people tend to rely more on database information. Disclaimers as to the content of the information may be easily ignored or skipped by the readers. Such information may be easily downloaded and re-used by the receiver of the information.

There may be another significant difference between the publisher of information in traditional form and the publishers of information in electronic form. Publishers in information in traditional form tend to have an opportunity to review the book before publication. However, Internet providers may have less opportunity to view the contents before such information is available on-line.

[b] England
[i] Physical Injury

Courts are reluctant to limit the liability for negligent misrepresentation when physical injury is involved. Lord Oliver in *Caparo Industries plc. v. Dickman*[261] indicated that mislabelling a dangerous medicine or negligent telephonic advice about the treatment of a sick child should be treated in the same manner as in cases where negligent acts cause physical injury.[262] Denning L.J. in *Candler v. Crane Christmas & Co.*[263] distinguished those

---

[260] *See* J. R. Anshel, *Improving Visual Comfort at a Computer Workstation, at* http://www.tifaq.com/articles/visual_comfort-jan99-jeffrey_anshel.html (reprinted from 34 The RSI Network (1999)).
[261] [1990] 2 A.C. 605 (H.L.(E.)).
[262] *Id.* at 636.
[263] [1951] 2 K.B.164 (C.A.).

cases from the cases involving the marine hydrographer.[264] The main reason supplied by Denning L.J. for such distinction rested in the way that the articles are distributed. In the case of a marine hydrography, there may be an indeterminate class of plaintiffs.[265] Another possible reason is that professional skills involved in medicine may directly affect personal health of a particular individual, as people act on such information.[266] However, there are also professional skills in undertaking marine hydrography, and marine hydrography may cause physical injury. Therefore, there is no difference between mislabelling of a dangerous medicine or negligent telephonic advice about the treatment, and marine hydrography.[267]

One of the characteristics of the computer program is that it can cause physical actions with the aid of hardware. Computer programs may be integrated as part of medical diagnostic devices that directly interact with patients. The court may not be able to impose products liability law with respect for the defective computer program itself, but will not hesitate to impose responsibility under products liability law for medical diagnostic devices. However, the software may be the essential cause of the injury. If navigational charts were considered "products" there is no reason not to consider computer programs as products.

[ii] **Economic Loss**
[A] **Special Relationship**

As stated above, *Hedley Byrne & Co. Ltd. v. Heller & Partners*

---

[264] *Id.* at 183.
[265] *Id.*
[266] *Id.* (stating, "He publishes his work simply for the purpose of giving information, and not with any particular transaction in mind at all.")
[267] *See* Saloomey v. Jeppesen & Co., 707 F.2d 671 (2d Cir. 1983); Halstead v. United States, 535 F. Supp. 782 (D. Conn. 1982); Aetna Cas. & Sur. Co. v. Jeppesen & Co., 642 F.2d 339 (9th Cir. 1981); *see infra* § 2.03 Theories Relevant To Imposing Liability [5] Strict Products Liability.

Ltd.,[268] established the rule regarding recovery of pure economic loss for making representations. The House of Lords held that a tortious duty of care with regard to making representations may also exist in circumstances other than those where a fiduciary relationship exists. It should be noted that in the *Hedley Byrne* context, which involved a statement as to the third - party debtor's creditworthiness, the only possibly foreseeable loss was economic.

In this case, advertising agents inquired of their own bank as to the credit-worthiness of a client, and the bank made inquiries of the client's bank. The client's bank gave a favourable reference, but disclaimed responsibility for it. Subsequently, the clients went into liquidation, and the advertising agent incurred monetary loss. If not for the disclaimer, the bank would have been found responsible for the statement made. In order to find liability, Lord Devlin stated that wherever there is a relationship equivalent to contract, there is a duty of care.[269] Lord Devlin also emphasised the importance of the voluntary assumption or undertaking of responsibility by the defendant.[270]

---

[268] [1964] A.C. 465 (H.L.(E.)).

[269] *Id.* at 530.

[270] *Id.* at 528-31; *see* Henderson v. Merret Syndicates Ltd. [1995] 2 A.C. 145, 181(H.L.(E.)). ("Furthermore, especially in a context concerned with a liability which may arise under a contract or in a situation "equivalent to contract," it must be expected that an objective test will be applied when asking the question whether, in a particular case, responsibility should be held to have been assumed by the defendant to the plaintiff.") Id. at 194 ("But, for present purposes more important, in the instant case liability can, and in my opinion should, be founded squarely on the principle established in Hedley Byrne itself, from which it follows that an assumption of responsibility coupled with the concomitant reliance may give rise to a tortious duty of care irrespective of whether there is a contractual relationship between the parties, and in consequence, unless his contract precludes him from doing so, the plaintiff, who has available to him concurrent remedies in contract and tort, may choose that remedy which appears to him to be the most advantageous.").

Lord Reid stated that there must be a special relationship between the parties where the plaintiff seeking the information and advice was trusting the defendant to exercise such a degree of care as the circumstances required, where it was reasonable for the defendant to do that, and where the defendant gave information or advice when the defendant knew or ought to have known that plaintiff might reasonably rely upon the defendant's representation.[271] Lord Morris stated that if a person possessed of a special skill undertakes, quite irrespective of contract, to apply that skill for the assistance of another person, and he or she knows or should know that another person relies upon such a skill, a duty of care would arise.[272] Therefore, the important question to be asked with regard to compensation for economic loss depends on whether there is a relationship supported by the voluntary implementation of special skills and reliance. It is not hard to imagine that such a relationship exists in the supply of bespoke software.

[B] Special Relationship -Scope of the Class of Plaintiffs and the Defendants

The special relationship required for the imposition of liability may be based on professional or special skills, in circumstances where the defendants were considered to have assumed responsibility and reasonable reliance. However, the actual scope of the class of plaintiffs and the responsible defendants needs to be defined in each case.

Denning L.J., in his dissenting opinion in *Candler v. Crane Christmas & Co.*,[273] provides a more detailed analysis regarding imposition of liability on professional persons. This case was later overruled by the *Hedley Byrne*[274] case and Denning L.J.'s

---

[271] [1964] A.C. 465, 486 (H.L.(E.)).
[272] *Id.* at 502-03.
[273] [1951] 2 K.B. 164 (C.A.).
[274] *Hedley,* [1964] A.C. at 507.

opinion was adopted. The *Candler* case held that a false statement carelessly made by one person to another causing financial loss was not actionable in the absence of any contractual relationship between the parties.[275] In this case, an investor in a limited liability company relied on accounts carelessly prepared by the defendant accountant. The limited liability company was wound up within a year. The plaintiff who incurred financial loss sued the defendant for misrepresentation. The recovery was denied under the theory of the tort of negligence.

Denning L.J., in his famous dissenting opinion, examined the issues as to which persons are under a duty to use care in their statements, apart from the contract itself, to whom these persons owe such duty, and to what extent the duty of care extends. He stated that the duty of care exists for professional persons such as accountants, surveyors, valuers and analysts, and that their duty is not merely a duty to use care in their reports. These professionals have a duty to take care in the work that results from their reports. Furthermore, their duty is not limited to their clients and employers, but also extends to any third person to whom they themselves show the work products, or to whom they know their employer is going to show the work products so as to induce him to invest money or take some other action on them.[276]

On the other hand, if the information is given in circumstances where it would be unreasonable for the recipient to act on it without checking the content, no duty of care arises.[277] With respect to the extent of the duty of care, he contends that it extends to the specific transaction and thus to the loss incurred by relying on the statement. He differentiated this type of professional liability with

---

[275] *Candler*, [1951] 2 K.B. at 201.
[276] *Id.* at 179-80.
[277] *See* Howard Marine and Dredging Co. Ltd. v. A Ogden and Sons (Excavations) Ltd. [1978] Q.B. 574, 594. (C.A.)(stating that the correct deadweight capacity could have been checked from the ship's document).

respect to a particular transaction from the liability of a scientist or expert, including a marine hydrographer who, in his opinion, should not be liable to his readers for careless statements in his published information.[278]

It should be noted that the *Hedley Byrne type* of case involved only banks and credit transactions; the only possible loss was financial and such financial loss to the determinate class of the plaintiffs was foreseeable with respect to this type of careless statement. However, in the marine hydrographer case, as discussed before, there can be physical or personal physical damages to the plaintiffs. Risks of physical injuries may be higher in the case of marine hydrography.

As mentioned by Denning L.J., accountants, surveyors or lawyers are no doubt regarded as having expertise or special skills. Furthermore, in England, the imposition of liability is not restricted to recognised professionals such as accountants and lawyers. Lord Reid and Lord Morris, in their dissenting opinions, took a flexible approach toward the skill of the defendants in *Mutual Life and Citizen's Assurance Co. Ltd. v. Evatt.*[279] The Privy Council held that the defendant insurance company was not liable for the financial loss incurred by the plaintiff, a policy holder in the defendant company, who relied on the defendant's advice on the financial stability of an associate company of the defendant. It was held that there is no duty of care unless the representor is in the business or profession of supplying information or advice, which calls for special skill and competence, such as surveyors and accountants, who claim to possess that degree of skill and competence and to be willing to exercise that degree of diligence which is generally possessed and exercised by persons who carry on the business or profession of giving advice of the kind. Furthermore, though not carrying on the business or profession

---

[278] *Candler,* [1951] 2 K.B. at 183.
[279] [1971] A.C. 793 (P.C.).

Chapter 2

generally, representors may be held liable when claiming to possess skill and competence in the subject-matter of the particular inquiry comparable to those who do carry on the business or profession.[280]

Lord Reid and Lord Morris stated that such specific skill or competence is not necessary to find liability. It was sufficient that the adviser is a businessman who, in the course of his business, is invited in a business context to advise on a certain matter and an individual chooses to accept that invitation to advise without warning or qualification.[281] The representor must realise whether the circumstance is such that he or she ought to have realised that the recipient intends to act upon the information or advice with respect to his or her property or of himself or herself in connection with some matter of business or serious consequence.

This broader interpretation, where the representors do not necessarily have to be in the business or profession of supplying the particular information or advice sought, was preferred and accepted in *Esso Petroleum Co. Ltd. v. Mardon*,[282] where the owner of a petrol-filling station was found liable for breach of a pre-contractual duty of care in advising on the profitability of investment with respect to the station. The court held that Mr. Mardon was entitled to recover damages either for breach of warranty or for negligent misrepresentation.[283] However, in this case, the contract resulted from the negotiation, and at present, the Misrepresentation Act 1967 provides for such cases regarding pre-contractual negotiation.

Such a broader interpretation was considered to have been confirmed in *Spring v. Guardian Assurance plc.*,[284] where Lord

---

[280] *Id.* at 805-06.
[281] *Id.* at 812.
[282] [1976] Q.B. 801, 833 (C.A.).
[283] *Id.*
[284] [1995] 2 A.C. 296, 318 (H.L.(E.)).

Goff emphasised the special skill of the defendant in preparing a reference with respect to an employee as an essential element to imposing liability. Such skill includes special knowledge, equivalent to the skill of preparing a bank reference, which fell within the expertise of the defendant bank in the *Hedley Byrne* case.[285]

Such broader interpretation seems appropriate, as the receivers of information may rely on the information as long as the representations made are reasonably within the scope of representor's special skills or special knowledge. The receivers of information may not be able to judge what is precisely within the scope of the profession or the business.

In most cases, parties seeking computer programs may be motivated to make contracts based on the special skills of the originators. Such parties are dependent on the special skills of the originators because in most cases there exists a disparity in expertise between the parties. Therefore, a person who acquires computer systems is entitled to rely on the representations of originators in the course of their business.

English law should not have any problem, as supported by the cases described above, in recognising that computer programmers have special skills and are expected to act in accordance with such skills.

[C] Liability of Accountants and Auditors

In the case of accountants or auditors, the scope of eligible plaintiffs has been restricted to avoid the imposition of liability on an indeterminate class of plaintiffs. The court normally finds it easier to impose liability in cases where information was offered to specific known plaintiffs for specific known purpose on which the plaintiffs relied, but which caused loss, as in the case of *Hedley Byrne*.[286] This specific issue has an implication for transactions

---

[285] *Id.*
[286] [1964] A.C. 465 (H.L.(E.)).

involving computer programs, as both transactions involve special skills in completing the tasks, the output of the computer programs may be distributed, and the plaintiff may act on such an output, suffering economic and possibly physical damage.

In *Caparo Industries plc. v. Dickman*,[287] the House of Lords held that an accountant auditing company accounts was not liable to investors who invested in the company by relying on those accounts and incurred damages. The court held that the purpose for which the audit report was supplied was not to make investments, and auditors are liable only if they know that their report is to be used by identified persons for a particular known purpose for which the audit report is supplied. Therefore, non-shareholders contemplating investment were not within the scope of eligible plaintiffs.[288]

Caparo Industries plc. v. Dickman distinguished *JEB Fastners Ltd. v. Marks, Bloom & Co.* on the facts,[289] where the court stated that it is possible to impose liability on auditors who negligently prepared audited accounts. Recovery would be allowed if the defendants knew or ought reasonably to have foreseen at the time the accounts were prepared, that the report was prepared for the purpose of being shown to the prospective take-over bidder of the company, and plaintiffs might suffer loss if the accounts were inaccurate, even though the defendants did not know specifically that the report would be shown to the plaintiff.[290] The accountant knew that financial support was needed and one of the foreseeable methods was a take-over, and by the time the audit was certified, the accountant knew the plaintiffs would be a possible source of finance.[291]

---

[287] [1990] 2 A.C. 605 (H.L.(E)).
[288] *Id.* at 662.
[289] *Id.* at 642.
[290] *Id.*
[291] [1981] 3 All. E.R. 289, 300-01.

Likewise, *Morgan Crucible Co. plc. v. Hill Samuel & Co. Ltd.*[292] held that there may be a relationship of proximity between the plaintiff, an identified bidder, and the defendants who intended that the plaintiff would rely on their audited financial statements to make an increased bid.[293]

With regard to transactions in information technology, if certain data were processed and the output of the computer program is relied on, plaintiffs in such cases may claim that they have incurred economic losses relying on such output. If the supplier of such computer programs knows that the output is to be used by known identified persons for a particular known purpose then liability may be imposed.[294] On the contrary, if such information is to be distributed to an unidentified public, then the scope of eligible plaintiffs may be considered too broad.

[D] Representations in Traditional Form with Respect to Information in Electronic Form

In *Professional Reprographic Services Ltd. v. DPS Typecraft Ltd.*,[295] the plaintiffs alleged that they were misled into leasing Apple Mac II computers by misrepresentation of the defendants. The plaintiffs leased the equipment from a third-party finance house, which purchased the equipment from the defendants. The plaintiffs were a company that conducted the business of typesetting. The defendants were a company that supplied computer equipment. There was no direct contractual relationship between the plaintiffs and the defendants. The plaintiffs claimed that they were misled into acquiring the Apple Mac II computer by representations that the computer could drive their existing Linotype 101 typesetter, notwithstanding the fact that it spoke a

---

[292] [1991] Ch. 295 (C.A.).
[293] *Id.* at 321, 324.
[294] *See* Esanda Fin. Corp. Ltd. v. Peat Marwick Hungerfords [1997] 142 A.L.R. 750 (H.C.).
[295] 15 February 1993 CA (unreported) LEXIS.

different computer language.

The plaintiffs expressly asked for a computer that could drive their existing Linotype 101 typesetter. The defendants expre-ssly represented that the Apple Mac II could drive the 101 so as to provide columns of type and, by implication, that it could drive tables and thus commercially viable material. Since the technology was relatively new and untried, the defendants did not know whether their representations as to the capabilities of the Apple Mac II were true. Nevertheless, the defendants made such representations assuring the suitability of the system and the plaintiffs had relied upon their representations.

The court stated that in negligence cases, a plaintiff must demonstrate the following; first, a duty of care owed by the defendant to the plaintiff and, second, a breach of that duty.

The defendants knew that the plaintiffs relied on the defendants' salesperson to answer accurately questions as to the equipment's capabilities. The defendants also knew that this was comparatively new and untried equipment and did not really know whether the relevant representations made were true but trusted in their own expertise to put any problems right. The defendants had a duty to investigate the viability of the proposed system for the specific technique which the plaintiffs had specifically identified. It was their duty to delve deeper, at least to the extent of checking with the company's own technical manger, whether the equipment was capable of the function to which the plaintiffs' inquiry was specifically addressed.

The plaintiffs relied on the representative's special knowledge or skill and the defendants departed from the standards of a reasonably competent supplier. Therefore, there was a special relationship based on special knowledge or skills between the parties. It was essential, for the existence of such a special relationship, that there was disparity in expertise between the parties.

[c] United States
[i] Physical Injury

In the United States, principles of free speech and free dissemination of information do not prevent the imposition of liability if speech is directed to inciting or producing imminent lawless action and is likely to bring, incite or produce such action.[296] Therefore, the imposition of liability is possible if a high degree of active use is anticipated. In *Weirum v. RKO General, Inc.*,[297] the court imposed liability on a radio station that conducted a contest rewarding the first contestant to locate a peripatetic disc jockey. The plaintiff's decedent was killed when his automobile was negligently forced off a highway by a listener of the radio station. The court, in examining whether the defendant owed a duty of care, which was a question of law, examined whether the risk was foreseeable, which was a question of fact for the jury. The court found that the defendant's youthful listeners, finding the prize had eluded them at one location, would race to arrive first at the next site and in their haste would disregard the demands of highway safety.[298] The court also stated that it is of no consequence that the harm to the decedent was inflicted by third parties acting negligently. The court stated that:

> If the likelihood that a third person may react in a particular manner is a hazard which makes the actor negligent, such reaction whether innocent or negligent does not prevent the actor from being liable for the harm caused thereby. Here, reckless conduct by youthful contestants stimulated by defendant's broadcast, constituted the hazard to which the decedent was

---

[296] *See* Brandenburg v. Ohio, 395 U.S. 444, 447 (1969); Herceg v. Hustler Magazine, Inc., 565 F. Supp. 802, 804 (S.D. Tex. 1983).
[297] 539 P.2d 36 (Cal. 1975).
[298] *Id.* at 40.

exposed.[299]

Such imposition of liability should also be possible if the information is on the Internet. Furthermore, as will be explained later, it might be useful in determining the degree of liability, to consider whether the information is used actively or passively.[300] With regard to transactions involving computer programs, computer programs are always used actively to perform certain functions. Computer programs are purchased for the purpose of achieving utilitarian functions.[301] It may be noted that the fact that there is active and intentional intervention by a third party does not change the liability of the person who made a statement.[302] This is the typical example of the third scenario where the intermediate party acts upon the information causing damage to a third-party victim.

[ii] Economic Loss
[A] Special Relationship -Liability of Auditors

In *Ultramares Corp. v. Touche*, a New York court held that in order to be liable for negligent misrepresentation, the accountant must be in privity of contract with the person seeking to impose liability or there must be a "bond that is so close as to approach that of privity, if not completely one with it." [303] In this case, the defendants, a firm of public accountants, were employed to prepare and certify a balance sheet at the end of the year. They

---

[299] *Id.*

[300] *See infra* § 2.03 Theories Relevant To Imposing Liability [5] Strict Products Liability [c] Reasons for Applying Strict Liability or Negligence for Information in Traditional Form and in Electronic Form [iii] Intended Use.

[301] *See* Braun v. Soldier of Fortune Magazine, Inc., 968 F.2d 1110 (11th Cir. 1992), *cert denied*, 506 U.S.1071 (1993)(holding a publisher liable for placing an advertisement of a sniper, who assassinated the plaintiff's father, because the advertisement on its face contained a "clearly identifiable unreasonable risk" of harm to the public).

[302] *See* § 2.02 Form of Injuries [1] Three Scenarios.

[303] 174 N.E. 441, 446 (N.Y. 1931).

had been regularly employed at the end of each of the three years to render such services. The auditors knew that the company was in need of capital, though the actual credit transactions were not communicated to them. The defendants knew that in the usual course of business the balance sheet would be shown to banks, creditors, stockholders, and purchasers but did not specifically know the plaintiff. The court stated, "If liability for negligence exists, a thoughtless slip or blunder, the failure to detect a theft or forgery beneath the cover of deceptive entries, may expose accountants to a liability in an indeterminate amount for an indeterminate time to an indeterminate class."[304] It probably helped the defendants' case that the purpose of preparing the balance sheet was not specifically confined to extending credits.[305]

Likewise, the New York court in *Credit Alliance v. Arthur Andersen & Co.*[306] held that accountants would be liable only if they were aware that financial reports were to be used for a particular purpose in furtherance of which a known party was intended to rely. The court found that the accountants did not prepare the audit report for the particular purpose in mind. The accountants did not specifically agree with the plaintiffs to prepare the report for the plaintiffs, for the use of or according to the plaintiffs' requirements and had not specifically agreed with the plaintiffs to provide them with a copy.[307] The court felt that the following rule should be applicable to find a "special relationship" to impose liability: (1) the accountants must have been aware that the financial reports were to be used for a particular purpose or purposes; (2) in the furtherance of which a known party or parties was intended to rely; and (3) there must have been some conduct

---

[304] *Id.* at 444.
[305] *See* JEB Fastners Ltd. v. Marks, Bloom & Co. [1981] 3 All E.R. 289, 293 (Woolf J.).
[306] 483 N.E.2d 110 (N.Y. 1985).
[307] *Id.* at 119.

on the part of the accountants linking them to that party or parties, which evinced the accountants' understanding of that party or these parties' reliance.[308]

However, some states find that the holding in the *Ultramares* case is too restrictive with respect to the scope of the duty of care. The North Carolina case, *Raritan River Steel Co. v. Cherry, Bekaert & Holland*,[309] specifically rejected the "privity or near-privity" approach in *Ultramares Corp. v. Touche* because "it provides inadequately for the central role independent accountants play in the financial world."[310] In the *Raritan* case, the court upheld the position taken by Restatement (Second) of Torts, section 552,[311] as applied to accountants, as follows,

> [A]n accountant who audits or prepares financial information for a client owes a duty of care not only to the client but to any other person, whom the accountant or his client intends the information to benefit; and that person reasonably relies on the information in a transaction, or substantially similar to it, that accountant or his client intends the information to influence.[312]

The accountants have to know of their clients' intentions as to whom their clients intend the information to benefit, at the time they audit to prepare the information.[313]

The court stressed the fact that there exists heavy public reliance on accountants' work and such reliance could be the basis of imposing liability on a non-contractual party; therefore;

---

[308] *Id.* at 118.
[309] 367 S.E.2d 609 (N.C.1988).
[310] *Id.* at 615.
[311] *See supra* note 239.
[312] *Raritan*, 367 S.E. 2d at 614.
[313] *Id.*

accountants should be liable to those persons or class of persons whom they know will reasonably rely on their work.[314] It is essential for the imposition of liability that the defendant auditors know that the statements would be used to represent the company's condition to creditors who would extend credit, and that the plaintiffs and other creditors would *rely* upon these statements. With such knowledge, the auditor could have, through purchase of liability insurance, set fees and adopted other protective measures appropriate to the risk.[315]

The court also rejected the approach upheld in some states, such as New Jersey,[316] Wisconsin,[317] and Mississippi[318] of holding accountants liable to all reasonably foreseeable plaintiffs.

The court distinguished the cases involving liability of auditors from the cases involving liability of designers and manufacturers in order to justify establishing a narrower class of plaintiffs to whom the auditors owe the duty of care.[319]

According to the *Raritan River* case, one difference between the audit report and the products concerned the control of the diffusion of the outcome of the work. Manufacturers and designers may be able to limit their potential liability by controlling the number of products they release in the market place. "Auditors, on the other hand, have no control over the distribution of their reports, and hence lack control over their exposure to liability"[320] This may be due to the fact that copying is relatively easy for

---

[314] *Id.* at 615.
[315] *Id.* at 616; *see supra* note 239.
[316] *See* Rosenblum v. Adler, 461 A.2d 138, 153 (N.J. 1983).
[317] *See* Citizens State Bank v. Timm, Schmidt & Co., 335 N.W.2d 361, 366 (N.J. 1983).
[318] *See* Touche Ross & Co. v. Commercial Union Ins., 514 So.2d 315, 322 (Miss. 1987).
[319] *Raritan*, 367 S.E.2d at 616.
[320] *Id.*

reports. Reproduction is also relatively easy in cases of computer programs. Furthermore, auditors necessarily rely on their clients for the content of their clients' records when rendering an opinion concerning the accuracy of such records. Therefore, there is a lack of control over some of the contents of the statements they assess.

Another difference is the expectation concerning the outcome of works done by manufacturers, designers and auditors. Manufacturers and designers can expect that their products will be used by a wide variety of unknown members of the public. Wider use would produce profits. On the other hand, accountants perform an audit pursuant to a contract with an individual client, therefore, wider distribution does not bring benefit to the accountants. Instead, wider distribution by copying, exposes their works to many whom they may have no idea will scrutinise their efforts. Therefore, their liability should be limited to those persons or class of persons whom they know will rely on their work.[321]

Even manufacturers and designers may not be able to control further distribution once the articles are made; nevertheless, they may be held liable only for products that they actually reproduce. It is technically easier for anyone to copy audit reports than products. No matter who is responsible for the copy of an audit report, the copy of the report indicates the name of the auditors responsible for creating the information. As a result, liability may be imposed on the accountants.

In any case, imposition of liability with respect to economic loss, whether concerning articles or statements, requires more than the more creation of such articles or statements. For instance, in *East River S.S. Corp. v. Transamerica Delaval, Inc.,*[322] recovery of eco-nomic loss caused by articles under tort theory was also restric-ted. Therefore, plaintiffs have to bring a claim that comes within the exceptions to the general rule against recovery of

---

[321] *Id.* at 616.
[322] 476 U.S. 858 (1986).

economic loss, including cases where there was express warranty or rendition of professional liability.[323]

In order to impose liability for both statement and articles, there should be a connection, between the manufacturers and the "injuring parties" which has been described as "a special relationship." The essential factors constituting such connection include, express warranties, exercise of special or skills or knowledge, disparities in expertise between the parties, and an assumption of responsibility coupled with concomitant reliance, which may give rise to a tortious duty of care irrespective of whether there is a contractual relationship between the parties, unless precluded by contract.[324] Such requirements apply irrespective of whether the damage is the consequence of the defective statements or articles. As discussed before, when determining the effect of the professional statements, it is hard to differentiate, as giving or not giving professional advice can also mean to giving or not giving instructions to act.

Results of operating computer programs, such as human-readable information in electronic form, may be reproduced more easily than those in traditional form. Just as knowledge of the purpose was required for an imposition of liability for the damage resulting from statements, knowledge of purpose may be required for an imposition of the liability for the damage resulting from information in electronic form.[325]

Finally, *Bily v Arthur Young & Co.*[326] illustrates an attempt

---

[323] *See supra* § 2.03 Theories Relevant To Imposing Liability [3] Negligence [c] United States [iv] Actions Based on Warranties and [v] Liability Based on Expertise.

[324] *See* Henderson v. Merrett Syndicates Ltd. [1995] 2 A.C. 145, 194 (H.L.(E.)).

[325] *See supra* § 2.03 Theories Relevant To Imposing Liability [3] Negligence [b] England [ii] Defective Articles, Compensation for Lack of Quality and [c] United States [iv] Actions Based on Warranties and [v] Liability Based on Expertise.

[326] 834 P.2d 745 (Cal. 1992).

by a United States' court to consider this issue. This court denied the possibility of recovery to investors against auditors on a theory of general negligence. However, it upheld the possibility of an auditor's liability to the investors under negligent misrepresentation theory under Restatement (Second) of Torts section 552.[327] The court held that auditors owe no general duty of care regarding the conduct of an audit to persons other than the client, and would not treat the mere presence of a foreseeable risk of injury to third persons as sufficient, standing alone, to impose liability for negligent conduct.

Under the *Bily* case, accountants can be held liable for negligent misrepresentations in an audit report to those persons who act in reliance upon those misrepresentations in a transaction which the auditor intended to influence in accordance with section 552. For instance, the auditor may be held liable to a third-party lender if the auditor is informed by the client that the audit will be used to obtain a $50,000 loan, even if the name of the specific lender is unknown to the auditors.[328]

Such a distinction between negligent acts and negligent statements may seem superficial in cases where specific or special skill is exercised, as discussed above. However, as has been stated previously, the United States' courts tend to restrict the recovery of economic loss to cases where claims based on negligent acts are involved. Therefore, recovery based on theories of negligent misrepresentation and fraud in inducement, as discussed above,[329] is useful in expanding the scope of recovery of economic loss without expanding the scope within the context of negligent act.

---

[327] *Id.* at 747 ; *see supra* note 239.
[328] *Bily,* 834 P.2d at 758.
[329] *See* § 2.03 Theories Relevant To Imposing Liability [2] Fraud.

[B] Representations in Information in Traditional Form with Respect to Information in Electronic Form -Distinction Between Negligent Misrepresentation and Fraud in Inducement

There are a number of cases where the cause of action is negligent misrepresentation regarding the supply of computer systems between the parties in privity. However, compared to the fraud in inducement cases discussed above,[330] negligent misrepresentation claims can be regarded as disguised breach of warranty claims. Furthermore, breach of warranty claims arising from misrepresentation are generally barred by a general merger clause or restricted by a limitation of the remedy clause. Therefore, the imposition of negligent liability for the mere failure of the computer system supplied may prove problematic. Furthermore, as discussed above, in the United States it is difficult to avoid the constraints of contractual terms because the statutory control over such terms is not as strong as in England.[331]

In the United States, claims based on negligence are generally said to require a special relationship between the parties.[332] The buyer-seller relationship, even if it involved computer programs, is not generally adequate to sustain a cause of action based on negligent misrepresentation. It should be noted however that the courts do not have much difficulty in holding defendants liable for fraud in inducement in the same cases.

---

[330] *See supra* § 2.03 Theories Relevant To Imposing Liability [2] Fraud [c] United States.

[331] *See supra* § 2.03 Theories Relevant To Imposing Liability [3] Negligence [b] England [iv] Implication of Restrictions on Contractual Terms.

[332] *See supra* § 2.03 Theories Relevant To Imposing Liability [4] Negligent Misrepresentation [c] United States [ii] Economic Loss [A] Special Relationship -Liability of Auditors.

In *AccuSystems, Inc. v. Honeywell Information Sys., Inc.*,[333] the New York court stated that a cause of action for negligent misrepresentation is not recognised in New York State unless there is a special relationship of trust or confidence between the parties.[334] As described previously in the section on fraud, the plaintiff entered into a transaction with the defendant based on a representation that the operating system had been extensively tested, had been installed in a number of other locations where it functioned well, and was capable of multitasking. The plaintiff also claimed that the defendant failed properly to service the system sold. The buyer-seller relationship was not enough to support a cause of action of negligent misrepresentation.

However, the court found that the action for fraud in inducement could be sustained because the representations made by Honeywell to the plaintiff prior to the agreement were known to be false or made recklessly, without knowing whether they were true or false, in order to induce plaintiffs to enter into agreement.[335]

Likewise in *Phoenix Technologies, Inc. v. Quotron Systems, Inc.*[336] causes of action for neg-ligent misrepresentation required a special relationship between the parties. The plaintiffs asserted claims of fraudulent inducement and negligent misrepresentation in misrepresenting the role of the Call-In Center. Under New York law, a general merger clause bars a claim for negligent misrepresentation arising under agreements that pertain to the

---

[333] 580 F. Supp. 474 (S.D.N.Y. 1984); *see supra* § 2.03 Theories Relevant To Imposing Liability [2] Fraud [B] In the Context of Professional Liability - Disparity of Expertise [B] New York Law (discussing Accusystems in detail).
[334] *Id.* at 480.
[335] *Id.* at 482.
[336] 1997 WL 220285 (E.D.Pa 1997), *aff'd* 135 F.3d 766 (3d Cir. 1997); *see supra* [2] Fraud [B] In the Context of Professional Liability - Disparity of Expertise [B] New York Law (discussing Phoenix Service in detail).

relationship of duty. Therefore, contracts bar any understanding or agreements extrinsic to the terms of the contract. Nevertheless, as in the case of *AccuSystems, Inc. v. Honeywell Information Sys., Inc.*,[337] the court held that the fraud in inducement claim could be considered separately from the contractual claim.

[C] Information in Electronic Form -Negligent Referral

The same principle concerning a special relationship was applicable with respect to negligent referral in *Pied Piper, Inc. (Pied Piper) v. Datanational Corp.* (Datanational).[338] Following a presentation by an IBM sales representative, Pied Piper purchased Datanational's customised software and IBM's computer system. An IBM representative recommended that the plaintiff purchase the computer system through the defendant, Datanational, an authorised IBM dealer. The defendant was referred to as IBM's "Business Partner." Following the installation of the computer system, customised software developed numerous "bugs" which greatly impeded Pied Piper's ability to conduct its retail business. Pied Piper alleged that IBM breached its duty to Pied Piper when it recommended Datanational as a seller to Pied Piper. It was held that the legal duty with respect to negligent referral exists when there is a fiduciary or special relationship of trust, and that such duties do not exist between commercial entities dealing with one another at arms' length, as compared to the situation where a physician can be liable for negligent referral.[339]

In the cases concerning referring physicians, they are liable if there is some control of the course of treatment, agency or concert of action, or negligence in the referral. Liability for negligent referral requires the actual knowledge of alleged incompetence. Determinate factors listed in cases regarding physicians in finding liability are the physician's: 1) actual knowledge of incompetence

---

[337] 580 F. Supp. 474 (S.D.N.Y.1984).
[338] 901 F. Supp. 212 (S.D.W.Va 1995).
[339] *Id.* at 214.

of the referred physician; 2) control or the right of control over the surgical process; 3) knowledge and skill to assess that proposed surgical procedure to be performed by the referred physician is outmoded; 4) fee received; 5) participation in diagnosis; and 6) physical presence during the surgery.[340]

Even in transactions between commercial entities involving computer consultants, if a "special relationship" is considered to exist it may be possible to impose liability for referral, provided that the same requirements were fulfilled.

[D] Content of Information in Electronic Form

In *Daniel v. Dow Jones & Co., Inc.*,[341] defects in the content of the information on the Internet were at issue. The subscriber to a computerised database was held not to have a special relationship with the provider, who merely transmitted the news, necessary to impose liability for negligent misstatements. The court stated that the "special relationship" required for an action for negligent misstatement must be greater than the relationship between the ordinary buyer and seller.[342] The plaintiff became a subscriber to the service of Dow Jones News/Retrieval offered by the defendant, a computer database provider. The plaintiff asserted that he relied on the pricing in the report to his detriment; the plaintiff did not realise that the prices referred to were in United States dollars, not Canadian dollars.

The court stated in a footnote "even though the exact nature of the 'contract' cannot be definitely determined on the record here, that does not effect the disposition."[343] In this case, it was not established that the agreement was formed between the parties and there was no proof that the plaintiff agreed to a limitation of the

---

[340] Reed v. Bascon, 530 N.E.2d 417, 422 (Ill. 1988).
[341] 520 N.Y.S.2d 334 (Cir. Ct. 1987).
[342] *Id.* at 338.
[343] *Id* at 337 n.1.

defendant's liability as a part of the on-line sign-up procedure.[344] The court held that the First Amendment precludes the imposition of liability for non-defamatory, negligently untruthful news. As the defendant's service was considered as a modern, alternative way the public may obtain up-to-the minute news, the court conferred the same protection as that provided for a more established means of news distribution. Imposition of such liability would place an intolerable burden of trying to satisfy a fact finder that its acts had been reasonable in determining the accuracy of the news items portrayed.[345]

Likewise, in *Cubby, Inc. v. Compuserve, Inc.*,[346] online service providers were considered more like a "distributor" than a "republisher," and they were liable for defamation on its system only where they knew or should have known of the defamatory statements.[347] A distributor was considered a passive conduit and would not be found liable in the absence of fault.[348] As discussed previously, it is easy to publish information on the Internet, and intermediaries, such as online providers here are not as involved in the content as publishers.

On the other hand, in *Stratton Oakmont, Inc. v. Prodigy Services Co.*,[349] the court found that Prodigy, the owner and operator of the computer network on which the defamatory statements appeared, was a publisher. Prodigy held itself out to

---

[344] *Id.*
[345] *Id.* at 340.
[346] 776 F. Supp. 135 (S.D.N.Y. 1991).
[347] RESTATEMENT (SECOND) OF TORTS § 581 (1976); *see also* Lunney v. Prodigy Services Co., 250 A.2d 230 (N.Y. App. Div. 1999) (holding that an Internet service provider was not a publisher and was not negligent in failing to prevent impostor from opening account using plaintiff's name).
[348] *See* Stratton Oakmont, Inc. v. Prodigy Serv. Co., 23 Media L. Rep. (BNA) 1794, 1995 WL 323710, *3 (N.Y. Sup. Ct. 1995) *renewal denied,* 24 Media L.Rep. (BNA) 1126, 1995 WL 805178 (N.Y. Sup. Ct. 1995).
[349] *Id.*

be controlling the content of its services and it used software automatically to pre-screen messages that were offensive or in bad taste. Publishers, such as newspapers, as compared to distributors such as newsagents, are more than a passive receptacle or conduit for news, comment and advertising. Prodigy exercised sufficient editorial control over its computer bulletin boards, by actively utilising technology and manpower to delete notes from the boards on the basis of offensiveness and "bad taste", to render it a publisher with the same responsibility as a newspaper. In this case, Prodigy's choice to gain the benefits of editorial control, exposed Prodigy to greater liability than other computer networks that made no such choice.[350]

In the United Kingdom, a libel case against an Internet service provider was settled before it was due to go to court. Demon Internet agreed to pay £15,000 for damages and an estimated £230,000 in costs to a physicist who was allegedly defamed by anonymous postings on the net. One of the postings was a forgery purporting to be from the physicist. The physicist protested repeatedly, but Demon Internet failed to remove the postings.[351] This case may imply that Internet service providers are subject to the same libel laws as newspapers and other media.

In both England and in the United States, Internet service providers may be required to withdraw messages as soon as a complaint is made, whether or not libellous.[352]

[d] Defences for Negligence

Contributory negligence is a defence to negligence. Recipients of information can be negligent in acting on reliance of information. As described in the second and third scenarios,[353] the issue of

---

[350] *Stratton*, 1995 WL 323710 at *3.
[351] THE GUARDIAN 31 March 2000.
[352] THE GUARDIAN 3 May 2000.
[353] *See supra* § 2.02 Form of Injuries.

contributory negligence is of importance when either victims or intermediate parties are acting on information.

For instance, in *Aetna Casualty & Surety, Co. v. Jeppesen & Co.*,[354] the court found that the relevant crew member was negligent in allowing himself to be misled by the variance in scale between the plan and the profile.[355] In transactions concerning information in machine-readable electronic form as compared to information in human-readable published form, the level of the end-users' skills and expertise tends to vary, giving greater divergence in determination of the contributory negligence.

In *Mackenzie Patten & Co. v. British Olivetti Ltd.*,[356] the court found that in addition to the fact that the computer system was not suitable for the plaintiffs' needs, it was also not suitable for operation for the plaintiffs' employees' needs. The defendants told the plaintiffs that the system was completely suitable and anyone with average intelligence could be taught to operate it. An expert witness affirmed that the system was out of date and obsolescent and considerable training for five days of an intelligent person by a competent installation programmer would have been required. With respect to a transaction involving computer technology, the users may need substantial training to operate the machines. Both the suitability of the system itself and support from the manufacturer may be essential for the users to use the system correctly and achieve the purpose for the acquisition, especially in cases such as this one where the plaintiffs were given assurance as to its suitability. As computer programs become increasingly common in the office environment, such office computer systems may be expected to be operated by average people without

---

[354] 642 F.2d 339 (9th Cir. 1981).
[355] *Id.* at 343.
[356] 11 January 1984 (Q.B.) (unreported) LEXIS; 1 C. L. & P. 92 (1984); 48 M.L.R. 344 (1985).

too much training unless the need for such training is clearly indicated.

It should also be noted that the courts have been emphasising disparity in expertise when allowing the cause of action to be based on fraud or misrepresentation, and that users are entitled to rely on the representation made by experts that the system would work.

[e] Comparison

In both England and the United States, with regard to negligent act or negligent misstatement, "special relationships" between the parties are required as the prerequisites for the imposition of liability for economic loss.

Courts have restricted the compensation for economic loss regarding negligent statements fearing the creation of a liability in an indeterminate amount for an indeterminate time to an indeterminate class. However, compensation may be available in circumstances where representors, with special skills, know or should know the purpose for which a report is prepared; for example, if the representors know the identifiable group of people to whom the report is to be shown and the likelihood of their reliance upon it.

With respect to transactions involving information in electronic form, reliance upon outputs from computer programs may cause damage. The purpose for which the information is offered and the range of recoverable plaintiffs are two of the important issues in allowing recovery.

The users of such outputs may be the parties who had acquired the computer programs from the supplier. In such cases, the court may first examine the contractual terms between the parties.

If there is no such contract, the court may consider the specificity of the computer programs. If the computer programs are custom-made for the users, it would be likely that the purpose is specific and an identifiable group of people is involved. If the computer programs are widely distributed for a general purpose such as calculation, the specific purpose is not known to the supplier. There may also be a problem in identifying a specific group of plaintiffs who would rely on the outputs.

The users of such outputs may not be the parties who had acquired the computer programs from the supplier. In such cases, it is rare to find contracts between the suppliers and the users of information. For instance, outputs of computer programs in an investment bank containing data for investment advice to clients may be relied on by the investors. If clients incur losses, a court would inquire, as requisites to finding liability, how specific the purpose of information was, and whether the supplier knew their clients' intentions, i.e. who the bankers or their clients intend the information to benefit. It would be considered favourable to finding liability that the suppliers knew that the investment bank was intending to target a specific group of people, for instance, a group working in a particular company.

With regard to negligent misstatements that induce the acquiring of computer systems, in England, it is not necessary to resort to fraud for the plaintiffs to avoid the application of contractual terms and obtain a remedy. Purchasers or users of computer systems are entitled to rely on the expertise of computer consultants. A special relationship would be likely to be created based on the special knowledge and skill existing between the parties.

In the United States, many courts do not recognise the special relationship for a cause of action based on negligent misrepresentation between the parties with respect to the purchase, referral and recommendation of computer systems. Between the parties to a contract, negligent misrepresentation claims can be regarded as ways to avoid the application of contractual terms. This is based on the idea that computer programmers or suppliers are not providing a "professional" service. The relationship between the parties is considered as a "buyer-seller relationship," not involving a professional service. Only a minority of courts recognises the existence of a special relationship between the parties, based on the special skills of computer suppliers or consultants. Such cases tend to call attention to the disparities in expertise between the parties.

In the United States, claims based on fraud in inducement and claims based on negligent misrepresentation are considered separately. Even if claims based on negligent misrepresentation are not allowed, the court may allow claims based on fraud in inducement claims, thus allowing the claimants to avoid the application of contractual terms. The court may find private autonomy may not work in cases where there is a huge gap in knowledge and bargaining power between the parties. Transactions involving computer systems need to be examined by considering these factors.

The general law against the recovery of economic loss is not applicable in transactions involving computer programs because of the specific nature of transactions involving computer programs. Computer programs are meant to perform certain functions and may produce some output or physical acts. In most of these transactions, there is reliance on special skill or knowledge in the supply of computer programs. Computer programmers, like accountants, exercise highly professional skills in creating computer programs. Unlike audit reports, computer programs are not normally distributed to indeterminate plaintiffs as suppliers attempt to control the distribution by licensing agreements to an identifiable class. Computer programs are transferred together with specifications and instructions, which represent the quality of the programs.

[5] Strict Products Liability
[a] Overview of Statutes in England and in the United States
[i] England

Donoghue v. Stevenson[357] removed the privity requirements in tortious claims for physical loss. Since then, statutory provisions have been implemented to impose liability, such as the Consumer Protection Act 1987[358] which implemented the EC's Product Liability Directive.[359]

Article 1 of the Directive states "The producer shall be liable for damage caused by a defect in his product." Article 3 provides that "'Producer' means the manufacturer of a finished product, the producer of any raw material or the manufacturer of a component part and any person who, by putting his name, trade mark or other distinguishing feature on the product presents himself as its producer." Furthermore, "any person who imports into the Community a products for sale, hire, leasing or any form of distribution in the course of his business shall be deemed to be a producer" and shall be responsible as a producer.

Sections 2(1) and (2) of the 1987 Act provide that where damage is caused wholly or partly by a defect in a product, the following persons shall be liable for the damage:

(a) the producer of the product;
(b) any person who, by putting his name on the product or using a trade mark or other distinguishing mark in relation to the product, has held himself out to be producer of the product;
(c) any person who has imported the product into a

---

[357] [1932] A.C. 562 (H.L.(Sc.)).
[358] 1987, c.43.
[359] Council Directive (EEC) 86/374 on Products Liability.

member State from a place outside the member States in order, in the course of any business of his, to supply it to another.

Section 1(2) of the Consumer Protection Act 1987 provides that "producer" in relation to a product, means:

(a) the person who manufactured it;
(b) in the case of a substance which has not been manufactured but has been won or abstracted, the person who won or abstracted it;
(c) in the case of a product which has not been manufactured, won or abstracted but essential characteristics of which are attributable to an industrial or other process having been carried out (for example, in relation to agricultural produce), the person who carried out that process.

Section 3(1) of the 1987 Act provides that there is a defect in a product "if the safety of the product is not such as persons generally are entitled to expect." " 'Safety' in relation to the product shall include safety with respect to products comprised in that product and safety in the context or risks of damage to property, as well as in the context of risks of death or personal injury." Section 3(2) provides that persons are generally entitled to expect that the product is as described. This expectation extends to "the manner in which, and the purpose for which, the product has been marketed, its get-up, the use of any mark in relation to the product and any instructions for, or warning with respect to, doing or refraining from doing anything with or in relation to the product."[360]

---

[360] Consumer Protection Act 1987 (c.43), s. 3(2)(a).

Article 6 of the Directive provides that:
(1) A product is defective when it does not provide the safety which a person is entitled to expect, taking all circumstances into account, including:
(a) the presentation of the product;
(b) the use to which it could reasonably be expected that the product would be put;
(c) the time when the product was put into circulation.
(2) A product shall not be considered defective for the sole reason that a better product is subsequently put into circulation.

Article 2 of the Directive provides that products are all movables. In the Consumer Protection Act 1987, a product is defined as any goods or electricity and "includes a product which is comprised in another product, whether by virtue of being a component part or raw material or otherwise."[361] Furthermore, under the 1987 Act, "goods" includes substances, and "substances" means "any natural or artificial substance, whether in solid, liquid or gaseous form or in the form of a vapour, and includes substances that are comprised in or mixed with other goods."[362] Information is not within the 1987 Act, even though information may be incorporated in tangible form in a book.[363] These definitions do not seem to incorporate a computer program as the subject matter of the products liability law,[364] although hardware embedding computer programs are considered "goods."

However, the European Court of Justice might be able to

---

[361] s. 1(2).
[362] s. 45(1).
[363] *See* ROGERS, *supra* note 115, at 342-43; S. Whittaker, *European Product Liability and Intellectual Products,* 105 L.Q.R. 125, 128 (1989).
[364] J. Stapleton, *Software, Information and the Concept of Product,* 9 TEL AVIV U. STUDIES IN LAW 147, 147-52 (1989).

adopt a flexible approach in treating software as goods if the product is defined as "something capable of money valuation and of being an object of commercial transactions."[365]

As stated above, software itself is not within the scope of the products liability law even if devices which integrate the software are within the scope of the law. The question arises as to whether it is appropriate to relieve the liability of computer programmers, despite the fact that the defective software may cause injury. It may be more appropriate for the courts to examine the characteristics and function of the subject matter of the transaction.[366] In the meantime, Glidewell J. in *St. Albans City & District Council v. International Computers Ltd.*[367] took the position, obiter, that instruction manuals were "goods" under the Sale of Goods Act 1979.[368]

As provided for in section 3(2)(a) in the 1987 Act and article 6 of the Directive, information surrounding products, such as instructions, warning, and representations are considered in determining the existence of the defect under the Act. It can be said that computer programs, when supplied with hardware, may be considered as an instruction to the hardware, and therefore, can be included in the scope of application.[369]

[ii] United States

Section 402A of the Restatement (Second) of Torts (1965) provides;

---

[365] J. STAPLETON, PRODUCT LIABILITY 334 (1994); *see also* Whittaker, *supra* note 363, at 128 (stating, "But, if we say that it is the defective information in the book, which causes the harm, rather than the defective book, why cannot we treat the information itself as a product for the purposes of the Directive? Information can be treated as property -"intellectual property" -and is so to different degrees and in different conceptual themes throughout the Community").

[366] *See* STAPLETON, *supra* note 365, at 334.

[367] [1996] 4 All E.R. 481 (C.A.).

[368] *Id.* at 493.

[369] *See* Stapleton, *supra* note 364, at 152.

(1) One who sells any product in a defective condition unrea-sonably dangerous to the user or consumer or to his property is subject to liability for physical harm thereby caused to the ultimate user or consumer, or to his proper property, if (a) the seller is engaged in the business of selling such a product, and (b) it is expected to and does reach the user or consumer without substantial change in the condition in which it was sold. (2) the rule stated in Subsection (1) applies although (a) the seller has exercised all possible care in the preparation and sale of his product, and (b) the user or consumer has not bought the product from or entered into any contractual relation with the seller.

Even though the scope of application is limited to "products," the courts are applying the products liability law to information in traditional form.

For instance, in *Halstead v. United States*[370] and in *Winter v. G.P. Putnam's Sons*,[371] it was held that a mass-distribution navigational chart was a product.

[b] Generic Policy Issues
[i] Products

As discussed in the previous section on statutes, the strict products liability law is applicable to transactions involving products. The strict products liability law is not intended to be applicable per se to information in either its traditional or electronic form, though the courts would not find it difficult to apply it to machines incorporating computer programs.[372] The

---

[370] 535 F. Supp. 782, 791 (D. Conn.1982).
[371] 938 F.2d 1033 (9th Cir.1991).
[372] *See* Lewis v. Timco, Inc., 697 F.2d 1252, 1253 (5th Cir. 1983); Kramer v. Lamb-Grays Harbor Co., Inc., 639 P.2d 649, 650 (Or. Ct. App. 1982).

courts would consider that the machines, which incorporate the computer programs as a whole, are products.

To date, there have not been many instances of litigation concerning the application of the strict products liability law to information in electronic form, though there are many cases related to repetitive stress injuries attributed to the use of computer keyboards.[373] This is mainly because of the fact that defects in information in electronic form are less likely to cause physical actions and more likely to induce economic loss rather than physical injuries.[374] Nevertheless, a minority of jurisdictions adopts the approach of eliminating a requirement of privity of contract even in relation to economic injuries.[375]

In the future, litigation of such a nature may increase due to the development of computer technology and information in electronic form, as applied to or as incorporated into various systems causing physical injuries. As discussed above, the current law emphasises the physical form of the subject matter rather than the actual functions of the subject matter of the transactions. This may lead to an arbitrary result. It is helpful to look beyond the physical characteristics of the subject matter and analyse the function of the subject matter in the light of the policy reasons justifying strict products liability law.

[ii] Policy Reasons

The policy reasons for applying the product liability law, as explained generally, are as follows: 1) unequal bargaining power; 2) mass-production; 3) consumer reliance; 4) impersonal distribution; 5) difficulty of proving negligence; 6) an ability on the part of the manufacturer to spread risk of loss through

---

[373] *See, e. g.,* Bowers v. N. Telecom, Inc., 905 F. Supp. 1004 (N.D. Fla. 1995).
[374] *See* TAPPER, *supra* note 39, at 228.
[375] *See supra* § 2.03 Theories Relevant To Imposing Liability [4] Negligence: Negligent Act Causing Economic Injury [b] United States.

numerous transactions;[376] and, 7) fair apportionment of the risks inherent in modern technological production.[377] Comment c of the Restatement (Second) of Torts section 402A (1965) states that:

> c. On whatever theory, the justification for the strict liability has been said to be that the seller, by marketing his product for use and consumption, has undertaken and assumed a special responsibility toward any member of the consuming public who may be injured by it; that the public has the right to and does expect, in the case of products which it needs and for which it is forced to rely upon the seller, that reputable sellers will stand behind their goods; that public policy demands that the burden of accidental injuries caused by products intended for consumption be placed upon those who market them, and be treated as a cost of production against which liability insurance can be obtained; and that the consumer of such products is entitled to the maximum of protection at the hands of someone, and the proper persons to afford it are those who market the products.

Manufacturers, by the use of mass advertising and merchandising practices, cause consumers to rely for their protection upon the skill and expertise of the manufacturers.[378] Consumers rely on sellers or manufacturers for guidance and information about the products due to their lack of specialised technical knowledge.[379]

---

[376] *See* La Rossa v. Scientific Design Co., 402 F.2d 937, 942 (3d Cir. 1968); NIMMER, *supra* note 39, at ¶10.14 [2][a].

[377] The Council Directive (EEC) 85/374 on Product Liability, preamble.

[378] J.E. Montgomery & D.G. Owen, *Reflections on the Theory and Administration of Strict Liability for Defective Products,* 27 S.C.L. REV. 803, 809-10 (1976).

[379] Henningsen v. Bloomfield Motors, Inc., 161 A.2d 69 (N.J. 1960).

It would be unfair to require consumers to trace the article they used to the original manufacturer and to prove acts of negligence remote from their knowledge.[380] On the other hand, professional services are not within the scope of strict liability. Traditionally, mass-production of professional services to a large body of distant consumers was rare.[381] However, at present, professional services may be provided in a mass-production context by large law firms or architecture firms. An attempt to create professional services in a mass-production context can be observed in the development of intelligent knowledge-based expert adviser systems.[382]

The emphasis on product for the purpose of applying products liability can be problematic. The products liability law is said to hold manufacturers liable to the end-users, but not to hold service providers, directly liable to the end-users. This is based on the presumption that the manufacturers of goods are supposedly in the best position to avoid unreasonable risks or hazards, and they can bear the cost of insurance. However, it is possible for service providers, such as designing firms, which are hired by the manufacturers, to be insured against the loss incurred by end-users. The present system would relieve the liability to end- users of designers who provided defective services when designing the system for the manufacturers.[383] Likewise, computer programmers, who provided the "defective service" to the assembler of the computer system, escape liability in relation to end-users. These "service providers" are like the manufacturers of goods supplied with the product. Here the concept of the defectiveness of goods overlaps with the concept of defective services.[384] Liability of the service providers, of course, could be pursued on different

---

[380] *La Rossa*, 402 F.2d at 942.
[381] *Id.* at 942.
[382] *See* TAPPER, *supra* note 39, at 262-68.
[383] Stapleton, *supra* note 364, at 149.
[384] *Id.* at 157.

theories including contract or negligence, and through a series of indemnifications. However, from the viewpoint of injured parties, the fact remains the same; the party is injured by the defective design.[385] Therefore, the distinction between "products" and "information" is not convincing as the categories of "defective goods" and "defective services" overlap, creating arbitrary results.

Furthermore, injury may be attributed to intangible "information"[386] but not the physical entity of the products. In this case, the influence of the information is far greater than its physical carrier, even though the physical carrier is a necessary adjunct to the information. Therefore, the question arises as to why there is a need to introduce the concept of "a good" as the essential element in imposing the strict products liability law.

In the context of products liability law, inadequacy of the information regarding products such as warnings or directions may provide grounds for strict liability even though the product itself is not defective. Breach of one's duty to warn could also be a basis for an action in negligence as well.[387] Many courts and

---

[385] *Id.* at 149.

[386] *See* H.L.A. HART & T. HONORE, CAUSATION IN THE LAW 133-35 (2d ed. 1985) (discussing the usage of the word "cause").

[387] *See* RESTATEMENT OF TORTS § 388 (1965)("One who supplies directly or through a third person a chattel for another to use is subject to liability to those whom the supplier should expect to use the chattel with the consent of the other or to be endangered by its probable use, for physical harm caused by the use of the chattel in the manner for which and by a person for whose use it is supplied, if the supplier

  (a) knows or has reason to know that the chattel is likely to be dangerous for the use for which it is supplied, and

  (b) has no reason to believe that those for whose use the chattel is supplied will realize its dangerous condition, and

  (c) fails to exercise reasonable care to inform them of its dangerous condition or of the facts which make it likely to be dangerous."); *see also* Consumer Protection Act 1987 (c. 43), s. 3(2)(a).

commentators argue that there is no practical difference between an action in negligence for breach of one's duty to warn and an action in strict liability for a product defect or inadequate warning or labelling.[388]

[iii] Core Information

It can be said that injury may result from products themselves or from peripheral information, such as instructions, which supplement or aid the way in which the products would be put into use. By the same token, injury may result from the content of the information itself ("core information") or from peripheral information, such as instructions. When the "core" information is supplied, there could be instructions, warnings, or explanations as to how, when, or in what manner the information should be put to use. However, it could be hard to differentiate in this case, what is the content and what is the instruction, warning or explanation. There could be layers of information surrounding "core" information in circumstances where recipients of the information are unfamiliar with the way to utilise certain information. The existence of peripheral information could be essential in some cases to avoid injuries caused by information. For instance, the navigational chart in *Aetna Casualty and Surety, Co. v. Jeppesen & Co.*,[389] might not have been deemed defective had there been a clearer indication or warning that a different scale was used. With respect to the utilisation of complex, high technology core information, the supply of peripheral information is essential to the utilisation of such core information.

Just as instructions or warnings with respect to products are already part of products for the purpose of the strict products liability law, some computer programs, particularly when supplied

---

[388] *See* Forest v. E.I. Dupont de Nemours, & Co., 791 F. Supp. 1460, 1462-63 (D. Nev. 1992); Sara Lee Corp. v. Homastote Co., 719 F. Supp. 417, 420 (D.Md. 1989).
[389] 642 F.2d 339 (9th Cir. 1981).

by the same supplier with hardware, can be considered as instructions for the hardware, and thus be included in the scope of the application for the strict liability law.[390] Programs such as operating systems are considered to communicate directly with hardware in this context. The relationships between packaged software such as Lotus 1-2-3 or Word 98 and hardware are not as direct as an operating system; nevertheless, software gives instructions to the hardware.

Information in electronic form, such as computer programs, is supplemented with instruction manuals. Such information is highly technical in nature and users are not always knowledgeable about the computer programs. Products liability law may be imposed on computer systems with instruction manuals provided that the computer systems, differentiated from the computer program itself, are considered as "products". The present legal system pertaining to products liability law imposes liability based on the existence of what are conventionally thought of as "products" and information supplied with such products. As previously described, computer programs are instructions which purport to execute certain tasks. If there is a defect in such instructions, it could directly, without any intervening act by the injuring party, cause an effect with the aid of peripheral devices, such as hardware. Therefore, in some cases, there is no difference in terms of causing injury, whether there is a product involved or not. The applicability of products liability law may need to be reconsidered taking the directness of effects into account.

[iv] Different Types of Defects

Defects in products are categorised into manufacturing defects, design defects, and failure to warn of defects. It may be hard to imagine manufacturing defects in information in the electronic form itself, as the information is digitally reproduced.

---

[390] *See* TAPPER, *supra* note 39 at 258; *see* Stapleton, *supra* note 364, at 152.

Therefore, manufacturing defects concern a physical medium. Computer programs can be defectively designed but, as mentioned above, they can also become defective when incorporated as part of the computer system. Specification, warnings or instructions concerning commuter programs directed to human beings may not be adequate to cover all the usages of the particular program for all levels of users. It may be impossible to cover all the aspects of the technology.

[c] Reasons for Applying Strict Liability or Negligence for Information in Traditional Form and in Electronic Form

[i] Similarity to Physical Products

In the United States, a federal court in *Halstead v. United States*,[391] held that a navigational chart was a product. Denying the defendant Jeppesen's argument that he was providing professional services in connection with a navigational chart rather than products, the court stated that Jeppesen was not a member of any recognised profession such as medicine, architecture or engineering, nor did Jeppesen provide any specialised service.

The court referred to other cases where plans and maps were considered goods, and held that they were not merely embodiments of intangible professional advice but "subjects of barter and sale, or capable of multiple uses."[392] The court was convinced that the classification of the Jeppesen chart as a product conforms to the rational of § 402A, considering Jeppesen's activity of mass-production and distribution of the charts. The court also stated that, if suitable for mass-marketing, the information is in some sense a fungible good.

---

[391] 535 F.Supp. 782, 789 (D. Conn.1982).

[392] *Id.* at 790; *see also* Wirtz v. A.S. Giometti & Assoc., Inc., 399 F.2d 738 (5th Cir. 1968); Shultz v. Merriman, 303 F. Supp. 1174, 1177 (D.N.H. 1969), *modified,* 425 F.2d 228, 229 (1st Cir. 1970).

On the other hand, in *Winter v. G.P. Putnam's Sons*,[393] the court denied the application of the products liability law to the content of the book *The Encyclopedia of Mushrooms*. The court rejected the plaintiff's argument that the strict product liability rules should be applied to books that give instructions on how to accomplish a physical activity and that are intended to be used as part of an activity that is inherently dangerous. The court found such a limitation illusory and stated that, while "How To" books are a special genre, it declined to attempt to draw a line that puts "How To Live A Good Life" books beyond the reach of strict liability while leaving "How To Exercise Properly" books within its reach.[394] However, the court separated navigational charts from the type of books described above. The court stated that:

> Aeronautical charts are highly technical tools. They are graphic depictions of technical, mechanical data. The best analogy to an aeronautical chart is a compass. Both may be used to guide an individual who is engaged in an activity requiring certain knowledge of natural features. The chart itself is like a physical "product" while the "How to Use " book is pure thought and expression.[395]

The opinion which considered an aeronautical chart or compass as "a physical 'product'" and distinguished it from "How to Use" book as pure thought and expression is not very helpful, since detailed charts can also be incorporated into a book or a cookbook to show the procedure in preparing meals. The reason for not imposing strict liability in this case should have been based primarily on the policy concerning freedom of speech and the principle of free dissemination of ideas. The court should

---

[393] 938 F.2d. 1033 (9th Cir. 1991).
[394] *Id.* at 1035.
[395] *Id.* at 1036.

ask whether the effect of application inhibits freedom of speech and the principle of free dissemination of ideas. Another concern should be the grave possibility of physical injury for using such information. As will be discussed later, the courts seem to consider, as one factor, whether the possibility of physical harm is high because of the intended "active use" of the information.

The product versus pure expression distinction could well be considered illusory. Both chart and "pure thought and expression" require being "read" or recognised and some physical action may be taken to cause their indirect effect.

The court found with aeronautical charts and a compass that "both may be used to guide an individual who is engaged in an activity requiring certain knowledge of natural features." Computer software, as well, was considered an example of a product involving information, which falls within the scope of the products liability law.[396] However, all the "How to" books also have such features.

Despite the arguments that computer software and certain information should be considered as a "product," as in the *Winter v. G.P. Putnam's Sons case*, computer programs have not been included within the scope of the products liability law.[397]

Glidewell J.'s *obiter* opinion in *St. Albans City & District Council v. International Computers Ltd.*[398] that instruction manuals were "goods" under the Sale of Goods Act 1979, takes the United States' view further with respect to liability for manuals. Glidewell J. stated that if manuals including instructions on the maintenance and repair of a particular make of car were wrong in important respects, and were likely to cause serious damage to the engine of the car, the manual would be considered "goods" within the mean-

---

[396] *Id.* at 1035.
[397] W.V.H. ROGERS, WINFIELD & JOLOWICZ ON TORT 342 (15th ed. 1998).
[398] [1996] 4 All E. R. 481, 493.

ing of the Sales of Goods Act 1979. The defective instructions would result in a breach of the implied terms in section 14 of the 1979 Act. This decision would have a great impact on any judgement determining whether or not certain information such as instruction manuals or the computer programs are "products." Therefore, in terms of application of the products liability law or sales law, the difference between instructions or computer programs and physical products is becoming increasingly ambiguous, and this distinction should be reconsidered with reference to the effect and potential damage the subject matter could cause.

[ii] Mass Distribution

Mass distribution coupled with creation, designing and manufacturing of the information, such as navigational charts, is one of the most important bases for finding certain information to be a "product." On the other hand, several courts have been careful not to include "mere provision of architectural design plans or any similar form of data supplied under individually-tailored service arrangement" as a "product."[399]

In *Saloomey v. Jeppesen & Co.*,[400] the court held that in accordance with the rationale of Restatement (Second) of Torts, section 402A,[401]

> Jeppesen undertook a special responsibility as seller, to insure that consumers will not be injured by the use of the chart.... This special responsibility lies upon Jeppesen in its role as designer, seller and manufacturer....the mass

---

[399] K-Mart Corp. v. Midcon Realty Group of Conn., Ltd., 489 F. Supp. 813, 818 (D.Conn. 1980); *see* La Rossa v. Scientific Design Co., 402 F.2d 937, 942-43 (3d Cir. 1968).

[400] *Saloomey*, 707 F.2d 671.

[401] *See* comment c (1965); *see supra* § 2.03 Theories Relevant To Imposing Liability [5] Strict Products Liability [a] Overview of Statutes in England and in the United States [ii] United States.

production and marketing of these charts requires Jeppesen to bear the costs of accidents that are proximately caused by defects in the charts.[402]

Therefore, mass production and marketing are the essential factors justifying responsibility of Jeppesen to bear the costs of accidents.

The United States federal court in *Halstead v. United States*[403] concluded that, since the official comments to Restatement (Second) of Torts section 402 A imply that the doctrine of strict liability was principally intended to impose a special liability on those who market defective products to the general public in a mass-distribution context, a mass-distribution navigational chart was a product.[404] The court further noted that:

> If suitable for mass marketing, the information is in some sense a fungible good for which the manufacturer placing it on the market assumes responsibility..... Jeppesen mass produced and distributed thousands of charts on the aviation market. Implicit in their presence on the market was the representation that the purchaser could rely on their information safely. Exposing defendant Jeppesen's conduct to strict products liability is thus entirely appropriate[405]

On the contrary, for an architect who designs a single set of plans and specifications for a single building, the imposition of products liability was considered inappropriate. This may arguably support extending strict products liability to mass-marketed design

---

[402] *Saloomey*, 707 F.2d at 677.
[403] 535 F. Supp. 791 (D. Conn. 1982).
[404] *Id.* at 791.
[405] *Id.*

and development of buildings.[406]

However, it should be noted that manufacturers are just as responsible for placing non-fungible goods on the market, even though those non-fungible goods are not readily available at the retail level for replacement.

It may true that a manufacturer of a mass-produced product may have superior bargaining power and thus be able to impose standard form contracts on consumers who are not well informed about the risks involved in products. They are also in the better position to spread the loss to mass consumers. It is relatively easy for a mass-produced product to be diffused to parties whose relationship to the manufacturer is remote. One of the purposes for having a products liability law is to allow remote consumers to seek compensation against upstream manufacturers. Imposition of products liability law may be justified in circumstances where there is no bargaining.[407]

Therefore, in a mass-distribution context, just as the manufacturer is held liable under strict product liability, designers may be held liable as well, unless, as rendering professional services, their duty is limited to exercising the skill and knowledge normally possessed by members of that profession or trade.[408]

The policy reasons behind the imposition of products liability law can be considered to favour the application of this law to certain types of information in electronic form, particularly to mass-market software.[409]

[iii] Intended Use

Unde products liability law, strict liability in tort is generally meant to protect the customer from the intended use of defectively

---

[406] *Id.*; *see also* K-Mart Corp. v. Midcom Realty Group of Conn., Ltd., 489 F. Supp. 813, 818-19 (D.Conn. 1980).
[407] *See* STAPLETON, *supra* note 365, at 116.
[408] RESTATEMENT (SECOND) OF TORTS § 299A (1965).
[409] *See* TAPPER, *supra* note 39, at 255 (4th ed. 1989).

produced merchandise. A plaintiff could recover for injuries caused by use of a product with a defective design that makes it unsafe for its intended use, so long as the plaintiff was unaware of the defect at the time of use.[410] This intended use theory is used as a justification not to impose liability on authors who write about any topic that might result in physical injury to the readers of books.

In *Walter v. Bauer*,[411] the court did not impose liability on a book publisher when a student was injured while doing a science project described in a textbook. The court determined that the book Discovering Science 4, which described a scientific experiment, could not be said to be a defective product, for the infant plaintiff was not injured by the use of the book for the purpose for which it was designed, i.e., to be read.[412]

However, this argument is not convincing in the sense that it cannot explain why some sorts of information such as a navigational chart were deemed to be products. Navigational charts also have to be "read" in order to be understood. In order for any information to be understood, it first has to be read. Reading is the only means by which the human being can understand the content of the information. As this argument fails to recognise the fact that any information has to be read to be understood by recipients, other theories are necessary to justify the imposition of strict products liability. One justification offered in the *Walter* case is that the imposition of strict liability in tort with respect to a science book would have a chilling effect on the First Amendment, freedom of speech. This opinion suggests that authors cannot be exposed to strict liability for writing on a topic such as how to cut trees or keep

---

[410] *See* Aetna Cas. and Sur. Co. v. Jeppesen & Co., 642 F.2d 339, 342-43 (9th Cir. 1981); Worrell v. Barnes, 484 P.2d 573, 575-76 (Nev. 1971); *overruled by* Calloway v. City of Reno, 993 P.2d 1259 (Nev. 2000); Restatement (Second) of Torts § 402 A (1965).
[411] 439 N.Y.S.2d 821 (Sup. Ct. 1981).
[412] *Id.* at 822.

bees which might result in physical injury.⁴¹³ Legal text books that contain precedents are other examples of information which may be relied upon.

With respect to the imposition of liability regarding published books, taking the First Amendment and issues regarding an "infinite number of victims" into account, it might be useful in determining the degree of liability to consider whether the use was an active or passive one. For instance, in the *Walter* case, the textbooks can be said to be actively used. If there is a description about the experiment in the textbook, it is intended to be actively used by the students. Likewise, information such as instruction and repair manuals for commodities is intended to be used actively. The difference between a text book and instructions manuals may not be so great. Instruction manuals are more actively used than a text book.

On the other hand, there are cases such as *Herceg v. Hustler Magazine, Inc.,*⁴¹⁴ where the defendant published a descriptive article on the practice of "autoerotic asphyxiation" entitled "Orgasm of Death," which allegedly caused the death of both the plaintiff's son and brother.⁴¹⁵ In this case, the primary reason for publication was not to incite the relevant activity. It was intended for passive use. People are not expected to act violently just because they watch a violent television program.

However, there may be certain information that may be too shocking for even passive audiences to bear and cause emotional distress.

It should be noted that principles of free speech and free dissemination of information do not prevent the imposition of liability if the speech is directed to inciting or producing imminent lawless action and is likely to bring it to incite or produce such

---

[413] *Id.* at 823.
[414] 565 F. Supp. 802 (S.D. Tex. 1983).
[415] Id. at 803.

action.[416]

This is illustrated in *Weirum v. RKO General, Inc.*,[417] described previously, where information was actively used by youthful listeners to find the prize at one location. The court held that it was foreseeable that defendant's youthful listeners, finding the prize had eluded them at one location, would race to arrive first at the next site and, in their haste, would disregard the demands of the highway.[418] In *Weirum v. RKO General, Inc.*, a certain act of a disc jockey *incited* youthful listeners to drive recklessly and cause an accident, harming another driver.

In comparison, computer programs are meant to execute certain intended tasks, causing precisely an intended effect. They are intended to be used "actively." Many computer programs have the same function as instructions or manuals for products. They are expected to be used to bring about certain results and such results can cause serious physical damage. Therefore, this should be taken into account when determining liability with respect to computer programs.

[d] England

In *St. Albans City & District Council v. International Computers Ltd.*,[419] Sir Iain Glidewell did not think that it was necessary to determine whether programs are goods to trigger the application of the Sales of Goods Act, as there was a clear breach of the expressed contractual terms. However, *obiter*, he considered that computer programs and an instruction manual on the maintenance and repair of a particular make of car are goods within the meaning of the 1979 Act.[420]

---

[416] *See* Brandenburg v. Ohio, 395 U.S. 444, 447 (1969); *Herceg*, 565 F. Supp. at 804.
[417] 539 P.2d 36, (Cal. 1975).
[418] *Id.* at 40.
[419] [1995] F.S.R. 686, [1996] 4 All E.R. 481 (C.A.).
[420] *St. Albans*, [1996] 4 All E.R. at 493.

Furthermore, despite the lack of physical presence, computer programs, as stated *obiter* at first instance by Baker J.,[421] may alter the contents of the hardware and be considered a product. However, Baker J.'s opinion that programs need to be contained in some physical medium is not appropriate. There are many ways in which the transaction can be executed in the light of current technology. The law does not need to depend upon the tangibility of the subject matter to determine which law is applicable to the particular transaction.[422]

[e] United States

In the United States, there has been no substantial litigation on the issue of computer programs. There are a number of cases that deal with machines that incorporate computer programs,[423] and many cases regarding defective design of the keyboard.[424]

Sparacino v. Andover Controls Corp.,[425] presents issues regarding computer programs manufactured by one party and then incorporated into a system by another manufacturer. In this case, the plaintiff filed a complaint against the defendants alleging that the defendants negligently sold, distributed and installed a dangerous and defective energy management system (EMS) and failed to give adequate warnings on the dangers of the inability

---

[421] *St. Albans*, [1995] F.S.R. at 699.

[422] C. Tapper, *Some Aspects of Contractual Licences for Software*, in CONSENSUS AD IDEM: ESSAYS IN THE LAW OF CONTRACT IN HONOUR OF GUENTER 283, 286 (Treitel ed. 1996).

[423] Lewis v. Timco, Inc., 697 F.2d 1252 (5th Cir. 1983); Kramer v. Lamb-Grays Harbor Co., Inc., 639 P.2d 649 (Or. *Ct. App.1982).

[424] *See* Bowers v. N. Telecom, Inc., 905 F. Supp. 1004 (N.D. Fla 1995) (citing expert testimony regarding "cumulative trauma disorders" sufficient to raise a genuine issue of fact in trial); Garessy v. Digital Equip. Corp., 980 F. Supp. 640 (E.D.N.Y. 1997) (upholding manufacturer's duty to warn regarding the risk of RSI).

[425] 592 N.E.2d 431 (Ill. App. Ct. 1992).

to override the safety exhaust system.[426] The defendants are the company that manufactured microprocessing equipment for building automation systems (Andover), and manufactured the EMS, and the company that incorporated the EMS into a heating, ventilating, air conditioning (HVAC) system and installed the system (CMC).

The HVAC system was designed by architects, energy consultants and design engineers. The plaintiff, a chemistry teacher, was injured because he could not activate the exhaust fan to draw out noxious chlorine gas to be used in experiment in the class room at 6:15 a.m. A computerised EMS in the exhaust fan was programmed not to operate until 6:30 a.m. The EMS was user-programmable and could be overridden by the wiring to particular switches. The EMS supplied by Andover to CMC was selected by CMC to meet the needs of architects and energy consultants. Andover did not know about the installation or the use of the EMS.[427]

For strict liability, the court considered whether the EMS was unreasonably dangerous and failed to perform in the manner reasonably expected in light of its nature and intended function. The court stated that it was up to the assembler of the system to install a safety device on a machine and that the manufacturer of a component part had no control over the part once it is sold and has no control over the final assembly of the machine.[428] Accordingly, Andover did not have a duty to foresee that CMC would integrate the user-programmable EMS in a dangerous or defective manner. It was CMC who programmed the EMS system in such a manner. The EMS was not dangerous as assembled, and the EMS did not

---

[426] *Id.* at 433.

[427] *Id.* at 434.

[428] *Id.* at 435; *see also* Jordan v. Whiting Corp., 212 N.W.2d 324, 328 (Mich. Ct. App. 1973), *modified [sic]* 240 N.W. 2d 468 (Mich. Ct. App. 1976).

fail to perform in the manner reasonably expected in light of its nature and intended function. Therefore, CMC may have owed a duty to warn but Andover's product was considered not defective or inherently dangerous. Therefore, strict liability was not imposed on Andover.[429]

For negligence, the court considered whether Andover had a duty to warn users of the potential dangers in connecting an exhaust fan to an EMS system without providing the ability for the user to override the system's control of the fan. It was held that, even assuming that Andover had known of the potential danger, it was not reasonable to expect that a chemistry experiment would be taking place in the school when no one was scheduled to be in the school; therefore, it was not foreseeable that the user of the exhaust fan would be injured in the manner in which the plaintiff was injured.[430] The specification that the EMS be programmed in an occupancy schedule is not unusual when the building is a school. Furthermore, EMS systems was user programmable and could have been overridden and Andover did not install or wire the EMS in a manner which would disable the exhaust fan. It was CMC who programmed and installed the EMS.[431]

The present law seems to emphasise the responsibility of assemblers who physically assemble the system rather than the manufacturers of components or the designer of the system. Even though the injury may be attributed to the components, it may be difficult to determine who is responsible for the injury in the complex system and the assembler can always be held responsible for not making the final products safer by overriding the system of each component. However, there is a danger that the technology to manufacture a computer program may be too complex for the integrator, who is not sufficiently knowledgeable to override or

---

[429] *Sparacino*, 592 N.E. 2d at 435.
[430] *Id.* at 436.
[431] *Id.*

re-design the programs to fit to whole system.

As computer programs can be used as components of many types of machines, a manufacturer of components should owe a duty fully to disclose information regarding the function of the components.

[f] Defences for Products Liability Law
[i] The Development Risk
[A] England

With respect to the strict products liability law, article 7(e) of the Product Liability Directive[432] provides that the producer shall not be liable as a result of the directive if he proves that the state of scientific and technical knowledge at the time when he put the product into circulation was not such as to enable the existence of the defect to be discovered. Section 4(1)(e) of the Consumer Protection Act 1987[433] provides as a defence to liability "that the state of scientific and technical knowledge at the relevant time was not such that a producer of products of the same description as the product in question might be expected to have discovered the defect if it had existed in his products while they were under his control."

There is a concern that if the development risk defence is used in the sense that it excludes liability not only in light of the state of the art at the time but also in light of reasonable foreseeability, then the liability under the Directive is no greater than in negligence. This largely depends on whether to allow the defendants to assert the defence only when the products' defects are undiscoverable given the state of the art, discoverable but only by extraordinary means, or discoverable by ordinary or "reasonable means."[434] In

---

[432] The Council Directive (EEC) 85/374 on Product Liability, preamble. [1985] OJ L210/29.
[433] c. 43.
[434] See STAPLETON, *supra* note 365 at 239.

European Commission v. United Kingdom,[435] the European Commission's approach was clarified when the Commission brought an action alleging that that the United Kingdom had failed to fulfil its obligation under the E.C. Treaty by adopting the subjective assessment. The European Commission asserted that the proper construction of article 7(e) concerns the objective state of scientific and technical knowledge, including the most advanced level of such knowledge. The court of justice dismissed this action. The court held that the wording of the directive implied that the objective state of scientific and technical knowledge, including the most advanced level of such knowledge, had to have been *accessible* at the time when the product in question was put into circulation.[436] Therefore, it would be unrealistic and unreasonable to expect a European product manufacturer to discover, for instance, research carried out by an academic in Manchuria published in a local scientific journal in Chinese, which does not go outside the boundaries of the region.[437]

The court found that the wording of section 4(1)(e) of the 1987 act placed "no restriction on the state of scientific and technical knowledge which was to be taken into account and it did not suggest that availability of the defence depended on the subjective knowledge of a producer taking reasonable care in the light of the standard precautions taken in the industrial sector in question." [438] As section 1(1) of the 1987 Act expressly provides that relevant provisions be construed in conformity with the Directive, there is no evidence to suggest that the English courts would interpret section 4(1)(e) of the 1987 Act inconsistently with the directive.

---

[435] [1997] 3.C.M.R. 923.
[436] *Id.* at 934.
[437] *Id.* at 934.
[438] *Id.* at 941.

[B] United States

Evidence that a product conformed to the then existing state of the art can be introduced as the defence in a number of jurisdictions in the United States. The state of the art in United States' law is generally defined as the level of scientific and technical knowledge available: however, it often includes evidence of industry custom or standards.[439]

Evidence of the state of the art could be admissible as an affirmative defence in some states.[440] Evidence of compliance with federal standards by the manufacturer was admissible in determining whether the product was defective or unreasonably dangerous.[441] Evidence of industry customs and the state of the art technology was admissible to establish the expectation of average users or consumers of the products.[442] In failure to warn cases, evidence of the state of the art was also admissible to show that manufacturers knew that their products posed health risks.[443] Evidence relating to compliance with industry standards and then existing technology was admissible for design defects cases in order to show whether the products had met consumer expectation.[444] Evidence of the state of the art technology was admissible to establish that the product was not unreasonably

---

[439] 47 A.L.R. 4th 621 (1986).

[440] *See. e.g.*, Ariz. Rev. Stat. Ann. §12,683 (2001) (stating, "a defendant shall not be liable if the defendant proves that 1. The defect in the product is alleged to result from inadequate design or fabrication, and if the plans or designs for the product or the methods and techniques of manufcturing, inspecting, testing and labelling the product conformed with the state of the art at the time the product was first sold by the defendant."); Mo. Ann. Stat. §537.764 (2000)(for failure to warn of the dangerous condition of a product).

[441] *See* Rucker v. Norfolk & W. Ry., Co., 396 N.E.2d 534 (Ill. 1979).

[442] *See* Keogh v. W.R. Grasle, Inc., 816 P.2d 1343 (Alaska 1991).

[443] *See* Lohmann v. Pittsburgh Corning Corp., 782 F.2d 1156 (4th Cir. 1986).

[444] *See* Sexton v. Bell Helmets, Inc., 926 F.2d 331 (4th Cir. 1991).

dangerous for normal use in its original condition.[445]

In *Roberts v. Rich Foods, Inc.*,[446] a motorist was injured by a car when the driver of the tractor-trailer was entering data in an "X-300" on board-computer manufactured by defendant company, Cadec Systems, Inc. (Cadec). This was to provide a computerised record of that road usage information for tax-reporting purposes. When the accident took place, the driver was either attempting to make the initial entry by depressing the button for the automatic computer records, making the follow-up entries for information in order to gather road usage, or gathering data for tax reporting purposes.

Under New Jersey law, the manufacturer shall not be liable if the characteristics of the product are known to the ordinary consumer or user, and the harm was caused by an unsafe aspect of the product that is an inherent characteristic of the product. However, such defence is not applicable if the plaintiff can prove that such danger could feasibly be eliminated without impairing the usefulness of the product. Impairing the usefulness of the product means "significantly diminishing its intended use."[447] For instance, to supply motorcycles with crash bars to avoid leg injuries would diminish the product's intended use. Even if it is technically possible, motorcycles are specifically designed as an open-air easily manoeuvrable, light-weight vehicle. The court held that whether the defendant could, without impairing the usefulness of the computer, feasibly have eliminated the dangers of X-300's being operable while in motion is a question for a jury to decide.[448]

With respect to fast - developing computer technology, it is

---

[445] *See* Berry v. Commercial Union Ins. Co., 565 So. 2d 487, 495 (La. Ct. App. 1990).
[446] 654 A.2d 1365 (N.J. 1995).
[447] *Id.* at 1373.
[448] *Id.* at 1374.

difficult to assess the standard practice of industry and the standard of care. The purpose of allowing the state of the art defence is based on the idea that it is not appropriate to impose liability when, given the state of scientific and technical knowledge, it was not possible to discover the existence of the defect.

If the state of the art defence is interpreted broadly, to include customary practices of the industry, it could be easier for computer manufacturers to escape liability. Therefore, it was appropriate to hold in *The T.J. Hooper* case that there were precautions so imperative that even their universal disregard would not excuse their omission, given that such equipment could have been obtained at small cost. On the contrary, if the state of the art defence is interpreted strictly, computer manufacturers are required to have the state of the art technology, the best technology available, in order to escape liability.

[ii] Defence for Manufacturers of Components
[A] England

Another important defence is provided for by the Directive article 7(f) that the manufacturer of a component is not liable "if the defect is attributable to the design of the product in which the component has been fitted or to the instructions given by the manufacturer of the product." In section 4(1)(f)(ii) of the Consumer Protection Act 1987, it is a defence if the defect constituted a defect in a product in which the product in question had been comprised; and "was wholly attributable to the design of the subsequent product or to compliance by the producer of the product in question with instructions given by the producer of the subsequent product."

[B] United States

Likewise, in the United States, *Littlejohn v. Stanley Structures, Inc.*[449] held that "evidence that a product complies with the design and manufacturing specifications of the purchaser may be relevant

---

[449] 688 P.2d 1130 (Colo. Ct. App. 1984).

to the issue whether the product is fit for the purpose for which it was intended."[450] Therefore, in transactions involving computer programs, manufacturers who integrate programs may be held liable if such defect was wholly attributable to the subsequent design, as in *Sparacino v. Andover Controls Corp.*[451] The court found that the manufacturer of a component part has no control over the part once it is sold and has no control over the final assembly of the machine. Therefore, it was up to the assembler of the system to install a safety device on the machine. As the EMS was not dangerous as assembled, there was no need to consider whether there was a duty to avoid injury to another. Furthermore, there was no need to consider whether manufactured components which were not in and of themselves dangerous or defective could become potentially dangerous to another when assembled.

[g] Comparison

In England, and in the United States, even though the computer program itself is not considered a "product," some courts have recognised that computer programs and instructions may be considered as "products."

In both jurisdictions, articles that incorporate computer programs are considered products. However, this analysis may pose difficulties because the party liable for supplying a defective computer program may not be held responsible under strict products liability law.

In the United States, a number of cases have analysed the reasons for separating products from other subject matter. The main reasons are similarity to physical products, mass-distribution and intended use. However, the reason based on similarity to physical products, for instance, characterisation of aeronautical charts as tools and differentiating from other "How to" books

---

[450] *Id.* at 1132.
[451] 592 N.E.2d 431 (Ill. App. Ct. 1992).

seems weak. With respect to intended use, as indicated in *St. Albans City & District Council v. International Computers Ltd.*,[452] instructions or any information which will be actively used and would be likely to cause damages may be considered products. The fact of mass-production may also be considered favourable to the imposition of strict liability. The original purposes for products liability law suggest that computer programs themselves, especially mass-market ones, be considered products.

It may be wiser for the courts to recognise that some types of information, either in traditional form or in electronic form, have the characteristics actively to induce acts, and therefore, should be considered in the same way as products, for the purpose of the strict products liability law.

§ 2.04 Liability in the Chain of Distribution

[1] Information in Traditional Form

The parties in the chain of distribution include parties who are involved in the creation of the information; parties who are involved in implementing the information; parties who are involved in distributing the information; parties who are using the information; and the third-party victim. In this section, I intend to consider the possible liability of the parties for injury, loss or damage at each stage.

[a] Negligence

[i] Authors, Publishers and Sellers of Books

The law concerning authors' liability for errors in information, such as content of books, designs, or drawings may depend on different factors, including the relationship between the parties, the nature of the publication, the method of distribution, intended use, intended audience, causation in fact, and the foreseeability of

---

[452] [1995] F.S.R. 686 (Q.B.D.), [1996] 4 All E.R. 481.

Civil Liability for Defects in Information in Electronic Form

damage.[453]

It is hard to imagine that all authors of the "How To" books will be held liable to all the readers for economic loss or physical injuries, especially with respect to "passive use," as described above.[454]

Compared to authors' liability, publishers' liability is said to have more clearly defined principles.[455] Unless publishers contributed to the content of the information, the court is reluctant to extend negligence liability to the publisher of information.[456]

The main reasons for not imposing liability based on negligent misrepresentation are as follows: 1) by imposing on a publisher a duty to examine the content of publication, the scope of liability would extend to an indeterminate number of potential readers, 2) the defendant's right to publish ideas free of fear of liability, and 3) the public's right of free access to ideas is guaranteed by the First Amendment.[457]

It could be assumed that a distributor's or a seller's liability should be less stringent than the publisher's liability in most cases, since the sellers are less involved in the content of books. The sellers of the books may be held liable in cases where they are responsible for the content or for the decisions as to distributing the books in a new district. For instance, in the case of a mushroom

---

[453] *See* Jones v. J.B. Lippincot Co., 694 F. Supp. 1216, 1216 (D.Md. 1988); Halstead v. United States, 535 F. Supp. 781, 791(D. Conn. 1982); Demuth Dev. Corp. v. Merck & Co., Inc., 432 F. Supp. 990, 993-94 (E.D. N.Y. 1977); *see supra* § 2.03 Theories Relevant To Imposing Liability.

[454] *See supra* § 2.03 Theories Relevant To Imposing Liability [5] Strict Products Liability [c] Reasons for Applying Strict Liability or Negligence for Information in Traditional Form and in Electronic Form [iii] Intended Use.

[455] *See Lippincot*, 694 F. Supp. at 1216 (D.Md. 1988).

[456] *See* Lewin v. McCreight, 655 F. Supp. 282, 283-84 (E.D.Mich. 1987); Alm v. Van Nostrand Reinhold Co., 480 N.E. 2d 1263, 1267 (Ill. App.Ct. 1985).

[457] *Alm*, 480 N.E.2d at 1267.

encyclopaedia, the book may describe the mushrooms in England. The distributor's decision to market the book in the United States may cause injury to the readers there. It could be possible that certain kinds of mushrooms described though not poisonous in England are poisonous in the United States.

[ii] Defamation
[A] England

Likewise, the publisher's liability is restricted in defamation cases in England. The Defamation Act 1996[458] imposes liability on authors, editors or publishers regarding defamatory statements. In defamation proceedings, a person has a defence if she or he shows that she or he was not the author, editor or publisher of the statement complained of, that she or he took reasonable care in relation to its publication, and that she or he did not know and had no reason to believe, that what she or he did caused or contributed to the publication of a defamatory statement.[459]

[B] United States

In *Lerman v. Chuckleberry Publishing, Inc.*,[460] the court stated, "With respect to distributors, the New York courts have long held that vendors and distributors of defamatory publications are not liable if they neither know nor have reason to know of the defamation."[461] In *Lerman v. Flynt Distributing Co.*,[462] it was explained that:

---

[458] Defamation Act 1996 (c. 31).

[459] s. 1.

[460] 521 F. Supp. 228 (S.D.N.Y. 1981), *rev'd* 745 F. 2d 123 (2d Cir 1994).

[461] *Id.* at 235, 745 F.2d 123, 133, 140-41 (2d Cir. 1994); *see also* Cubby, Inc. v. Compuserve, Inc., 776 F. Supp. 135, 138-40 (S.D.N.Y. 1991); RESTATEMENT (SECOND) OF TORTS § 581 cmt. d. (1976) ("News dealers. Under the rule stated in this Section, a news dealer is not liable for defamatory statements appearing in the newspapers or magazines that he sells if he neither knows nor has reason to know of the defamatory article. The dealer is under no duty to examine the various publications that he offers for sale to ascertain whether they contain any defamatory items. Unless there are special circumstances that should warn the

Obviously, the national distributor of hundreds of periodicals has no duty to monitor each issue of every periodical it distributes. Such a rule would be an impermissible burden on the First Amendment. At the same time a distributor as an integral part of the movement of information from the creator to the reader--the distributor here was to receive 46% of the profit from the sale of the magazine--cannot be entirely immune from liability. When a distributor acts with the requisite scienter in distributing materials defaming or invading the privacy of a private figure it must be subject to liability.[463]

It seems appropriate to impose a different level of liabilities for authors, publishers and distributors. Basically, the same principle that governs information in traditional form may be used for the law in information on the Internet, however, there are some differences described above.[464]

[b] Products Liability Law

Information can be designed, created and distributed by different sources, such as distributors, sellers, publishers, designers and computer programmers.

As discussed above[465] in *Saloomey v. Jeppesen & Co.*[466] and

---

dealer that a particular publication is defamatory, he is under no duty to ascertain its innocent or defamatory character. On the other hand, when a dealer offers for sale a particular paper or magazine that notoriously persists in printing scandalous items, the vendor may do so at the risk that any particular issue may contain defamatory language.")

[462] 745 F.2d 123 (2d Cir. 1984), *cert denied*, 471 U.S. 1054, (1985).

[463] *Id.* at 139.

[464] *See supra* § 2.03 Theories Relevant To Imposing Liability [4] Negligent Misrepresentation [a] Negligent Misrepresentation and Information in Electronic Form.

[465] *See supra* § 2.03 Theories Relevant To Imposing Liability [5] Strict Products Liability [ii] Mass Distribution.

Halstead v. United States,[467] it was easy to determine that Jeppesen was strictly liable for the damage because parties were responsible for publishing and selling charts in a mass-scale production context. *Halstead v. United States* stated that from the presence on the market established from mass-marketing, it was implied that there was a "representation that the purchaser could rely on their information safely"[468] In *Saloomey v. Jeppesen & Co.*, it was stated that the mass-production and marketing of the charts required Jeppesen to bear the costs of accidents that are proximately caused by defects in the charts.[469] Those opinions suggest the possibility of the imposition of strict products liabi-lity with respect to design and development of buildings mass-marketed to the public.[470]

However, in the case of designers or computer programmers who may be considered as rendering professional services, their duty is limited to exercising the skill and knowledge normally possessed by members of that profession or trade.[471] In order to hold them liable for the same type of strict products liability, such parties must expressly warrant that there are no defects in such services. For manufacturers, it could be possible to separate deliberately the designing division from the manufacturing divisions in order to evade the application of the product liability law.

One of the reasons for imposing strict products liability is based on the idea that the entrepreneurs who make and sell products have the capacity to distribute the losses of the few among the many who purchase the products. There is an assumption that

---

[466] 707 F.2d 671 (2d Cir. 1983).
[467] 535 F. Supp. 791 (D. Conn.1982).
[468] *Id.* at 791.
[469] *Saloomey*, 707 F.2d at 677.
[470] *Halstead*, 535 F. Supp. at 791 ; *see also* K-Mart Corp. v. Midcon Realty Group of Conn., Ltd., 489 F. Supp. 813, 818-19 (D.Conn. 1980).
[471] RESTATEMENT (SECOND) OF TORTS § 299 A.

the manufacturer can shift the cost of accidents to all purchasers by charging higher prices for the products.[472] The product liability law is based on the idea that liability should be based on "deep-pocket, loss-spreading and best-insurer goals," however, liability is not necessarily imposed on this class of defendants,[473] for instance, designer firms may be just as resourceful as manufacturers, and manufacturers may deliberately split off design divisions.

This danger may be especially acute in relation to the provision of mass-marketed software.

[2] Information in Electronic Form

[a] Negligence

Contrary to the cases involving human readable information in traditional or electronic form, the courts are not concerned with interfering with the right to publish ideas free of fear of liability and the right of free access to ideas with respect to computer programs. Publishers of books do not generally have a duty to examine the contents of the publication, since such a rule would be an impermissible burden on the First Amendment.[474]

Publishers or online providers of information on the Internet, could be performing functions analogous to publishers or sellers. Their responsibilities differ in accordance with their involvement.

In England, under section 1 (3)(e) of the Defamation Act 1996, a person shall not be considered the author, editor, or publisher of a statement if she or he is only involved "(e) as the operator of or provider of access to a communications system by means of which the statement is transmitted, or made available, by

---

[472] *See* W.L. PROSSER & W.P. KEETON, PROSSER & KEETON ON TORTS 692-93 (5th ed. 1984).

[473] *See* STAPLETON, *supra* note 365, at 94.

[474] Lerman v. Flynt Distrib. Co., 745 F.2d 123, 139 (2d Cir. 1984), *cert denied*, 471 U.S. 1054 (1985).

a person over whom he has no effective control."

As discussed previously, in *Daniel v. Dow Jones & Co., Inc.*,[475] the court did not impose liability on a provider of news services for misrepresentation who merely transmitted the news and in *Cubby Inc. v. Compuserve, Inc.*,[476] online service providers were considered more like a "distributor" than a "republisher" and they were liable for defamation on its system only where they knew or should have known of the defamatory statements.[477]

On the other hand, in *Stratton Oakmont, Inc. v. Prodigy Services Co.*,[478] if the operators of a computer network hold themselves out to be controlling the content of its services, they are considered "publishers" and may be held liable if they fail to monitor the contents.[479]

[b] Products Liability

In *Yoder v. Honeywell Inc.*,[480] the court held that the parent company of the manufacturer of computer keyboards was not liable under the "apparent-manufacturer" theory to the plaintiff who allegedly suffered repetitive stress injuries.[481] The court denied the liability of the parent company based on the fact that the parent company was not a seller or distributor of the keyboard, even though the parent company designed and copyrighted the printed circuit board.[482]

In applying the products liability law, it is unlikely that

---

[475] 520 N.Y.S.2d 334 (Civ. Ct. 1987).
[476] 776 F. Supp. 135 (S.D.N.Y. 1991).
[477] RESTATEMENT (SECOND) OF TORTS § 581 (1976).
[478] 23 Media L. Rep. (BNA) 1794, 1995 WL 323710 (N.Y. Sup. Ct. 1995) *renewal denied*, 24 Media L. Rep. (BNP) 1126, 1995 WL 805178 (N.Y. Sup. Ct. 1995).
[479] *Id.* at *7.
[480] 104 F.3d 1215 (10th Cir. 1997).
[481] *Id*, at 1224; *see also* RESTATEMENT (SECOND) OF TORTS § 400 (1965)("One who puts out as his own product a chattel manufactured by another is subject to the same liability as though he were its manufacturer.").
[482] *Yoder*, 104 F.3d at 1223.

designers, architects or computer programmers would be considered as suppliers of products. If these parties are considered as rendering professional services, their duty is limited to exercising the skill and knowledge normally possessed by members of their profession or trade.[483] However, it is doubtful whether such characterisation is appropriate considering mass-production, the active use, and functional aspect of computer programs.

[3] Some Issues with Respect to the Liability in the Chain of Distribution

The involvement of parties in the chain of complex distribution affects liability. For human-readable information in electronic form, the liability of intermediaries, such as online providers differs in accordance with their roles in distribution as publishers or distributors. Generally they are not expected to monitor the content of the information unless expressly assuming such responsibility, or they are explicitly warned with respect to the contents whether libellous or not. Internet providers tend to be less involved in the content of the information than ordinary publishers.

However, for machine-readable information in electronic form, service providers', such as computer programmers', obligations are limited to exercising reasonable skills, irrespective of the fact that computer programs may be mass-marketed, or computer firms may have the capacity to distribute the losses of the few among the many who purchase the products.

§2.05 Issues Regarding Tort and Contract

[1] Overview

The substance of this topic has already been introduced in previous sections, however, I attempt to summarise and clarify

---

[483] *See supra* [5] Strict Products Liability [b] Generic Policy Issues.

some of the issues prior to the discussion of contract law. One of the important issues regarding a tortious claim with respect to information in electronic form is whether a tortious claim is allowed when there is a contractual relationship between the parties. The reasons for plaintiffs to bring tortious claims are mainly to evade application of 1) contractual terms which disclaim warranties, limit or exclude remedies available to the users, and 2) contractual statute of limitation which is likely to be shorter than the one in tort.

With regard to contractual remedies, a party should be put in the position in which he or she would have been placed had the contract been enforced whereas, for tortious remedies, a party should be put in the position in which he or she would have been placed had the tortious act not been committed.

The disparity in bargaining position and in expertise in transactions involving computer programs causes difficulties for a number of plaintiffs. Allowing the tortious claim may save ordinary users who may not have the bargaining power to negotiate the terms of the agreements. Even if the users can negotiate the terms, it may be difficult for an unskilled user to estimate correctly the risks involved in purchasing the computer systems. It may also be difficult to discover latent defects in a computer in order to bring a suit under the contractual claim provided that the period of the statute of limitations for breach of contract is shorter than the one for tort.[484]

[2] England
[a] Information in Traditional Form
With respect to economic loss incurred by relying on statements, as discussed above, *Henderson v. Merrett Syndicates Ltd.*,[485]

---

[484] *See* Henderson v. Merrett Syndicates Ltd. [1995] 2 A.C. 145, 185 (H.L.(E.)) (Lord Goff).
[485] *Id.*

described in § 2.03 Theories Relevant To Imposing Liability [3] Negligence [b] England [iii] Rendering Services showed a flexible approach to concurrent remedies in contract and tort.

Lord Goff stated that the contracts for services did contain an implied promise to exercise reasonable care and skill in the performance of the relevant services.[486] He argued that if the existence of a contract between a surgeon and his patient did not preclude the existence of a tortious duty to the patient in negligence, there was no reason why a tortious duty should not co-exist with a contractual duty. As assumption of responsibility coupled with the concomitant reliance may give rise to a tortious duty of care, irrespective of whether there is a contractual relationship between the parties, unless contract precludes doing so, the plaintiff may choose the remedy which appears to him to be the most advantageous.[487] In this case, the tortious remedy was preferable for the purpose of the statute of limitation. Furthermore, the whole scheme may have been deliberately set up to avoid privity between the parties.

[b] Information in Electronic Form

In *Henderson v. Merrett Syndicates Ltd.*,[488] Lord Goff stated that in the broad duty of care recognised following the generalisation of the tort of negligence in the 20th century, concurrent remedies in tort and contract should be available not only against medical professionals but also against members of different professions.[489] In transactions involving computer programs, the court may find that transactions involve special skills of the computer suppliers and there exists the assumption of responsibility coupled with concomitant reliance. There are many cases where

---

[486] *Id.* at 193 (Lord Goff).
[487] *Id.* at 194 (Lord Goff).
[488] *Id.* at 185 (Lord Goff).
[489] *Id.* at 192. (Lord Goff)

manufacturers attempt to licence the programs rather than sell them. In these cases, manufacturers ordinarily have the bargaining power to determine the contractual terms. They also have the expertise that users do not have.

Stephenson Blake (Holdings) Ltd. v. Streets Heaver Ltd.,[490] seems to illustrate such arguments in the context of transactions involving computer programs. In England, as stated previously, there is a general consensus that computer consultants providing special skill and concurrent liability in this context should not present any difficulties. However, if there is a contractual relationship as well, to what extent the contractual limitations restrict the claims in tort remains problematic.

As discussed before, attempts by manufacturers to limit or exclude remedies are strictly regulated by the Sale of Goods Act 1979, the Supply of Goods and Services Act 1982, the Unfair Contract Terms Act 1977 and Unfair Terms in Consumer Contracts Regulations 1999. Therefore, in England, there may be less need for plaintiffs to invoke tortious claims than in the United States.

[3] United States
[a] Information in Traditional Form
Recovery under the tort theory of negligence is problematic in cases where the tortious duties imposed on defendants are considered completely to overlap with contractual duties.[491] The court often considers that such a tortious claim is simply a disguised breach of warranty claim brought in an effort to circumvent the restrictive terms of the contract, especially where the integrated purchase contract specifically disclaims prior representations and warranties.[492] The courts would be likely to deny recovery where

---

[490] Q.B.D. (O.R.) H.H.J.Hicks Q.C., 2 March 1994 (unreported).
[491] *See* TAPPER, *supra* note 39, at 239-40.
[492] *See, e. g.*, Ritchie Enter. v. Honeywell Bull, Inc. 730 F. Supp. 1041, 1050-51 (D.Kan. 1990).

the representations alleged in counts for negligence were precisely the representations alleged in counts for breach of warranties, and where fraud was not argued.[493]

Allowing a concurrent claim may be considered to disrupt the bargain principle between the parties.[494] The parties are supposedly entitled to limit their liabilities in relying on the scope of the contractual terms. The parties presumably have negotiated and drafted the agreement; therefore, allowing a tortious claim may undermine commercial stability. However, as discussed previously, the theory of fraud in inducement helps to take the plaintiffs' claims out of the contractual restrictions.

Therefore, a majority of jurisdictions hold that recovery in tort is limited to personal injury cases or cases where property damage was incurred either to property other than the property sold, or to the property sold when rendered useless by some violent occurrence.[495]

Sommer v. Federal Signal Corp.[496] illustrates how the courts deal with such concerns. With respect to physical damage caused by negligent acts, the court found that a fire-alarm company could be held liable in tort to other defendants for contribution in a suit by the owner of a building against all the defendants to recover for property damage due to fire. Exculpatory and limitation of liability clauses in the alarm monitoring company's contract with

---

[493] *See* Rio Grande Jewelers v. Data Gen. Corp., 689 P.2d 1269, 1270-71 (N.M.1984).

[494] *See* Computerized Radiobiological Serv. Inc. v. Syntax Corp., 595 F. Supp. 1495, 1504 (E.D.N.Y. 1984), *aff'd in part rev'd in part,* 786 F.2d 72 (2d Cir. 1986), *overruled by,* Hosp. Computer. Sys. v. Staten Island Hosp., 788 F. Supp. 1351 (D.N. J. 1992).

[495] *See* Rockport Pharmacy, Inc. v. Digital Simplistics, Inc., 53 F.3d 195, 198 (8th Cir. 1995); R.W. Murray Co. v. Shatterproof Glass Corp., 697 F.2d 818, 828-29 (8th Cir. 1983).

[496] 593 N.E. 2d 1365 (N.Y. 1992).

the building owner could be considered ineffective due to the gross negligence of the alarm monitoring company.[497]

The court listed two controlling factors that New York courts rely on to separate contract from tort:

> (1) whether there is a legal duty independent of contractual obligations as an incident of the parties' relationship; and
>
> (2) the nature of the injury.[498]

With respect to the first factor, the court noted that a duty to perform their contractual duties may be imposed on professionals or common carriers and bailees as well as a duty of reasonable care independent of its contracts. The nature of their services and of their relationship with customers was considered to represent significant public interests. With respect to the second factor, the manner in which the injury occurred and the resulting harm was considered. The injury was caused due to a fire that had spread out of control causing extensive damage to the building. Such an "abrupt, cataclysmic occurrence" was thought to be more familiar to the law of tort than to that of contract.[499]

Therefore, the court concluded that the manner in which the injury arose in the case and the resulting harm allowed tortious claims separate from contractual claims. However, it was noted that a duty of reasonable care independent of its contracts may be imposed on professionals or common carriers and bailees, as well as a duty to perform contractual duties.[500]

---

[497] *Id.* at 1370.
[498] *Id.* at 1369.
[499] *Id.* at 1369-70.
[500] *Id.* 1369.

In transactions involving computer programs, the important issue may be whether computer programmers are considered to exercise professional or special skills.

[b] Information in Electronic Form

In *Rockport Pharmacy, Inc. (Rockport) v. Digital Simplistics, Inc.*,[501] the Eighth Circuit, under Missouri law, denied a cause of action in tort from a buyer of a computer system against a seller to recover economic loss. The plaintiff sought compensation for the original cost of the computer system, including maintenance and replacement expenses under the negligence theory.

The economic loss doctrine provides that "where a purchaser's expectations in a sale are frustrated because the product he bought is not working properly, his remedy is said to be in contract alone, for he has suffered only 'economic losses.'"[502] The fact that the parties entered into a maintenance agreement as part of the sale did not help to establish that there was a cause of action for the negligent performance of professional service. Rockport argued unsuccessfully that the economic loss doctrine was not applicable in an action based on the negligent rendition of services by professionals. On the contrary, the court held that the contract between Rockport and Digital was not primarily for services, but rather for the sale of goods.[503] The purpose of the "economic loss" rule is to keep the law of contract and tort separate and distinct, and that the courts should maintain the separation in the allowable remedies. Another purpose of this rule is to sustain the reliability of commercial transactions. Once the contract has been made, the parties should be governed by it. The doctrine is considered to shield a defendant from unlimited liability for all economic consequences of a negligent act, particularly in a commercial

---

[501] 53 F.3d 195 (8th Cir. 1995).
[502] Kennedy v. Columbia Lumber & Mfg. Co., 384 S.E.2d 730, 736 (S.C. 1989).
[503] *Rockport*, 53 F.3d at 198.

setting, thus keeping the risk of liability reasonably calculable.[504]

As discussed above,[505] in New York, a cause of action for negligent misrepresentation is not recognised unless there is a special relationship of trust or confidence between the parties that is more than the buyer-seller relationship. A seller of a computer system is not considered to have a special relationship with its buyers.[506]

The court should consider that buyers would be likely to rely upon the special skills of their suppliers in transactions involving computer systems. As discussed above, disparity in expertise is an important factor in imposing responsibility on computer suppliers, as many consumers are not sufficiently expert to judge whether the systems offered are suitable.

However, even if a cause of action based on negligent misrepresentation is not sustained, a cause of action based on fraud in inducement may be sustained in some courts, as in the *AccuSystems* case regarding capabilities of an operating system. The court found that, in a dynamically growing industry, the plaintiffs' reliance on the defendants' representation with respect to the operating system was reasonable. The remedies available in contract were time-barred; on the other hand, an action for fraud may be brought within six years from its commission.[507]

---

[504] *See* Huron Tool v. Precision Consulting Servs., Inc., 532 N.W.2d 541. 545 (Mich. Ct. App. 1995).

[505] *See supra* § 2.03 Theories Relevant To Imposing Liability [2] Fraud [c] United States [ii] Information in Electronic Form [B] New York Law, in New York.

[506] *See* AccuSystems, Inc. v. Honeywell Info. Sys., Inc., 580 F. Supp. 474 (S.D.N.Y. 1984); Daniel v. Dow Jones & Co., Inc., 520 N.Y.S.2d 334 (Civ. Ct. 1987).

[507] *See* Phoenix Techs., Inc. v. Quotron Sys., Inc, 1997 WL 220285 (E.D.Pa 1997) (holding that under New York law, a general merger clause in a contract bars any negligent misrepresentation claims arising under the contract, the court held that the fraud in the inducement claim could be considered separately from the contractual claim.).

Possibility of recovery under the theory of fraud in inducement was also allowed under Michigan law in a more restrictive manner. In *Huron Tool v. Precision Consulting Services, Inc.*,[508] fraud in inducement was said to represent a special situation where parties to a contract appear to negotiate freely, which normally would not constitute grounds for invoking the economic loss doctrine, but where in fact the ability of one party to negotiate fair terms and make an informed decision is undermined by the other party's fraudulent behaviour. In contrast, where the only misrepresentation by the dishonest party concerns the quality or character of the goods sold, fraud and breach of contractual claims are factually indistinguishable. The other party is still free to negotiate warranty and other terms to account for possible defects in the goods.[509] However, it may be difficult to distinguish between the fraudulent behaviour and fraud concerning the quality or character of the goods sold. It is the quality or character of the goods that is the basis of the bargain. For instance, in the *AccuSystems*[510] case, the claim based on fraud in inducement was allowed on the basis that Honeywell issued a document which maintained that the TL operating system had been extensively tested, had been installed in a number of other locations where it was functioning well, and that it was capable of multitasking.[511]

[4] Comparison

Both in England and in the United States, the concurrent responsibility of professionals has been upheld. However, the kind of service considered "professional service" is not clearly defined at present. In England, the court takes a flexible approach as to the

---

[508] 532 N.W.2d 541 (Mich. Ct. App. 1995).
[509] *Id.* at 544-45.
[510] 580 F. Supp. 474 (S.D.N.Y. 1984).
[511] *Id.* at 482.

cases where special skills are exercised,[512] whereas in the United States, such claims are difficult unless the nature of their services exercised are within the recognised professions.

Under English law, computer consultants are generally held to possess special skills and are expected to be competent in the field of their skills, and concurrent liability is allowed where there is an assumption of duties with special skills and such skills are relied upon.

In the United States, such a special duty is not widely recognised. However, application of the fraud in inducement theory is possible for plaintiffs to avoid the application of contractual terms limiting or excluding remedies available to them. This has to be due to the fact that even though services provided by manufacturers are not within the scope of a recognised profession, the users are entitled to rely on the representation, such as the capability of the operating system, made by the manufacturers.

§ 2.06 Imposition of Liability with Respect to Information

I attempted to describe the law of tort relating to liability for injury caused by published information, and to ascertain whether there is any indication in these relevant authorities of their likely impact upon publication or dissemination in electronic form, particularly computer programs or information on the Internet or online database.

One of the important issues in this chapter dealt with circumstances where the court allows tortious claims for recovery of economic loss independent of contract in transactions involving computer programs or human-readable information on the Internet or online database.

---

[512] *See supra* § 2.03 Theories Relevant To Imposing Liability [3] Negligence [b] England [vi] Transactions Involving Special Skills and [vii] Professional Liability of Computer Programmers.

With regard to the supply of computer programs and other ancillary services, the plaintiffs often claim that they were induced into transacting by misrepresentation, and that the suppliers provided negligently designed computer programs or negligent support or maintenance.

In England, if there is a contract between parties, statutory control over contractual terms excluding or limiting remedies available to plaintiffs is stricter than in the United States. Therefore, there is less need to resort to tortious remedies. The significance of distinctions between negligent acts and negligent statements is diminishing, especially in the context where professional skills were involved. It was held in *Henderson v. Merrett Syndicates Ltd.*,[513] that if someone has special knowledge which he undertakes to apply for the assistance of another and that other person relies upon such skill, the *Hedley Byrne & Co. Ltd. v. Heller & Partners Ltd.*[514] principle extends beyond the provision of information and advice to include the performance of other services. Such special skills include computer programming. The plaintiffs are entitled to rely on the special knowledge or skills of computer suppliers and are able to bring an independent cause of action separate from contractual claims, as in *Stephenson Blake (Holdings) Ltd. v. Streets Heaver Ltd.*[515]

In the United States, claims based on fraud in inducement and claims based on negligent misrepresentation are considered separately. Claims based on negligent misrepresentation generally require a special relationship between the parties. Many courts do not recognise the special relationship between the parties with respect to the purchase, referral, and recommendation of computer systems. Between the parties to a contract, negligent misrepresen-

---

[513] [1995] 2 A.C. 145 (H.L.(E)).
[514] [1964] A.C. 465 (H.L.(E.)).
[515] Q.B.D. (O.R.) H.H.J.Hicks Q.C., March 2, 1994 (unreported).

tation claims can be regarded as ways to avoid the application of contractual clauses. This is based on the idea that computer programmers or suppliers are not providing a "professional" service. The relationship between the parties is considered as a "buyer - seller relationship."

In the United States, the majority of courts restrict recovery of economic loss in tort, under *East River S.S. Corp. v. Transamerica Delaval Inc.*[516] When discussing recovery of economic loss, the United States' courts tend to discuss the restriction of recovery under either negligence or products liability and have not explored in depth the possibility of imposing liability in negligence as in England. Therefore, in order to recover economic loss, plaintiffs have to bring a claim that comes within the exceptions to such a general rule, including the cases where there was express warranty and rendition of professional liability. However, the majority of the United States' courts allow professional liability claims only for a recognised profession, which does not extend to include computer programmers. The theory of negligent misrepresentation of the Restatement (Second) of Torts section 552 (1976) or supply of computer systems by a recognised profession, such as accountancy, may help to widen the scope of plaintiffs in professional liability claims in tort, which can be claimed as independent from contractual claims. Claims based on fraud in inducement in the United States are also helpful for plaintiffs who have relied on the expertise of computer suppliers to avoid the application of contractual terms excluding or limiting the remedies available.

With respect to cases where the output of computer programs or human-readable information on the Internet or online databases is relied upon and causes damage, the purpose for which the information is offered and the scope of recoverable plaintiffs

---

[516] 476 U.S. 858 (1986).

are two of the important issues in allowing recovery. Human-readable information on the Internet or in online databases shares the same concern as cases on the output of computer programs; however, there are additional concerns, discussed previously, to be considered in determining liability.

With respect to the applicability of products liability law to information in electronic form, certain types of information, including navigational charts, instruction manuals or computer programs, when considered in the light of intended use and distribution, may be included within the scope of application. This is justified especially because instructions including computer programs can be considered either effective or ineffective, with respect to the results they create; however, instructions cannot be considered true or false, obscene or defamatory as in information in traditional form. Therefore, there is no danger in suppressing freedom of expression when liability is imposed for defective instructions including computer programs.

One of the essential bases in determining tortious liability is representation with regard to the subject matter or particular information. Representations here include a wide variety of information which makes up the whole subject matter, such as sales brochures, advertising, instructions, manuals, stock price lists, computer programs and information on the Internet. These representations can be attached to a particular product, or be independent for the purpose of transactions.

Such representations are part or the whole of the subject matter. When considering the imposition of liability with respect to representations, it is essential to consider how specific the representation is or how specifically targeted the receivers are, and the existence of special or specific skills. Such factors are helpful in justifying a higher duty of care by representors and reliance by the receivers of information.

Chapter 3 The Law of Contract Relating to Liability for Injury Caused by Information in Electronic Form

§ 3.01 Introduction

In this chapter, I focus on the law of contract relating to liability for injury caused by information in electronic form. Within the type of information in electronic form, I will examine the supply of computer programs and other services such as data processing and business consultancy related to the supply of computer programs and supply of human-readable information in electronic form. This human-readable information includes information on the Internet and online databases.

In order to achieve this, I will first examine the difficulties in classifying contracts for information in general. Second, I will explore the effect of classification, different factors considered in determining classification, and evaluation of such factors. Third, I will examine different factors considered in determining classification with respect to transactions involving information in electronic form and how the classification of contracts affects the outcome of actual cases. Between the contracting parties, the classification of the contract is crucial in determining the level of liability imposed in relation to the subject matter. Contractual liabilities may differ in accordance with the legal form or classification of a given transaction as sale of goods, supply of services, etc. As my main concern is the standard or quality of performance for transactions in information in electronic form, my analysis is restricted to those aspects of contracts relevant to the standard or quality of performance.

Fourth, I will focus on the creation, exclusion or limitation of contractual obligations. I will examine creation or exclusion of express and implied obligations, limitation or exclusion of remedies. Last, I will discuss statutory control by the reasonableness test, the doctrine of unconscionability and statutory control of standard form or consumer contracts.

By conducting a comparative analysis of law in England and the United States, I will attempt to articulate the purpose of classification in transactions involving information in electronic form and evaluate the relevant provisions in the newly enacted Uniform Computer Information Transaction Act (U.C.I.T.A.) in the United States.[517]

§ 3.02 Classification of Contracts

[1] Classification of Contracts

[a] The Structure of the Classification

Certain forms of information, such as computer programs and databases play essential roles in modern society. Such new subject matter questions the validity of the existing law as applied to them. The purpose of this chapter is to consider the role of the classification of contracts in relation to contracts for information in electronic form, especially computer programs, in England and in the United States, and to compare the way in which both countries have dealt with the issues of classification.

The important question to be asked is, why does the law distinguish between contracts? Prior to answering this question, it is helpful to look at the structure of how the present law classifies contracts in accordance with their subject matter, and the process by which the subject matter is supplied.

The classification of the contract is crucial in determining the level of liability imposed in relation to the subject matter. Those categories relevant to information in electronic form are, 1) contracts for goods, 2) contracts for services, and possibly, 3) contracts for information. There are two types of injuries in relation to these subject matters. One is injury based on the quality of the subject matter itself, and the other relates to the process by which the subject matter is supplied.[518]

[b] Contracts for Goods

Contracts for goods are placed at one end of the category

---

[517] (2001).

of default rules providing imposition of liability. Default rules in statutory laws provide for an implied term or warranty as to the quality of the product.[519] There are variations depending on how widely those goods are diffused. Specifically-made goods are placed in a stricter category than are mass-marketed goods, and there are separate rules for this category of goods in terms of an implied term or warranty.[520]

[c] Contracts for Services

Under the common law principle, the supplier has a duty to carry out services with reasonable care and skill.[521] There are no

---

[518] U.C.I.T.A. § 403 cmt. 2 (2001). ("The implied warranty of merchantability comes from one of three different legal traditions associated with computer information transactions. The **first**, the source of this warranty, is the Article 2 world of the sale of goods and focuses on the quality of the result (product) delivered, establishing an implied assurance that this product will conform to ordinary standards for products of that type. The **second**, from common law dealing with licenses, services and information contracts, focuses on the process or performance effort, rather than the result, establishing standards such as that the work will be performed in a workmanlike manner. The **third**, from common law, pertains to services and information contracts in some states, rejecting any implied obligation in a contract other than one involving a special relationship of reliance.").

[519] Sales of Goods Act 1979 (c. 54), as amended in 1994, s.14; U.C.C. § 2-314 (1998).

[520] Sales of Goods Act 1979 (c. 54); as amended in 1994, s.14(3); *see* Slater v. Finning Ltd. [1997] A.C. 473 (H.L.(Sc.)) (holding that implied condition for fitness was not breached where the failure of the goods to meet the intended purpose arises from an abnormal feature or idiosyncrasy, not made known to the seller by the buyer); U.C.C. § 2-315 (1998).

[521] *See* Supply of Goods and Services Act 1982 (c.29), s.14, as amended in 1994; Milau Assoc., Inc. v. N. Ave. Dev. Corp., 368 N.E.2d 1247, 1250 (N.Y. 1997); S. WILLISTON, A TREATISE ON THE LAW OF CONTRACTS § 1012C (3d ed. 1961); RESTATEMENT (SECOND) OF TORTS § 299A (1965)("one who undertakes to render services in the practice of a profession or trade is required to exercise the skill and knowledge normally possessed by members of that profession or trade"); RESTATEMENT (SECOND) OF TORTS § 552 (1976).

implied terms or warranties as to the result of the subject matter supplied.[522] Contracts, which contain both elements of services and goods, are neither pure contracts for goods, nor services. There are different ways to find applicable statutes for these types of mixed contracts. English law treats the two elements separately in accordance with the different principles of law.[523] A majority of the United States' cases asks whether goods or services predominate in a mixed goods and services contract as a whole.[524] The basis of such determination is not always clear. In the United States, careful drafting of U.C.I.T.A. was necessary specifically for information in electronic form in order to avoid making this determination.[525]

[d] Contracts for Information

As discussed in the introduction, information here involves both machine-readable information in electronic form and human-readable information in traditional form and in electronic form.

A significant part of the contracts to supply information, however, belongs to the categories of sale of goods or supply of services. For instance, information supplied in the form of software is deemed "goods" in many cases in England and the United States.[526]

On the other hand, parties may agree to provide legal services or accounting services, where information is created as a result of the rendition of such services.[527]

---

[522] *See* Supply of Goods and Services Act 1982 (c. 29), s. 4(1).

[523] *See supra* Supply of Goods and Services Act 1982.

[524] *See infra* § 3.02 Classification of Contracts [6] United States.

[525] *See infra* § 3.03 Express Terms or Warranties [7] The Effect of the Enactment of the U.C.I.T.A. -Basic Concepts.

[526] *See* § 3.02 Classification of Contracts [5] England and § 3.02 Classification of Contracts [6] United States.

[527] RESTATEMENT (SECOND) OF TORTS § 552 (1976)("One who, in the cause of his business, profession or employment, or in any other transaction in which he has pecuniary interest, supplies false information for the guidance of others in their business transactions, is subject to liability for pecuniary loss caused to them by

However, contracts for supplying contents of information contained in newspapers, books or magazines, and information on the Internet, distributed to the public, seem to involve different obligations from contracts for goods and services. Neither the immediate suppliers nor the publishers may be subjected to implied obligations as to the accuracy of the content of the publication or duty to exercise reasonable care.

For instance, a contract "to provide an encyclopaedia obliges the party to deliver that type of work, but that is simply a matter of defining the basic contractual promise."[528] The courts have to consider the effect on the dissemination of speech in determining liability for such publications.[529] The fact that there may be a contract does not alone create the obligations as to the accuracy of the content of information provided.

There may also be a difference in the level of liability regarding content for immediate suppliers and the publishers. Physical properties of books and the information they contain have two distinct characteristics. The readers may have direct contractual relationships with the immediate distributors. The immediate suppliers "sell" these newspapers, books or magazines as tangible, physical properties. A distributor may be considered a passive conduit and a newspaper is more than a passive conduit for news, comment and advertising.[530] Therefore, though

---

their justifiable reliance on the information, if he fails to exercise reasonable care or competence in obtaining or communicating the information.").

[528] U.C.I.T.A. § 402 cmt. 8 (2001).

[529] *Id. See also* Daniel v. Dow Jones & Co., Inc. 520 N.Y.S. 2d 334 (Civ. Ct. 1987).

[530] Stratton Oakmont, Inc. v. Prodigy Serv. Co., 23 Media L. Rep. (BNA) 1794, 1995 WL 323710 (N.Y. Sup. Ct. 1995), *renewal denied,* 24 Media L. Rep. (BNP) 1126, 1995 WL 805178 (N.Y. Sup. Ct. 1995) (concerning defamatory statement); Cubby, Inc. v. Compuserve, Inc. 776 F.Supp. 135 (S.D.N.Y. 1991)(concerning defamatory statement).

the immediate suppliers may be liable for physical defects in newspapers and magazines, they are not to be held liable for the content of the information, unless they know or have reason to know the content of the information.[531]

Publishers of newspapers or magazines may not have a direct contractual relationship with their readers. Publishers distribute information in different ways. For instance, publications such as the Wall Street Journal may be distributed by intermediate distributors to members of the general public.[532] Publishers of loose-leaf summaries of the business operations and finances of a large number of corporations, containing information on securities, may have direct subscription agreements with readers to supply

---

[531] *See* Cardozo v. True, 342 So.2d 1053, 1055-56 (Fla. Dist. Ct. App. 1977)("The definition of 'goods' under the U.C.C. is sufficiently broad to include books." "....As such Ellie's (a retail book dealer) is held to have impliedly warranted the tangible, physical properties; i.e., printing and binding of books. But, at this point it becomes necessary to distinguish between the tangible properties of these goods and the thoughts and ideas conveyed thereby...." "It is unthinkable that standards imposed on the quality of goods sold by a merchant would require that merchant, who is a book seller, to evaluate the thought processes of the many authors and publishers of the hundreds and often thousands of books which the merchant offers for sale."); Lerman v. Flynt Distrib. Co., 745 F.2d 123, 139 (2d Cir. 1984), *cert. denied,* 471 U.S. 1054 (1985)(concerning defamatory publication); Lerman v. Chuckleberry Publ'g, Inc., 521 F. Supp. 228, 235 (S.D.N.Y. 1981) (concerning defamatory publication "With respect to distributors, the New York courts have long held that vendors and distributors of defamatory publications are not liable if they neither know nor have reason to know of the defamation."); Cubby, Inc. v. Compuserve Inc., 776 F. Supp. 135 (S.D.N.Y. 1991); RESTATEMENT (SECOND) OF TORTS § 581 cmt. d. (1976).

[532] *See* Gutter v. Dow Jones, Inc., 490 N.E.2d 898 (Ohio 1986) (holding that a publisher of the Wall Street Journal is not liable for negligent misrepresentation to a subscriber who relied on non-defamatory false statement of fact in making securities investment).

supplements each month.[533] Publishers may also provide specific investment recommendations directly to their readers.[534] However, even if there are contracts between readers and publishers, such as subscription agreements, the courts are not likely to find any implied obligations on a news service or a publisher for a negligent false statement for the accuracy of the content of the information supplied[535] in the absence of a breach of contractual obligation or trust, or amounts to a deceit, libel, or slander.[536] It may be feared

---

[533] *See* First Equity Corp. of Florida v. Standard & Poor's Corp., 869 F.2d 175 (2d Cir. 1989)(holding that a publisher is not liable for negligent misstatements for describing the terms of the indenture relating to securities).

[534] *See* Gale v. Value Line, Inc., 640 F. Supp. 967 (D.R.I. 1986) (holding that the publisher of Value Line is not liable to the subscriber who purchased warrants in reliance on incomplete summary of warrant).

[535] *See* Jaillet v. Cashman, 189 N.Y.S. 743 (Sup. Ct. 1921)(holding that a stock ticker is analogous to a newspaper and a publisher of a ticker is not liable for publishing the erroneous report. A customer in a broker's office having ticker service suffered losses after relying upon a false report on a stock ticker). *But see* Rosenstein v. Standard and Poor's Corp., 636 N.E.2d 665 (Ill. App. Ct. 1993) (holding that it may be possible for an option trader to recover the loss against a company which erroneously incorporated the closing price of a particular stock in indexes. The company was an official source for calculating and disseminating the closing values of indexes); De La Bere v. C.A. Pearson, Ltd. [1908] 1 K.B. 280 (C.A.)(holding that the proprietors of a newspaper, which advertises the offering of advice with reference to investment, are responsible for taking reasonable care to name a good stockbroker to a reader who wished to know of one).

[536] *See* Langworthy v. Pulitzer Pub. Co., 368 S.W.2d 385, 390(Mo. 1963); *Jaillet*, 189 N.Y.S. at 744; *Gutter*, 490 N.E.2d at 899-900("The general veiw is that "[n]o action for damages lies against a newspaper for merely inaccurate reporting when the publication does not constitute libel."); 58AM. JUR. 2D 148 (Newspapers, Periodicals & Press Assns., Section 22) (1971) ("In the absence of a contract, fiduciary relationship, or intentional design to cause injury, a newspaper publisher is not liable to a member of the public to whom all news is liable to be disseminated for a nagligent misstatement in an item of news, not amounting to libel, published by the publisher, unless he wilfully originates or circulates it knowing it to be false, and it is calculated to and does, as the proximate cause,

that, unless the liability is limited, the publisher may become liable to an undefined, infinite class of readers.[537]

The development of technology has altered the method of distribution. Information is increasingly provided on line, without intermediate distributors. The readers may have a direct contractual relationship with the publishers to gain access to the online databases. Still, the change in the technology does not seem to affect the approach taken by the courts. The relationship between the information provider and an on-line subscriber was not adequate to find the provider liable in *Daniel v. Dow Jones Co., Inc.*[538] discussed above. The court determined that the "special relationship" required for an action for negligent misstatement must be greater than the relationship between the ordinary buyer and seller.[539] The court stated in a footnote that "even though the exact nature of the 'contract' cannot be definitely determined on the record here, that does not effect the disposition." In this case, it was not established that the agreement was formed between the parties and there was no proof that the plaintiff agreed to a limitation of the defendant's liability as a part of the on-line sign-up procedure.[540]

On the contrary, the courts may not be able to deny the existence of a direct contractual relationship in the cases of LEXIS or WESTLAW subscriptions. Despite the existence of such a contractual relationship, it is unlikely that the court will find a

---

result in injury to another person.").

[537] *See* Ultramares Corporation v. Touche, 174 N.E. 441, 444 (N.Y. 1931).

[538] 520 N.Y.S.2d 334 (N.Y. Civ. Ct. 1987); *see supra* § 2.03 Theories Relevant To Imposing Liability [4] Negligent Misrepresentation [c] United States [ii] Economic Loss [D] Content of Information in Electronic Form.

[539] *Daniel*, 520 N.Y.S.2d at 338.

[540] *Id.* at 337 n.1.

"special relationship."[541] As shown in the diagram below, authorities tend to refer to a "special relationship" without differentiating whether or not there was a contract between the parties. The reason may be that they are placed in the same category of contractual relationship, which does not create liability. Therefore, for information made available to the public in substantially the same format, the same discussion as to whether tortious liability exists with respect to such subject matters[542] may be applicable to the existence of contractual liability.[543]

Comment 3b to Section 404 of the U.C.I.T.A., gives an example in which there is no implied warranty for a website which contains published informational content on restaurants. Information systems that are analogous to newspapers, magazines, or books are treated as such for purposes of the law of contract. However, some online databases tend to be relied on, and are believed to be kept up to date. Online databases are easily transferred for further secondary use. Therefore, not all online database suppliers may become free from liability for supplying defective information.[544]

Likewise in England, in *Hedley Byrne & Co. Ltd. v. Heller & Partners Ltd.*,[545] Lord Reid stated that there must be a special

---

[541] *See supra* note 527; AccuSystems, Inc. v. Honeywell Info. Sys., Inc., 580 F. Supp. 474 (S.D.N.Y. 1984), (holding that a cause of action for negligent misrepresentation is not recognised unless there is a special relationship of trust of confidence between the parties. The buyer-seller relationship was not enough to support a cause of action); Phoenix Techs., Inc. v. Quotron Sys., Inc., 1997 WL 220285 (E.D.Pa 1997) *aff'd*, 135 F.3d 766 (7th Cir. 1997).
[542] *See supra* § 2.03 Theories Relevant To Imposing Liability [4] Negligent Misrepresentation.
[543] *See* U.C.I.T.A. § 102(51)(2001).
[544] *See* § 2.03 Theories Relevant To Imposing Liability [4] Negligent Misrepresentation [a] Negligent Misrepresentation and Information in Electronic Form.
[545] [1964] A.C. 465 (H.L.(E.)).

relationship between the parties such that the defendant knew or ought to have known that the plaintiff might reasonably rely upon the defendant's representation.[546] Therefore, suppliers of information in a special relationship even without contracts may be held liable for the content of the information.

However, any attempt to expand the scope of a special relationship for the imposition of liability outside the contract may open doors to a liability to an indeterminate amount for an indeterminate time to an indeterminate class.[547] This concern is equally applicable to the category of cases where there is a contractual relationship but not a special relationship. Considering the determination of liability issues, the type of information and the process by which it is supplied seem to be important factors. The law is reluctant to impose liability based on relationships other than those in the special or fiduciary category.

The diagram below shows the structure describing the "special relationship" within both contractual and tortious relationships.

As far as the default rule is concerned, the standard of performance differs in accordance with the category into which the particular contract falls. However, the position fluctuates by various terms or conditions agreed upon between the parties. Express terms or warranties as to the quality of the services can impose additional liability on the suppliers of service contracts. Suppliers of information may charge a higher price for supplying accurate information. Clients rely more on the information when they pay a higher price for the accuracy of the information supplied. On the contrary, if suppliers of information charge a low price, a lesser duty may be imposed. This categorical classification seems

---

[546] *Id.* at 486; Raritan River Steel Co. v. Cherry, Bekaert & Holland, 367 S.E.2d 609 (N.C. 1988).
[547] *See* Ultramares Corp. v. Touche, 174 N.E. 441, 444 (N.Y. 1931); *see supra* § 2.03 Theories Relevant To Imposing Liability [4] Negligent Misrepresentation.

to provide a clearer and more unambiguous set of rules regarding goods and services than those rules regarding information. Rules concerning information cannot be fully incorporated into this structure.

Contractual Relationship	Tortious Relationship
Special Professional Attorney Accountant	**Relationship** *Hedley Byrne & Co. Ltd. v. Heller & Partners Ltd.*[548] *Raritan River Steel Co. v. Cherry, Bekaert & Holland*[549]
No Special Newspapers, magazines (contractual relationship with the distributor; no direct contractual relationship with the publisher) On-line databases	**Relationship** *Caparo Industries plc. v. Dickman*[550] *Ultramares Corp. v. Touche*[551]

---

[548] [1964] A.C. 465 (H.L.(E.)).
[549] 367 S.E.2d 609 (N.C. 1988); *see also* Bily v. Arthur Young & Co., 834 P.2d 745 (Cal. 1992); RESTATEMENT (SECOND) OF TORTS § 552 (1976).
[550] [1990] 2 A.C. 605.
[551] 174 N.E. 442, 444 (N.Y. 1931).

[2] The Effect of Classification

[a] The General Purpose

In this section, I intend to clarify why it might matter whether a particular contract is classified as one for sale of goods or supply of services. There are mainly three reasons why classification may affect the transactions: evidence; limitation period; and, implied obligations.

[b] Evidence

The Statute of Frauds imposed formal requirements for only some types of contracts. In England and Wales, written evidence for contracts for the sale of goods of ten pounds and more was required in accordance with the Sale of Goods Act 1893.[552] Even before 1893, the buyers were able to plead lack of written evidence in an action by the supplier to recover the contractual price for specifically-made goods.[553] Under the present law, as provided in the Sale of Goods Act 1979, no written formalities are required in relation to contracts for sale of goods.[554] On the other hand, in the United States, section 2-201 of the U.C.C. provides that a contract for the sale of goods for the price of 500 dollars or more is not enforceable unless there is some writing indicating that the contract for sale has been made between the parties. Therefore, it is possible, in the United States, to claim that a contract for the sale of goods is not enforceable because of the statute of frauds.[555]

[c] Limitation Period

In England and Wales, the Limitation Act 1980[556] provides that an action founded on tort or simple contract should be brought within six years from the date on which the cause of action

---

[552] Sale of Goods Act 1893, s. 4.
[553] Lee v. Griffin (1861) 1B & 272.
[554] Sale of Goods Act 1979 (c. 54), s. 4.
[555] *See* Wharton Mgmt. Group v. Sigma Consultants, Inc., 1990 WL 18360 (Del. Super. Ct. 1990), *aff'd*, 582 A.2d 936 (Del. 1990).
[556] c. 58, ss. 2 and 5.

accrued. For personal injury caused by negligence, nuisance, or other breach of duty, the limitation period is three years from either the occurrence of the damage or the "date of knowledge" of the injured party.[557] In the United States, the limi-tation period varies in accordance with state laws. Ordinarily, the statute of limitations in tort starts to run at the time of damage or at the time claimants discovered the damage. Therefore, claimants in tort may be entitled to a longer statute of limitation.[558] Section 2-725(1) of the U.C.C. provides that an action for breach of any contract for sale must be commenced within four years after the cause of action has accrued.

[d] Implied Obligation

In England, if the contract is construed as sale of goods, the Sale of Goods Act 1979 is applicable unless expressly excluded or varied. Under Section 14(2), as amended in 1994, if the seller sells goods in the course of a business, there is an implied term that the goods supplied under the contract are of satisfactory quality. Under Section 14(3), if a seller sells goods in the course of a business and a buyer's particular purpose is made known so as to show reliance on the seller's skill and judgement, there is an implied term that goods supplied under the contract are reasonably fit for that purpose.

If the contract is classified as a mixed contract of goods and services the Supply of Goods and Services Act 1982 is applicable. Section 4(2) of the 1982 Act, as amended in 1994, provides that there is an implied condition that the goods supplied for the contract for the transfer of goods in the course of a business are of satisfactory quality. Sections 4(4) and (5) provide that if a particular purpose is made known to the transferor, and the transferee relies, or it is reasonable for the transferee to rely, on

---

[557] *Id.* s. 11(2).
[558] *See* AccuSystems, Inc. v. Honeywell Info. Sys., Inc., 580 F. Supp. 474 (S.D.N.Y. 1984).

the skill or judgement of the transferor in the course of a business, there is an implied condition about quality or fitness for that particular purpose. Section 13 of the 1982 Act provides that there is an implied term that the supplier will carry out service with reasonable care and skill, provided that the supplier is acting in the course of a business.

Therefore, in English law, under both contracts for sale of goods and mixed contracts of goods and services, there is an implied obligation that the goods supplied under the contract are of satisfactory quality.

If the contract is construed as one for the supply of services, the reasonable care and skill standard under section 13 is applicable.

In the United States, if the contract is classified as one for services, the common law is applicable. A party can refuse to proceed with performance if the breach is material. Substantial performance is performance without a material breach.[559] If the contract is classified as one of sale, U.C.C. Article 2 is applicable.[560] Article 2 provides for an implied warranty that the goods be merchantable under section 2-314, and an implied warranty that goods be fit for the intended purpose where the seller had a reason to know of any particular purpose for which the goods were required, under section 2-315.

If the contract is classified as one for mixed goods and services, the courts have to determine which type of law is applicable. In determining the type of law, the majority view asks whether the contract is predominantly or primarily a contract for the sale of goods or the supply of services, and the minority view asks whether the underlying action is brought because of alleged

---

[559] *See* E. A. FARNSWORTH, FARNSWORTH ON CONTRACTS §8.16 at 442-43 (2d ed. 1990).
[560] 1998 Official Text.

defective goods or because of the quality of service rendered.[561] In the latter view, if the gravamen of the action focuses on goods, then the U.C.C. governs. If the focus is on the quality of the services rendered, then the common law applies.[562]

In both jurisdictions, if the contract is classified as one for sale of goods or for the transfer of property in goods,[563] a result-oriented term or warranty is attached; if the contract is classified as one for supply of services, there is no result-oriented term or warranty. The supplier of the services owes solely a process-oriented duty of care to perform with reasonable care.[564] Therefore, the main difference of the classification is whether there is a "guarantee" as to the result of the transaction.

However, the classification is obviously not important if the court finds that an express duty is breached.

A contract involving a supply of information which is distributed to the members of the public in substantially the same form neither involves implied obligations for the accuracy of information nor the obligation to take reasonable care.

[e] Comparison

In England, there is no difference in the outcome in terms of the issues involving evidence and the limitation period. With respect to implied obligation, English law treats separately two elements of one contract, the sale of goods and the supply of services, in accordance with the different principles of law.[565]

However, in the United States, the outcomes of the cases are different in terms of the issues involving evidence, the limitation

---

[561] *See infra* § 3.02 Classification of Contracts [6] United States.
[562] *See* W. D. HAWKLAND, UNIFORM COMMERCIAL CODE SERIES §2-105:01 (1995); *see* R. T. NIMMER, THE LAW OF COMPUTER TECHNOLOGY ¶ 6.02 [1] 6-4 to 6-9 (1992).
[563] *See* Supply of Goods and Services Act 1982 (c. 29).
[564] *See supra* note 518.
[565] *See* Supply of Goods and Services Act 1982 (c. 29).

period, and the implied obligations. With respect to the issues of the implied obligations, the majority of the cases treat an entire contract as one object, consisting of either a transaction entirely in goods or one entirely involving services.[566]

[3] Uncertain Nature of the Criteria in Classification- Examples of Actions by Suppliers to Recover Payment for the Work Done in Cases Where Customers Refuse to Accept

[a] General Factors Considered in Classification

Of the contracts involving computer programs, many can be classified either as contracts for the sale of goods or as contracts for the supply of services. The courts consider different factors in determining classification. The main factors are: the nature of the subject matter created, the process of performance, and the methods of distribution.

Before discussing the cases regarding defects in computer programs, I intend to enumerate the basic reasoning for classification in earlier and relatively uncomplicated English cases. This is to examine whether there has been a definite and clear standard in determination, whether the same factors are used in determining the classification in relation to transactions involving computer programs, and whether the factors should be reconsidered in the light of the development of computer technology. Another important question to be asked, subsequent to the discussion of the cases regarding defects in computer programs, is whether the basic categories of contract law, the sale of goods, the supply of services and information, are still valid as applicable to information in electronic form.

---

[566] *See infra* § 3.02 Classification of Contracts [6] United States.

[b] Delivery of a Chattel

In *Lee v. Griffin*,[567] in determining that the contract to make artificial teeth was a contract for the sale of goods, Crompton, J. stated that:

> The distinction between these two causes of action is sometimes very fine; but where the contract is for a chattel to be made and delivered, it clearly is a contract for the sale of goods. There are some cases in which the supply of the materials is ancillary to the contract, as in the case of a printer supplying the paper on which a book is printed.[568]

However, in some service contracts, for instance, a contract to paint a portrait, a chattel is to be made and delivered. Furthermore, the court did not clarify as to when the supply of the materials is ancillary to the contract.

In England, if the contract were construed, as one for sale of goods and the defence was the statute of frauds, recovery of compensation for labour and materials was not possible until 1954. On the other hand, if the contract were construed as one for skill and labour, the statute of frauds did not apply, so recovery of compensation for the work done was possible. For instance, recovery for the full amount of the agreed fee minus expenditure saved might be available to the plaintiff-supplier.[569]

---

[567] *Lee*, (1861) 1B & S at 275; *see also* Robinson v. Graves [1935] 1 K.B. 579.

[568] *Lee*, (1861) 1B & S at 275. For U.S. case, *see* Schmidt v. Rozier, 98 S.W. 791, 792 (Mo. Ct. App. 1906) (following Lee v. Griffin. "[T]he subject matter of the contract being a coat and vest, chattels, to be afterwards delivered, it is the opinion of the court that the cause of action is for goods sold, etc., notwithstanding the peculiar pattern of the garments mentioned, and it therefore falls within the statute of frauds as such rather than without that statute as a cause of action for work, labor, and materials furnished.").

[569] *Robinson*, [1935] 1 K.B. at 588.

[c] Substance of the Contract

In *Robinson v. Graves,* determining that the contract to paint a portrait was a contract for work and labour,[570] Greer L.J. stated:

> If you find, as they did in *Lee v. Griffin,* that the substance of the contract was the production of something to be sold by the dentist to the dentist's customer, then that is a sale of goods. But if the substance of the contract, on the other hand, is that skill and labour have to be exercised for the production of the article and it is only ancillary to that there will pass from the artist to his client or customer some materials in addition to the skill involved in the production of the portrait, that does not make any difference to the result, because the substance of the contract is the skill and experience of the artist in producing the picture.[571]

The court could not use the reasoning based on the fact that "the contract is for a chattel to be made and delivered" used in *Lee v. Griffin,*[572] as the painting of a portrait was to be delivered, and it also had difficulty in clarifying the "substance" of the contract and the standard to differentiate the contracts.

In *J. Marcel Ltd. v. Tapper,*[573] the court found that even though skill, labour and materials were required to make the fur coat, the transaction involving specifically ordered materials was still the sale of goods. In the absence of a memorandum, the transaction was not enforceable for lack of writing.[574]

---

[570] *Id.*
[571] *Id.* at 587.
[572] *Lee,* (1861) 1B & S at 275.
[573] [1952] 1 Q.B.D. 15.
[574] *Id.* at 16.

[d] Analysis of the Different Approach and the Statute of Fraud Defence

The courts seemed to have difficulties in clearly articulating what the standard is, and neither the "chattel to be made and to be delivered" argument nor "substance of the contract" seems to provide clear guidance when applied to cases other than those with a relatively simple subject matter. As regards sale of goods, the requirement of a written memorandum ("the statute of frauds defence") was repealed in 1954. There was thus no longer a need to classify for this purpose in England. The situation is different in the United States, as section 2-201 of the U.C.C. requires a writing for the sale of goods for the price of 500 dollars or more.

[e] Different Factors of Consideration and Contracts Relating to Information in Electronic Form

Different factors are considered significant in the determination of classification. The most traditional and obvious factor concerns the nature of the subject matter created; whether it is an artistic or functional object, or whether it is tangible or intangible. The second factor concerns the process of performance. The third concerns the method of distribution.

First, the court considers whether the chattel was to be made and to be delivered. With regard to this factor, if the subject matter is considered an artistic object, such as a sculpture, it may be difficult to question the performance standard in reference to the final result. Therefore, it may be more suitable to judge the standard of the performance by reference to the process by which the work was performed. If a subject matter is considered a functional object, such as a washing machine, it is more suitable to judge the standard of the performance by reference to the result of the performance. In a contract to clean a house or to play a musical instrument, there is no tangible result, therefore, it may be more suitable to judge the standard of performance by reference to the process by which the work was performed. However, the criteria in determining the performance standard under a contract to clean and a contract to play a musical instrument are quite different.

Second, the courts may consider whether the process of performance involves the special skill of the supplier, continuing reference to the customer's needs or whether no other contact is required. When considering this factor, it may not be possible to judge the standard of performance by reference to one part of the performance rather than the whole.

Third, the courts may consider whether the method of distribution is mass or unique delivery. Most of the mass-delivered subject matters are supplied with standardised terms of contract, and there is no opportunity for users to negotiate the terms.

However, no one factor is definitive. A commissioned portrait can also be mass distributed. An intangible artistic music performance may be mass distributed in the form of a cassette tape due to the development of recording technology. Musical performance may also be uniquely distributed in the form of a cassette tape to a client who commissioned the music from the composer. There might not be so much difference between the portrait and the made-to-order fur coat in terms of the process of performance and in terms of the methods of distribution.

This means that classification may be construed in a flexible manner in unprecedented cases. Therefore, the courts may be able to draw conclusions that seem most appropriate to do justice, based on the facts of the cases.

In a transaction involving computer technology, a tangible or intangible thing, hardware, software, or a combination of both may be delivered. Subject matter can be mass delivered or uniquely delivered from beginning to end of the transactions, with or without a maintenance or support service. Considerable knowledge or skill may be involved in the whole transaction. Software itself is intangible, but it can perform visible tasks.

Therefore, these transactions may contain all the elements of the manufacturing of artificial teeth, the painting of a portrait or the cleaning of houses, especially in cases of the supply of customised computer systems. This is part of the reason why classification may be difficult in some cases.

[4] Nature of Licensing Agreements -Relationship With Intellectual Property

Transactions involving computer technology often, though not necessarily, involve the transfer of intellectual property rights. Transactions regarding computer programs and other digitised information ordinarily take the form of licensing agreements. However, discussion as to whether the software is a good and whether the software is protected by intellectual property should be separated when considering a liability issue alone, as this fact does not weaken the responsibility of the licensor of the intellectual property. The fact that intellectual property law protects certain software is relevant only in relation to determining the enforceability of the licence clauses restricting the use of intellectual property rights and other rights, including the right to transfer the intellectual property rights regarding the subject matter.[575] In any case, the end user of the subject matter should be allowed to utilise the subject matter permitted under the principles of intellectual property law, irrespective of the intention of the licensor.[576]

There are possibly two contracts to which end-users may be a party in the transaction involving information in electronic form. One is between the end-user and the immediate supplier and the other is between the end-user and the proprietor of the information. In order to understand the complex nature of such transactions, it is useful to distinguish the "supply" side of the transaction from the "licence" side.

---

[575] *See* NIMMER, *supra* note 562, at ¶ 6.02[2], 6-9 - 6-11.

[576] Vault Corp. v. McQuaid Software Ltd., 655 F. Supp. 750 (E.D.La. 1987) aff'd, 847 F.2d 255 (5th Cir. 1988) (holding that the Louisiana statute validating the prohibition on reverse engineering conflicts with federal policy and is unenforceable).

The immediate supplier is mainly involved with the supply element of the transaction involving computer technology. The immediate supplier may supply the black box "package" to the user; however, the immediate supplier may not have any control over the terms of the licensing agreements attached to the "package".[577]

The proprietor of the intellectual property has control over the terms of the licensing agreement both in terms of the supply and the licence elements. This "licence" element of the transaction is concerned with the use or transfer restrictions of the intellectual property. The "supply" element is concerned with the performance of the subject matter in general.[578]

Liability issues are concerned with the "supply" element of the transaction, in which both the immediate supplier and the proprietor are concerned.[579] Therefore, the fact that intellectual

---

[577] *See supra* note 531.

[578] C. Reed, *Liability, in* COMPUTER LAW 86 n.8 (C. Reed ed., 3d ed.1996) (arguing that there are two contracts, one is the contract supplying the package, which is between the dealer and the user and could well be a sale, and the other is the licence of intellectual property rights granted by the software house which is not a sale. "Where the software house supplies the package directly to the user it will be both licensing and supplying; here there is no reason why the supply element of the transaction should not be a sale......" "It is analogous to the seller of a prerecorded cassette tape arguing that the tape is not defective because the only fault is that the music is distorted whilst the tape itself is perfect. The reason that the purchaser pays more for a prerecorded than a blank tape is precisely because it has information (music) on it." *Id.* It may be more appropriate to refer to "two elements" of the subject matter of the contract than to two contracts. It may be noted that the difference between computer programs and the music tape is that the computer program can be "defective" in the sense that it does not function, even if the content and the physical medium are both in their intended condition and not "distorted".).

[579] *See* R. T. Nimmer, *Breaking Barriers: The Relation Between Contract and Intellectual Property Law* (1998), *at* http://www.2BGuide.com/docs/rncontract-new.html (arguing that there are three basic issues in an information contract; 1) Product Issues: Defining the informational subject matter of the transaction,

property is involved should not be used to weaken the responsibility for defects in transactions. In this book, as I am mainly concerned with the supply element of the transaction, it is not necessary to examine the legal nature of the licensing aspect of the transaction.

[5] England
 [a] Effect of Classification -Samuels v. Davis
Samuels v. Davis[580] is helpful in considering the effect of classification in England prior to the consideration of actual computer program cases. Scott L.J stated that "it is a matter of legal indifference whether the contract was one for the sale of goods or one of service to do work and supply materials."[581] The plaintiff was a dental surgeon, who sued to recover the price of making a denture for the defendant's wife. The defendant claimed that the denture was so unsatisfactory that his wife was unable to use it. The defendant also claimed that the contract was for the sale of goods or alternatively for work done and materials supplied. In either case, there was an implied condition that the denture was reasonably fit for the purpose. The court agreed with this assertion. The court stated that, by reason of the relationship between the parties, and the purpose for which the contract was entered into, the contract must import terms that the dentist would achieve reasonable success in the work done, provided that there was

---

what rights are transferred or withheld, and what fee, loyalty, or price is charged for that product, 2) Liability Issues: Defining the allocation of risk for errors, defects, third-party claims for libel, defamation or the like, associated with the information subject matter, 3) Performance Issue: Defining how the transaction will be performed, when it will be completed, what laws apply and other issues associated with establishing the relationship between the parties. He also argues that copyright or other intellectual property law does not control the second and the third issue).

[580] [1943] 1 K.B. 526.
[581] *Id.* at 527.

reasonable co-operation from the patient.[582]

Even if the contract was not for goods, the court seemed to have imposed the duty to create a result-oriented outcome by reason of the specific relationship between the parties. In this case, the dentist was "contracting to make a denture which will fit the patient's mouth" and "he is bound to take reasonable care and to show such skill as may be expected from a qualified practitioner."[583] If the supplier has the special skill and such skill was expected from the supplier, the imposition of the duty to attain a result-oriented outcome is possible. This position does not seem to have been changed in some of the more recent cases.

The same can be said regarding the materials provided for repair work done to a car in *G.H. Myers & Co. v. Brent Cross Service Co.*[584] Du Parcq J. stated that "a person contracting to do work and supply materials warrants that the materials which he uses will be of good quality and reasonably fit for the purpose for which he is using them, unless the circumstances of the contract are such as to exclude any such warranty."[585] The same principle can be applied to transactions involving the repair and the maintenance of computer programs.

[b] Classification and Application of Statute

In *Saphena Computing Ltd. v. Allied Collection Agencies Ltd.*,[586] the court stated that the law governing these contracts regarding software was precisely the same whether they were contracts for the sale of goods or for supply of services.[587] This statement should have been made on the presumption that the software itself is a good. Both the Sale of Goods Act 1979 and the

---

[582] *Id.*
[583] *Id.* at 530.
[584] [1934] 1 K.B. 46.
[585] *Id.* at 55.
[586] [1995] F.S.R. 616.
[587] *Id.* at 652.

Supply of Goods and Services Act 1982 impose the same implied obligations for goods.

In this case, a plaintiff entered into a contract for the supply of certain hardware and software for use in the defendant's business of debt-collection. The plaintiff supplied and installed software for batch operation and on-line software, but both sets of software had defects. The software for batch operation was corrected and the on-line software was in the process of getting repaired. Before the repair, the contract was terminated by mutual consent after the instalment of on-line software.

The plaintiff sued the defendant for breach of contract and copyright infringement. The plaintiff claimed that the defendant had not paid for the on-line software and had retained and used copies of the software's source code to enhance the software provided. The defendant counterclaimed for damages for breach of implied terms that the software be reasonably fit for its purpose.

The recorder found that there was an implied term as to the fitness of the software for the purposes for which it was required. Software had to be "reasonably fit for such purposes as had been notified to the suppliers before the orders were placed or were notified subsequently and accepted by suppliers." The recorder also found that this obligation had not been fulfilled by the suppliers when the parties agreed to end their relationship. However, as "software is not a commodity which is delivered once, only once and for all, but one which will necessarily be accompanied by a degree of testing and modification,"[588] when the purchaser decided to terminate the contract, the reasonable time in which the suppliers should have the right to test and modify the software supplied had not expired. Therefore, the suppliers were no longer obliged to do any more work on the software and the plaintiffs were not liable for the cost of repairing defects.[589] The court denied the defendant's

---

[588] *Id.*
[589] *Id.* at 653.

counterclaim for damages for breach of an implied term that the software would be reasonably fit for its purpose because both parties terminated the agreement by mutual consent. Thus, the termination of a contractual relationship, before the necessary time for adjustments or corrections lapses, may deprive the plaintiff of power to render the software fit for its purpose.[590]

Likewise in *St. Albans City & District Council v. International Computers Ltd.*,[591] the classification did not seem to matter. The court stated that the same principle of law for transfer of goods with respect to implication of terms as to quality or fitness for purpose should be applicable to contracts for supply of services in relation to computer programs. The court held *obiter* that in the absence of any express term as to quality or fitness for purpose, or any term to the contrary, a contract for the transfer into a computer of a program intended by both parties to instruct or enable the computer to achieve specified functions is "subject to an implied term that the program will be reasonably fit for, ie reasonably capable of achieving, the intended purpose."[592] It can be said in this case as well, by reason of the relationship between the parties, and the purpose for which the contract was entered into, the contract must import terms that the computer programmer would achieve reasonable success in the work done, provided there was a reasonable co-operation by the user.

As computer programs are ordinarily supplied to achieve certain functions, any transactions involving computer programs

---

[590] *Id.*; *see* I.J. LLOYD, INFORMATION TECHNOLOGY LAW 424 (2d ed.1997).

[591] [1995] F.S.R. 686 (Q.B.D.), [1996] 4 All E.R. 481. (C.A.); *see also* Micron Computer Sys. Ltd. v. Wang (U.K.) Ltd., 9 May 1990 (Q.B.D)(unreported)(holding that in the computer industry, the occasional failure of the system is normal and to be expected. After determining that a "computer system" was a good, the court found that the system was fit for the purpose for which it was sold and was merchantable.).

[592] *St. Albans*, [1996] 4 All E.R. at 494.

may become subjected to an implied term that the program will be reasonably fit for its intended purpose in England.

The court seemed to consider that computer programmers, like dentists, are expected to exercise expertise and special skills to achieve specified functions, if they represented themselves capable of achieving such a result-oriented outcome and their expertise was relied upon. The consequence of this statement made by Sir Iain Glidewell has the effect of construing a computer program as a good, thereby adopting the performance standard applicable to goods under the Sales of Goods Act 1979, as amended in 1994 and in the Supply of Goods and Services Act 1982, as amended in 1994.

[c] *Obligation Specific to Contracts Involving Computer Programs*

Both in *St. Albans City & District Council v. International Computers Ltd.,*[593] and in *Saphena Computing Ltd. v. Allied Collection Agencies Ltd.,*[594] a contract for the transfer of software to achieve a specific, known purpose was subject to an implied term that the program will be reasonably fit for the intended purpose. As stated in *Samuels v. Davis,*[595] by reason of the relationship between the parties, and the purpose for which the contract was entered into, the contract must import terms that the supplier would achieve reasonable "success" in the work done.[596]

However, it is also stated in *Saphena Computing Ltd. v. Allied Collection Agencies Ltd.,*[597] that mere delivery of customised software does not constitute a complete performance, and that the suppliers are allowed the time to make any necessary modifi-

---

[593] [1996] 4 All E.R. 481, 494 (*obiter*, Sir Iain Glidewell) (C.A.).
[594] [1995] F.S.R. 616, 651.
[595] [1943] 1 K.B. 527.
[596] *Id.* at 527.
[597] [1995] F.S.R. 616.

cation.[598] In this case, the supply first started in September 1985 and by 11 February 1986, the reasonable time had not expired.[599]

In transactions involving computer technology, performance may be judged by reference to the outcome of work done; however, continuous performance for a reasonable time may be needed to complete the performance.

[d] Physical Medium and Intangibles

In *St. Albans City and District Council v. International Computers Ltd.*,[600] Sir Iain Glidewell stated that the contract was not a sale of goods because the transfer of a disk or any other tangible thing was not involved. It is not acceptable to use the tangibility of the subject matter as the sole criterion to determine which law is applicable to a particular transaction, because there are many ways in which a transaction could be executed in the light of current technology.[601]

There may be two elements physically involved in the transaction involving computer programs, one is the physical medium or hardware and the other is the software or intangible code. However, this distinction is not useful, as transactions to transfer software do not require any physical medium. Furthermore, the same function of computer programs can be achieved either by the hardware or the software. As the computer programmers or manufacturer may distribute the software on the Internet, there may be only one contract between the proprietor and the customer.

In the Australian case of *Toby Constructions Products Ltd. v. Computer Bar Sales Pty Ltd.*, it was stated:[602]

---

[598] *Id.* at 652.
[599] *Id.* at 653.
[600] [1996] 4 All E.R. 481, 493 (C.A.).
[601] *See* C. Tapper, *Some Aspects of Contractual Licences for Software in* CONSENSUS AD IDEM: ESSAYS IN THE LAW OF CONTRACT IN HONOUR OF GUENTER 283, 286 (Treitel ed. 1996).
[602] [1983] 2 N.S.W.L.R. 48.

It would be too simplistic altogether to say that the supply of the system was a sale of goods merely because the bulk of the cost related to the hardware. Rather I think it is necessary to look at all the features of the object of the sale and the various ingredients such as price, the nature of the material which was to be supplied, the terms of installation, and the work which the system was designed to effect.[603]

The court also suggested that mass-production was a relevant criterion in determining whether there was a sale of goods.[604] The court determined that the sale of a computer system, comprising both hardware and software, constituted a sale of goods.[605]

The English case of *Eurodynamics Sys. plc. v. General Automation Ltd.*,[606] seems to have the same approach as the *Toby* case in the sense that it focused on the "reality of the transaction."

Although the ideas and concepts involved in software remained [the defendant's] property, the reality of the transaction is that there has been a transfer of product.[607]

---

[603] *Id.* at 51.
[604] *Id.*
[605] *Id.* at 54.
[606] 6 September 1988 (Q.B.) (unreported).
[607] However, this comment is not necessarily stating that there were two contracts, one for physical manifestation and the other for the grant of license involved in the transaction between licenser and licensee, as stated in Beta Computers (Europe) Ltd. v. Adobe Sys. (Europe) Ltd., [1996] S.L.T. 604, 608 (O.H.) ("It is submitted with respect that this is correct, and that where software is licensed there are effectively two contracts between the licenser and licensee: a contract for the supply of the physical manifestation of the software, and secondly the grant of a licence to use the software." *Id.* The court in *Eurodynamics* merely stated that the

Lord Penrose in the Scottish case of *Beta Computers (Europe) Ltd. v. Adobe Systems (Europe)Ltd.*,[608] stated that the supply of proprietary software for a price is a contract sui generis which may involve elements of nominate contracts such as sale, but would be inadequately understood if expressed wholly in terms of any of the nominate contracts. He also stated that it is unattractive to consider that software contracts involve two distinct contracts, one for supply of the storage devices containing the software and a second for licensing the use to which these could be put, as such an idea emphasises the role of the physical medium, and relates the transaction in the medium to the sale or hire of goods.[609] In this case, the defendants tried to return the shrink-wrap package unopened and the plaintiff argued that the contract was made prior to the point in time at which the conditions were presented to the defenders on delivery of the product they ordered. The court determined that the supplier tendered goods with an offer to complete the bargain in terms of the conditions derived from the author and the defendants were entitled to reject the software.[610]

As discussed above, it may be helpful to think that there are two elements involved in transactions involving computer technology. However, this idea does not necessarily emphasise the role of the physical medium, as these two elements are not the supply of storage devices and licence. The two elements are the "supply" element and the "licence" element of computer technology, where the former element is concerned with the performance of the subject matter including express or implied

---

transaction as a whole, is construed as a contract for a transfer of product, though there may be two different elements or aspects in the same contract, one aspect for the supply of the subject matter, including software as well as hardware, and the other for the grant of licence).

[608] [1996] S.L.T. 604.
[609] *Id.* at 608-09.
[610] *Id.* at 612.

terms, and the latter element is concerned with the grant and the restriction to use the proprietary right.

The owners of the intellectual property and the immediate suppliers are both involved in the "supply" element of the transaction, and the "licence" element of the transaction does not weaken the obligations in relation to the "supply" element.

[e] Breach of Express Duties

As mentioned above, the classification does not matter if express duties are breached. In *Eurodynamics Sys. plc. v. General Automation Ltd.,*[611] the court determined that it was not critical to decide whether software was a good, as the breach of *implied* terms of merchantability and fitness for purpose alleged had not been established. Instead, the court found that the *express* obligation of the supplier was breached. Eurodynamics Systems Plc. (ED) sued General Automation (GA), for damages for material misrepresentations or, alternatively, breach of contract. ED designed and developed bespoke computer application software for small to medium mainframe computers. ED specialised in business/technical and accounting software and wanted to expand its business and to sell both its own software and the computers on which the software was designed to operate. In order to accomplish this purpose, ED became a franchisee of GA with a view to purchasing computers and associated programmes.

The express provisions of the franchise agreement imposed an obligation on GA to support COBOL software. After the agreement, GA started both to refuse to meet the extant technical complaints and to provide future support for COBOL-based software to ED. The court found that GA was in breach of express terms and awarded the sum of £ 94,500 based on the estimate that, during the relevant period, ED would have succeeded in selling at least seven turnkey systems and seven application packages.

---

[611] 6 September 1988 (Q.B.) (unreported).

[f] Professional Liability

In *Stephenson Blake (Holdings) Ltd. v. Streets Heaver Ltd.,*[612] the court held that the defendant, who was in the business of providing specialised computerised information systems and a business planning consultancy, was under a contractual duty to exercise skill and due care to ensure that the system which it recommended conformed to that description or, if it became impossible to recommend such a system, to warn the plaintiff in plain terms of that fact and its likely consequences, in supplying the software and hardware regarding the acquisition of a computerised accounting system. The court imposed professional liability as the plaintiff, having no knowledge of computer technology, relied on the defendant's expertise and advice. It stated that, "once advice on the subject had been given and accepted....it would be part of the duty of the defendant to use due care and skill to ensure that the system which they recommended conformed to it."

This obligation to exercise a duty of reasonable care is similar to the obligations characterised in *St. Albans City & District Council v. International Computers Ltd.,*[613] and in *Saphena Computing Ltd. v. Allied Collection Agencies Ltd.*[614] In this case, the court is clearly imposing special liability based on the expertise of computer programmers.

[g] Classification and Implied Terms and Express Terms

In England, uncertainty as to the criteria in classification of the contract does not seem to hinder the solution of problems involved in transactions for computer programs. This is due to the fact that there are implied terms that goods supplied for a contract for the transfer of goods in the course of business are of satisfactory quality under the Sale of Goods Act 1979 and the Supply of Goods and Services Act 1982. The common law

---

[612] Q.B.D. (O.R.) H.H.J.Hicks Q.C., March 2, 1994 (unreported).
[613] [1995] F.S.R. 686, [1996] 4 All E.R. 481.
[614] [1995] F.S.R. 616, 650.

tradition and the statutes support this. Cases in England consider that computer programs are intended to perform specific tasks; suppliers offer expertise in computer technology and consumers rely on such expertise. In many transactions involving the supply of computer systems that are customised to the client's needs, there is an understanding by both parties that computer programmers are supplying programs with special skills and knowledge for a special business purpose, and that clients are relying on such skills and knowledge. The courts seem to uphold parties' intentions for the purpose of such contracts.

This approach, as stated in *Samuels v. Davis*,[615] emphasises "the reason of relationship between the parties and the purpose for which the contract was entered into" in incorporating the term in the contract.[616]

With respect to express terms, courts are able to hold suppliers responsible for express representations, regardless of the classification; and the application of the Unfair Contract Terms Act 1977 ensures this.

Therefore, the holding in *Stephenson Blake (Holdings) Ltd. v. Streets Heaver Ltd.*,[617] that it was the duty of computer programmers to use due care and skill to ensure that the system which they recommended would work, is consistent with the case law in England.

[h] Contracts for Information

Contracts to transfer information can include licensing agreements to transfer intellectual property rights. The Unfair Contract Terms Act 1977 schedule 1(c) provides that sections 2 to 4 of the Act do not extend to "any contract so far as it relates to the creation or transfer of a right or interest in any patent, trademark, copyright, registered design, technical or commercial information

---

[615] [1943] 1 K.B. 527.
[616] *Id.* at 527.
[617] Q.B.D. (O.R.) H.H.J.Hicks Q.C., March 2, 1994 (unreported).

or other intellectual property, or relates to the termination of any such right or interest." However, this provision covers only sections 2 to 4 and does not cover issues relating to standard of performance. As I am focusing on the performance standard in this book, it is not necessary to go into the legal analysis of the licensing agreements.

As discussed above,[618] with respect to the content of the information, the same discussions as to whether tortious liability exists with respect to such subject matters where information is made available to public in substantially the same format, may be applicable to the discussions with respect to contractual liability.[619]

[6] United States
[a] Different Tests for Classification
As many of the contracts involving computer programs are mixed contracts for services and goods that involve the exercise of personal skills and labour and the supply of materials or equipment,[620] there are mainly two tests in distinguishing contracts for services and goods. One is the predominant purpose test and the other is the gravamen of the action test. The predominant purpose test treats an entire contract as one object, consisting of either a transaction entirely in goods or one entirely involving services.[621]

---

[618] *See supra* § 3.02 Classification of Contracts [d] Contracts for Information.

[619] *See supra* § 2.03 Theories Relevant To Imposing Liability [4] Negligent Misrepresentation [a] Negligent Misrepresentation and Information in Electronic Form.

[620] *See* Kearsarge Computer, Inc. v. Acme Staple Co., 366 A.2d 467, 471 (N.H. 1976) (concerning a contract for computer data processing services).

[621] *See* HAWKLAND, *supra* note 562, at § 2-102:04; NIMMER, *supra* note 562, at ¶ 6.02[1] 6-4 - 6-9.

In *Milau Assoc. v. North Avenue Devel. Corp.*,[622] the court stated that it is not possible conceptually to sever the sale of goods aspects of the transaction when the transaction is for the predominant purpose of rendering services. Unless the parties have contractually bound themselves to a higher standard of performance, then reasonable care and competence owed generally by practitioners in the particular trade or profession defines the limits of an injured party's justifiable demands.[623]

The predominant purpose test is often said to misapply goods-related rules to the service elements of a mixed contract. The gravamen of the action test applies different rules for different parts of the same relationship, and therefore is said to create uncertainty in the law applicable to the transaction.[624] However, as suggested by Hawkland, the gravamen of the action approach is useful in dealing with mixed contracts involving goods and services.[625] For example, in *Worrell v. Barnes*:[626]

---

[622] 368 N.E.2d 1242(N.Y. 1977).

[623] *Id.*, at 1249-50 (stating that there is a need to assess all hybrid transactions along the sales-services continuum both legally and pragmatically." The fact that in Perlmutter our 'service predominates' analysis led to a conclusion of law which was also supported by policy considerations peculiar to the impure blood cases does not strip its analytic approach of vitality. The court made no attempt to mask the fact that reallocating the risk of loss by imposing warranty liability on no greater proof than the adverse result itself would place untoward economic and health-care burdens on hospitals and patients alike."); *see also* Perlmutter v. Beth David Hosp., 123 N.E.2d 792, 793-94 (N.Y. 1954) (oncerning the supply of impure blood plasma).

[624] *See* NIMMER, *supra* note 562, at ¶ 6.02[1] 6-4 to 6-9.

[625] *See* HAWKLAND, *supra* note 562, at § 2-105:01.

[626] 484 P.2d 573 (Nev. 1971) (Nev., 1971), *overruled by* Calloway v. City of Reno, 993 P.2d 1259 (Nev. 2000); *See also* Anthony Pools, a Div. of Anthony Indus., Inc. v. Sheehan, 455 A.2d 434, 441(Md. 1983) ("The gravamen test of Dean Hawkland suggests the vehicle for satisfying the legislative policy. Accordingly, we hold that where, as part of a commercial transaction, consumer goods are sold which retain their character as consumer goods after completion of the performance promised

[I]f the gas escaped because of a defective fitting or connector, the case might be characterized as one involving the sale of goods. On the other hand, if the gas escaped because of poor work by Barnes the case might be characterized as one involving services, outside the scope of the UCC.[627]

As shown in this case, there is no reason why less obligation is imposed in relation to goods just because the transaction involves both goods and services.[628]

The approach taken by the English law seems to offer more certainty in application than in the gravamen of the action approach, by not depending on the origin of defects.

[b] Predominant Test, Contract for the Sale of Goods
[i] Turn-Key Computer System

Neilson Business Equipment Center, Inc. v. Monteleone[629] seems to reinforce the preconceived assumption regarding the effect of classification. The defendant, Neilson Business Equipment Center, Inc. (Neilson) agreed to customise the computer system to

---

to the consumer, and where monetary loss or personal injury is claimed to have resulted from a defect in the consumer goods, the provisions of the Maryland U.C.C. dealing with implied warranties apply to the consumer goods, even if the transaction is predominately one for the rendering of consumer services. The facts of the instant case, however, make it unnecessary for us presently to decide whether § 2-316.1 would require that U.C.C. based, implied warranties also extend to consumer goods which are used up in the course of rendering the consumer service to the consumer.").

[627] *See* HAWKLAND, *supra* note 562, at §2-102:04 (1995) (arguing that it might be more sensible and facilitate administration, at least in the area in which contracts involving provisions of both goods and service do not readily fall into one category or the other, to abandon the "predominant factor" test, and focus instead on whether the gravamen of the action involves goods or services.).

[628] G.H. Myers & Co. v. Brent Cross Serv. Co. [1934] 1 K.B. 46.

[629] 524 A.2d 1172 (Del. 1987).

meet the plaintiff's, Monteleone's needs. In addition to the lease, the parties had a separate maintenance agreement. The plaintiff chose to lease the equipment in order to obtain a favourable cash flow and tax benefits. The lease agreement for "turn-key" hardware and software equipment was considered a sale of goods. The court applied a "predominant" test in determining:

> When a mixed contract is presented, it is necessary for a court to review the factual circumstances surrounding the negotiation, formation and contemplated performance of the contract to determine whether the contract is predominantly or primarily a contract for the sale of goods... Neilson contracted to supply a turn-key computer system; that is, a system sold as a package which is ready to function immediately. The hardware and software elements are combined into a single unit - the computer system-prior to sale.[630]

The court seems to have made the determination based on the fact that the hardware and software elements are combined into a single unit, as a "computer system." Any consulting services rendered by the *Neilson* case were considered ancillary to the contracts.

As the transaction was considered a sale of goods, there was an implied warranty of merchantability and an implied warranty of fitness for a particular purpose. In order for the computer system to be merchantable, the system must have been capable of passing without objection in the trade under the contractual description, and be fit for the ordinary purpose for which it was intended. The supplied computer system failed regarding merchantability because it did not meet the plaintiff's expressed record and book-keeping needs. The court found that the plaintiff, having no prior experience

---

[630] *Id.* at 1174.

in acquiring computer technology, relied on Neilson's professional expertise to develop and deliver a satisfactory computer system for the plaintiff's specific needs.[631]

One of the important factors in determining the liability of the supplier was that the defendant was an expert in computer technology and should have performed satisfactorily with the defendant's skills and knowledge. Therefore, even if the contract were construed as one for services, the court may have imposed liability, based on the fact that the supplier, the expert in computer technology, did not perform with reasonable skill. In cases where the court finds that the suppliers are considered "experts" in the field and such expertise is relied on by the customers, the court may impose liability based on the notion that the suppliers should be held to a higher standard of care. In such cases, it is likely that the "performance standard" of the result-oriented outcome of the performance and the process-oriented outcome of the performance would be closer than in cases where the court does not find such expertise.

Although, instalment of turn-key systems requires a substantial amount of time for analysis, feedback and correct instalment, as the final product is supposed to be in immediate operation,[632] it can be said that the purpose of contemplating such a transaction is on the "completeness" of the final product. Delivery of a "turn-key" system is more likely to involve the transfer of both software and hardware than merely software alone, as the users would be likely to implement new powerful hardware to process as much information as possible, as more speedy and powerful hardware is continuously developed and distributed in the market. The users would probably expect to use both old and new systems at the beginning to ensure that the new systems function properly. It

---

[631] *Id.* at 1176.
[632] *See* Triangle Underwriters, Inc. v. Honeywell, Inc., 457 F. Supp. 765, 767 (E.D.N.Y. 1978), *aff'd. in part, rev'd. in part,* 604 F.2d 737 (2d Cir. 1979).

was appropriate to apply the sale of goods standard to such a transaction to ensure a satisfactory result. This case represents a typical example where there is a gap between the knowledge of a skilled supplier and the ignorance of an unsophisticated user.[633] In these cases, the suppliers had reason to know their recommendations were to be relied on and the users were justified in relying on the recommendation of the suppliers.

[ii] Customised (Bespoke) Software

In *RRX Industries, Inc. v. Lab-Con, Inc.*,[634] the Ninth Circuit determined that an agreement to supply a software system for use in medical laboratories and to correct any malfunctions or "bugs" that arose in the system was considered a contract for goods. The court applied a "predominant" test and found that the sales aspect of the transaction predominated, and that employee training, repair services, and system upgrading were incidental to the sale of the software package and did not defeat characterisation of the system as goods.[635] The software system supplied turned out to be unreliable and defects continued to exist after some attempts to repair bugs. The court found "the default of the seller so total and fundamental that its consequential damages limitation was expunged from the contract."[636] In this case, the court could not consider whether hardware was transferred or not, in order to find there was a transaction involving goods, as no hardware was involved, the defendant solely installed the software system.

---

[633] *See also* USM Corp. v. Arthur D. Little Sys., Inc., 546 N.E.2d 888, 891 n.4 (Mass. App. Ct. 1989) (holding that a contract involving developing, marketing, and installing "turn-key" computer system is a contract for the sale of goods. The court found that there was an express promise that the response time, which was defined as "the amount of time between entry of a command into the system and the appearance on the screen of the requested output" would not be substantially excessive, and such a promise had been breached.).

[634] 772 F.2d 543 (9th Cir. 1985).

[635] *Id.* at 546.

[636] *Id.* at 547.

It seems acceptable to hold that a transaction for software alone is the sale of goods as in the cases of hardware, even if the transaction involves substantial service elements and a considerable amount of time to customise software for specific business purposes. It might be reasonable for the user to expect a result-oriented outcome, for instance, in terms of implied warranties, in transactions involving customised computer programs, as the purpose of the transaction is to supply a workable system, especially in cases of a "turn-key" system.

[c] Predominant Purpose Test, Supply of Services

In the United States, a contract for the supply of services generally requires "substantial performance." The test for substantial performance is whether the performance meets the essential purpose of the contract.[637]

In *Data Processing Services, Inc. v. L.H. Smith Oil Corp.,*[638] an agreement to develop computer software and to develop and implement a data processing system to meet specific needs for an accounting system was considered a contract for services. However, despite such classification, the recognition by the court, of the programmer's expertise imposed the higher duties of care of professionals on the supplier of the computer programs.

Data Processing Services, Inc. (DPS) was in the business of computer programming and L.H. Smith Oil Corporation (Smith) sold petroleum products. Smith stopped payment after paying several billings submitted by DPS and DPS sued for breach of contract and open account. In determining the classification, the court stated:

> DPS sold no "hardware" to Smith. Instead, DPS was retained to design, develop and implement an electronic data processing system to meet Smith's specific needs,

---

[637] *See* Plante v. Jacobs, 103 N.W.2d 296, 298 (Wis. 1960).
[638] 492 N.E.2d 314 (Ind. Ct. App. 1986).

... Although the end result was to be preserved by means of some physical mani-festation such as magnetic tape, floppy or hard disks, etc., which would generate the recordkeeping computer functions DPS was to develop, it was DPS's knowledge, skill, and ability for which Smith bargained. The sale of computer hardware or generally-available standardized software was not here involved. ... The mere means by which DPS's skills and knowledge were to be transmitted to Smith's computers was incidental. The situation here is more analogous to a client seeking a lawyer's advice or a patient seeking medical treatment for a particular ailment than it is to a customer buying seed corn, soap, or cam shafts. While a tangible end product, such as floppy disks, hard disks, punch cards or magnetic tape used as a storage medium for the program may be involved incidentally in this transaction, it is the skill and knowledge of the programmer which is being purchased in the main, not the devices by which this skill and knowledge is placed into the buyer's computer. The means of transmission is not the essence of the agreement.[639]

The court also commented on the expertise of the computer programmers stating:

Those who hold themselves out to the world as possessing skill and qualifications in their respective trades or professions impliedly represent they possess the skill and will exhibit the diligence ordinarily possessed by well informed members of the trade or profession.[640]

---

[639] *Id.* at 318-19.
[640] *Id.* at 319.

As DPS represented itself to have the necessary expertise to do the work and knew it lacked the skill and expertise, DPS should have foreseen the loss to be incurred by Smith. The court found that DPS breached its implied promise of having the reasonable skill and ability to do the job for which it had contracted.[641] Here, the representation of skill and expertise was the essential factor in holding the defendant liable to display reasonable skill and ability to do the job.[642] As the transaction was deemed one for the supply of services, no result-oriented warranties were imposed. Nevertheless, the court stated that "DPS was to act with specific regard to Smith's need."[643] This case shows that the professional skills of the computer programmers and reliance of their customers are the factors that blur the boundary between the classifications of the contract.

As the courts impose such higher standards of care for computer programmers, the duty to supply with reasonable care tends to be elevated, close to being a duty to supply subject matter that actually works properly in accordance with the customer's needs. Therefore, in such cases, the effect of classification becomes less obvious.

The court calculated the sum Smith paid to DPS for services in the development of a system, additional employee time involved due to the failure of DPS's program to perform, and the cost of hiring of at least one additional employee. The court found that the amount of judgement rendered within the parameters of the evidence presented to the trial court. Although the trial court's conclusion that the transaction for goods to which Article 2 of the UCC applied was clearly erroneous, reversal was not necessary, as the findings of fact were sufficient to support the judgement on

---

[641] *Id.* at 320.
[642] *Id.*
[643] *Id.* at 318.

common law principles.[644]

The court correctly stated that "the means of transmission is not the essence of the agreement." In addition, the fact that the court did not find that the reversal of the trial court's decision to classify the transaction as the sale of goods was necessary, clearly indicates that the imposition of the higher standard of care for computer programmers is the factor that blurs the boundary between transactions for goods and services.

However, the court also stated that DPS sold no hardware to Smith and the sale of computer hardware or generally available standardised software was not involved. Technically speaking, hardware can incorporate skills and knowledge, although it is relatively easier to incorporate a required specification to meet the client's needs into software.[645] The mere fact that the hardware was included as a part of the transaction should not transform a transaction into one for sale of goods. As stated above, many transactions involving customised software are considered sale of goods. If the result oriented result is considered, there is no need to consider the process oriented outcome. However, it is more reasonable to think that the development side of the transaction should be considered, as in England, a contract for the supply of services and be treated accordingly.

In contrast, *Micro-Managers, Inc. v. Gregory*,[646] reached a different result. The contract to develop a new programmable controller to replace the existing equipment, where payment was to be made based on the time spent at stated rates, was deemed a contract for the supply of services. The user claimed that the software was virtually useless, that the user received no benefit

---

[644] *Id.* at 319.

[645] *See supra* § 3.02 Classification of Contracts [5] England [d] Physical Medium and Intangibles. It may be noted that almost anything that can be done by software can also be done by hardware.

[646] 434 N.W.2d 97 (Wis. 1988).

from it, that the contract was not substantially performed, and that the software developed did not substantially meet or conform to the specifications mutually agreed upon. The court determined this argument to go to the quality of the work product, and not to whether the supplier used its expertise and skill to develop the software. Such an inquiry would be relevant if this were a contract for goods under the U.C.C. but, since it was not, no such inquiry was required.[647] The court found that the supplier substantially performed its contract by using its expertise and skill.[648]

However, the main purpose of contracts to transfer computer technology is primarily a functional one. Contracts to develop and design computer programs to assist business operations, are fundamentally different from contracts to hire an artist to paint a portrait. Therefore, as discussed above, it may not be possible completely to separate the process by which the work is done from the outcome of the work in the case of contracts to transfer computer technology. As this case shows, the "predominant purpose" test may create harsh results for the users, by emphasising solely the labour part of the bargain. In this case, the software might have been useless even though expertise and skill were exercised. The English approach, to impose satisfactory quality, may be preferred to avoid such consequences.

[d] Gravamen of the Action Test, Contract for the Supply of Services

In *Herbert Friedman & Assoc., Inc. v. Lifetime Doors, Inc.*,[649] in determining whether the UCC applies to a mixed goods-services contract, the court applied the gravamen of the action test,[650] as the Michigan court, unlike the majority of courts, has not expressly adopted a predominant purpose test.

---

[647] *Id.* at 104.
[648] *Id.*
[649] 1989 WL 157487 (N.D. Ill. 1990).
[650] *See* HAWKLAND *supra* note 562, at §2-105:01.

Herbert Friedman & Associates, Inc. (Friedman), a designer and installer of computer software systems, had an agreement with Lifetime Doors, Inc. (Lifetime) to deliver "packages" of software as it completed the required modifications, and Lifetime to make periodic payments. Friedman sued Lifetime after Lifetime terminated the agreement before Friedman had finished installing a computer software system at Lifetime.

The court looked at whether the contract contained a single price which covered both the installation and sale of goods, and whether the claim was based "entirely on deficiencies in the rendition of services for which the contract contained a separate price, rather than on a defect in the goods themselves."[651] As explained in *In re Trailer & Plumbing Supplies*,[652] this test simply asks whether the underlying action is brought because of alleged defective goods or because of the quality of the service rendered. If the gravamen of the action focuses on goods, then the U.C.C. governs. If the focus is on the quality of the services rendered, then the common law applies.[653] The court found that the fixed cost of the contract was $250,000 for the software including the custom modifications and there was an estimated per diem charge of $550 for consulting.[654] Friedman's damages were primarily claimed for failure to pay for the software it delivered rather than for the consulting services it rendered. In these circumstances, the Michigan court applied the U.C.C. to this transaction.[655]

In this test, if the action were based on the way the service was rendered, the court would have applied the law pertaining to the supply of services. However, as in this case, not all transactions are separable. If the plaintiff's claim was based on both defective

---

[651] *Herbert Friedman*, 1989 WL 157487 at * 8.
[652] 578 A.2d 343 (N.H. 1990).
[653] *Id.* at 345.
[654] *Herbert Friedman*, 1989 WL 157487 at * 8.
[655] *Id.*

goods and quality of service rendered, it is not clear whether the court may select both laws in relation to the contract. If the court was to consider both laws on defective goods and quality of the service, the approach is similar to the one in England.

The court found that Lifetime was justified in cancelling further performance because Friedman did not perform its contractual obligations within a reasonable time.[656] However, Lifetime had to pay for the software it had accepted. The court found that the accepted package was not substantially impaired because the entire package of software had not been installed. The court also found that Lifetime's complaints were partly based on the misconception about what the software could achieve and that these were not communicated sufficiently to Friedman.[657] Even though the software was supposed to be customised to the client's needs, what Friedman meant by "custom" was not a complete fabrication from scratch, but rather an adaptation of the defendant's software to meet a customer's needs within the parameters of the defendant's software's basic structure.[658] Therefore, the software here was considered standardised rather than customised.[659]

The court seemed to have examined the brochures very carefully; however, the effect of advertisement should be considered more carefully in light of the relative knowledge of the customer. For instance, definition and usage of the word "customised" should be considered sensitively so that customers with no prior experience would not be misled.

As stated above, this test seems to give a flexible approach to the complex nature of the transactions involving computer technology. However, not many authorities have adopted this test. The test is criticised for creating uncertainties as to which law is

---

[656] *Id.* at *10.
[657] *Id.* at *5.
[658] *Id.* at *1.
[659] *Id.* at *5.

applicable to the transaction.[660] Compared to this approach, English law seems to offer clear and comprehensive ways for separating the supply of goods and services elements in this respect.

[e] Factors Considered in the Classification

[i] Important Factors

The factors relevant in determining the classification are mainly categorised as follows: the physical configuration of the subject matter, the process of performance, the method of distribution, and the remuneration. They are basically the same factors as discussed above in earlier cases.

[ii] Physical Configuration

In *Advent Sys., Ltd. v. Unisys Corp.*,[661] the court stated that computer programs are the products of intellectual property but, once implanted in a medium, the program is tangible, moveable, available in the market place and widely distributed to computer owners.[662] However, this analysis is weak, since programs do not need to be implanted in a medium to be distributed. Nevertheless, the characteristics of computer programs available in the market and widely distributed to computer owners may be a relevant factor in terms of the method of distribution. U.C.C. § 2-102[663] provides that transactions subject to the Code be "in goods." "Goods" are defined in § 2-105(1)[664] as "all things which are movable at the time of identification to the contract for sale other than the money in which the price is to be paid, investment securities and things in action." This definition is a broad one, and the focus of the definition of goods is whether the thing is movable or not rather

---

[660] NIMMER, *supra*, note 562, at ¶ 6.02[1], 6-4 to 6-9.
[661] 925 F.2d 670 (3d Cir. 1991).
[662] *Id.* at 675.
[663] 1998 Official Text.
[664] *Id.*

than whether the thing is tangible or not.[665]

In many cases, the courts seem to be making determinations by considering factors other than physical tangibility. In *Neilson Business Equipment Center, Inc. v. Monteleone*,[666] and in *USM Corp v. Arthur D. Little Systems Inc.*,[667] a turn-key computer system, sold as a package ready to function immediately and in which the hardware and software elements were combined into a single unit,[668] was considered a good. However, as stated above, it may also be possible to argue that the emphasis was on "ready to func-tion immediately"[669] for unskilled users, rather than on the physical configurations, in order to impose a result-oriented outcome; the gap between the knowledge of the supplier and user may have also been a contributing factor.

In *Wharton Management Group v. Sigma Consultants, Inc.*,[670] the court found that Sigma had not sold "hardware," but also stated that Sigma was retained after preparing a study of Wharton's existing operations, to design, develop, and install computer software which would meet Wharton's specific needs and objectives.[671] It was Sigma's knowledge, skill and ability for which Wharton bargained, therefore, the contract was for the *services* rendered.[672]

Consideration of the physical elements, namely transfer of hardware, has often been used as an important factor to distinguish

---

[665] *See* Fickeisen v. Wheeling Elec. Co., 67 W.Va. 335, 336(1910); J. M. Conley, *Tort Theories of Recovery Against Vendors of Defective Sortware*, in PLI Order No. G4-3855 PRACTISING LAW INSTITUTE, PATENTS, COPYRIGHTS, TRADEMARKS, AND LITERARY PROPERTY COURSE HANDBOOK SERIES 701, 705(1990).
[666] 524 A.2d 1172 (Del. 1987).
[667] 546 N.E.2d 888 (Mass. App. Ct. 1989).
[668] *Neilson*, 524 A.2d at 1174.
[669] *Id.*
[670] 1990 WL 18360 (Del. Super. Ct. 1990), *aff'd*, 582 A.2d 936 (Del. 1990).
[671] *Id.* at *2.
[672] *Id.* at *3.

between contracts for goods and services. However, as discussed above, this "traditional factor" does not seem to provide a fully valid justification in deciding the reasoning for the classification. Technically speaking, the hardware can incorporate as much skill and ability as the software, although it is more common to modify or alter software rather than hardware to satisfy the customer's specific needs. Therefore, the courts should not consider computer programs in the same way they consider other tangible materials.

[iii] **Process of Performance**

In determining that the contract was for the supply of services, in the *Wharton* case, the court considered that Sigma prepared a study of Wharton's existing operations, before designing, developing, and installing computer software to meet Wharton's specific needs, and that it was Sigma's knowledge, skill and ability for which Wharton bargained.[673]

However, both in the *Neilson* case, and in the *USM* case, the contracts were deemed the sale of goods, despite the fact that these transactions involved analysis of the present system and custom-designing of the new turn-key computer systems. Likewise, many years of data processing servicing, and the development and the customisation of the software was considered merely as a support to an "Insurance Machine" in accommodating the business practice of the plaintiff consisting of a "computer software product" in *Colonial Life Insurance Inc. v. Electronic Data Systems Corp.*[674]

A number of cases seems to consider that transactions involving software can be a sale of goods, regardless of whether or not a substantial service element to customisation is involved.[675]

---

[673] *Id.*

[674] 817 F. Supp 235 (D.N.H. 1993).

[675] *See* Advent Sys., Ltd. v. Unisys Corp., 925 F.2d. 670 (3d Cir. 1991); RRX Indus., Inc. v. Lab-Con, Inc., 772 F.2d 543 (9th Cir. 1985); Chatlos Sys., Inc. v. Nat'l Cash Register Corp., 635 F.2d 1081 (3d Cir. 1980); Triangle Underwriters, Inc. v. Honeywell, Inc., 604 F.2d. 737 (2d Cir. 1979)

Therefore, the type of service rendered for customisation is not particularly helpful in classification unless the role of the supplier is clearly an advisory one, such as analysis or collection of business data. The courts seem to be making arbitrary decisions as to what is, or is not, the predominant element of the transaction. If the contract is deemed one for the supply of services, there is no implied obligation for the results achieved by the software or hardware supplied. If the courts impose a higher standard of care for computer programmers, a duty to supply with reasonable care tends to be elevated, close to being a duty to supply subject matter that actually works properly in accordance with the customer's needs. However, there is no reason to distinguish goods supplied with services and without services.[676] The gravamen of the action approach and the English approach may offer solutions to this problem, as the users are just as justified in expecting a certain level of performance in terms of a result-oriented outcome.

[iv] Method of Distribution

In *Data Processing Services, Inc. v. L.H. Smith Oil Corp.*,[677] in determining that the transaction was the supply of services, the court stated that the sale of computer hardware or generally available standardised software was not involved.[678] Standardised software is not manufactured for specialised purposes, there is no contact between a user and a supplier, and it is distributed to the general public. Even though only the software may be transferred in such transactions, there are no individualised services involved in order to justify the classification as the supply of services.[679]

---

[676] *But see* Milau Assoc., Inc. v. No Ave. Devel. Corp., 368 N.E.2d 1247, 1249-50 (N.Y. 1977).
[677] 492 N.E.2d 314 (Ind. Ct. App. 1986).
[678] *Id.* at 319.
[679] *Id.*

[v] Remuneration

The cost of labour does not seem to be a determinate factor in determining the predominant factor. However, the fact that the remuneration is paid based on the time spent for the services provided seems highly relevant. The court stated, in *Advent Systems, Ltd. v. Unisys Corp.*,[680] that the comparison of the relative costs of the materials supplied with the costs of the labour may be helpful but is not dispositive.[681]

In *Conopco, Inc. v. McCreadie*,[682] the court considered the way remuneration was paid to the defendant, in addition to examining the nature of the subject matter acquired and other ancillary services rendered. The defendants, the partners of Ernst & Young (E & Y), had an agreement with Faberge Inc., which was subsequently assigned to the parent company of Conopco Inc. This agreement was considered a contract for services. The court considered that even if the defendant was involved in the selection and installation of hardware, the defendant's role was considered an advisory one, performed in conjunction with the plaintiff's staff. In addition, the defendant was compensated for each day of employee service it provided; the defendant's remuneration was not tied at all to the provision of goods.[683]

Likewise, in *Micro-Managers, Inc. v. Gregory*,[684] the contract to develop a new programmable controller to replace the existing equipment was deemed a contract for the supply of services. In making the determination, the court considered the fact that the payment was to be made based on the time at stated rates.[685] If remuneration is paid specifically for labour or services rendered

---

[680] 925 F.2d 670 (3d Cir.1991).
[681] *Id.* at 676.
[682] 826 F. Supp. 855 (D.N.J. 1993), *aff'd*, 40 F.3d 1239 (3d Cir. 1994).
[683] *Id.* at 870.
[684] 434 N.W.2d 97 (Wis. Ct. App. 1988).
[685] *Id.* at 100.

and this is expressly stated in the contract between the parties, there is strong evidence that the contract was for the supply of services.

[vi] Comparison with Traditional Subject Matters

Essentially, there are no differences between factors considered for traditional subject matter, discussed above[686] and subject matter involving computer technology. However, the tangibility factor is of little use in transactions involving computer technology. Furthermore, most of such transactions involve skilled suppliers and continuing performance, which are typical characteristics of the supply of services contracts. This makes it even harder to classify using traditional factors. The drafting of the U.C.I.T.A. was necessary to clarify such uncertainties involved in classification.

[f] Contracts for Information

For contracts for information, see discussion above in § 3.02 Classification of Contracts [1] Classification of Contracts [d] Contracts for Information.[7] Explanation of the Difference between English Law and United States Law.

The difference between English law and United States law in relating to the classification of the contract for sales and services law is based on the fact that English law considers that the obligations of a supplier in relation to the goods supplied should be, as nearly as possible, the same, whatever kind of contract is employed.[687] The Law Commission Report stated that:

> It seems reasonably clear that at common law the obligations of the supplier in respect of materials supplied were regarded as the same whether the contract was classified

---

[686] *See supra* [3] Uncertain Nature of the Criteria in Classification -Examples of Actions by Suppliers to Recover Payment for the Work Done in Cases Where Customers Refuse to Accept.

[687] *See* Law Commission, *Law of Contract: Implied Terms in Contracts for the Supply of Goods* (Law Com. No. 95, 1979) para. 33, at 11.

as one of sale or of work and materials, and in either case whether the supplier worked on, or with, the materials or whether he did not.[688]

Lord Upjohn in *Young & Marten Ltd. v. McManus Childs Ltd.*[689] stated that:

> The distinction between a contract for the sale of goods and a contract for the provision of work and materials is one which depends on the particular nature of each individual contract, as was said as long ago as 1856 in *Clay v. Yates*[690] and it is frequently a question of fine distinction. It would be most unsatisfactory, illogical, and indeed a severe blow to any idea of a coherent system of common law, if the existence of an implied obligation depended upon such a distinction...Indeed, for my part I think, as a matter of common sense and justice, one who contracts to do work and supply materials ought to be under at least as high, if not a higher, degree of obligation with regard to the goods he supplies and the work he does than a seller who may be a mere middleman or wholesaler.[691]

Therefore, the same principle of law for transfer of goods with respect to implication of terms as to quality or fitness for purpose is applicable to contracts for supply of services in

---

[688] *Id.*, para. 57, at 17; *see also* Dodd and Dodd v. Wilson and McWilliam [1946] 2 All E.R. 691.
[689] [1969] 1 A.C. 455 (H.L. (E.)).
[690] (1856) 1 H. & N. 73.
[691] *Young & Marten,* [1969] 1A.C. at 472-74.

transactions regarding computer programs.[692] In English law, under both contracts for sale of goods and mixed contracts for goods and services, there is an implied obligation that the goods supplied under the contract are of satisfactory quality.

Both in *St. Albans City & District Council v. International Computers Ltd.*,[693] and in *Saphena Computing Ltd. v. Allied Collection Agencies Ltd.*,[694] a contract for the transfer of software, to achieve a specific, known purpose was subject to an implied term that the program would be reasonably fit for the intended purpose. As customised software is almost always made to be fit for a specific purpose, any transaction involving customised software may fall within the scope of Section 14(3) of the Sale of Goods Act 1979 and Sections 4(4) and 4(5) of the Supply of Goods and Services Act 1982. These sections provide that if the special purpose is known to the supplier, there is an implied term that the goods will be fit for the intended purpose.

On the other hand, the predominant purpose test in the United States treats an entire contract as one object, consisting of either a transaction entirely in goods or one entirely involving services.[695] Therefore, if the contract is construed as one for supplying services, the U.C.C. is not applicable, and thus there are no result-oriented implied warranties. As discussed above in *Micro-Managers, Inc. v. Gregory*,[696] the court held that the argument as to the quality of the work product and as to whether the supplier used its expertise and skill to develop the software, were completely different.[697]

---

[692] St. Albans City & District Council v. In'l Computers Ltd. [1995] F.S.R. 686 (Q.B.D.), [1996] 4 All E.R. 481; Saphena Computing Ltd. v. Allied Collection Agencies Ltd. [1995] F.S.R. 616.
[693] [1995] F.S.R. 686 (Q.B.D.), [1996] 4 All E.R. 481.
[694] *St. Albans*, [1995] F.S.R. at 650.
[695] *See* NIMMER, *supra* note 562, at ¶ 6.02[1], 6-4 to 6-9.
[696] 434 N.W.2d 97 (Wis. 1988).
[697] *Id.* at 104.

However, as in *Data Processing Services, Inc. v. L.H. Smith Oil Corp.*,[698] if the courts impose such a higher standard of care for computer programmers, the duty to supply with reasonable care tends to be elevated, almost to being a duty to supply the subject matter which actually works properly in accordance with the customer's needs. Therefore, in such cases, the effect of classification becomes less obvious.

The English approach in adopting the same principle of law for transfer of goods with respect to implication of terms as to quality or fitness to contracts for supply of services and to contracts for goods seems more sensible in considering the functional characteristics of computer programs.

[7] The Effect of the Enactment of the U.C.I.T.A. -Basic Concepts

[a] Basic Terms

The Article 2B project in the United States started with the presumption that the current classification approach to distinguishing goods and services in relation to computer technology is seriously outdated.[699] At first, the National Conference of Commissioners on Uniform State laws and the American Law

---

[698] 492 N.E.2d 314 (Ind. Ct. App. 1986).

[699] *See* PART 1 CONTEXT: LAW REFORM AND THE U.C.C., Modern Economy and Law Reform, U.C.C. 2B (August 1, 1998 proposed draft), citing R. REICH, THE WORK OF NATIONS 85-86 (1991)(stating, "The distinction that used to be drawn between 'goods' and 'services' is meaningless, because so much of the value provided by the successful enterprise ... entails services [and information].");U.C.C. § 2B-103 cmt. 3(February 1, 1999 proposed draft)("Transactions in computer information differ from sales or leases of goods because the focus of the transaction is on the information, its content or capability, rather than on the tangible items that contain the information is delivered. In a sale of goods, the buyer obtains ownership of the subject matter of the contract (e.g., the specific toaster or television). That ownership creates exclusive rights in the subject matter (e.g., the toaster). In contrast, a person in a transaction whose subject matter

Institute attempted to integrate the transactions in intangibles to the U.C.C. Article 2 and 2A framework. However, a transaction with respect to information is quite different from that to tangible goods, and cannot be appropriately integrated into the U.C.C. framework. Therefore, it was determined that Article 2B should not remain a project within the Uniform Commercial Code. The new Act is called the Uniform Computer Information Transaction Act. The Act was approved and recommended by the National Conference of Commissioners on Uniform State Laws at its annual conference meeting in July 1999. It represents a serious attempt to foresee problems, provide flexible tools for solving them, provide some predictability of 'outcome', and reconcile opposing interests.

With respect to warranties, the U.C.I.T.A. is said to blend three categories of laws: the law regarding the sale of goods, which focuses on the quality of the product; the law regarding the supply of services which focuses on the process; and the law regarding supply of informational content which disallows implied obligations of accuracy in information.[700]

The U.C.I.T.A. is to be applicable to computer information transactions.[701] "'Computer information transaction' means an agreement or the performance of it to create, modify, transfer, or

---

involves obtaining the computer information and that acquires a copy of computer information may obtain ownership of the copy but does not, and cannot reasonably expect to, own the information or the rights associated with it. ...Transactions in computer information differ from transactions in other information because of the nature of the information involved. Information capable of being processed in a computer is more readily susceptible to modification and to perfect reproduction than information in other form such as printed books or magazines. Indeed, to use computer information, one must copy it into a machine."); Stenograph v. Bossard, 46 U.S.P.Q.2d 1936 (D.C. Cir. 1998); MAI Sys. Corp. v. Peak Computer, Inc., 991 F.2d 511 (9th Cir. 1993).

[700] *See supra* note 518.
[701] U.C.I.T.A. § 103(a) (2001).

license computer information or informational rights in computer information."[702] "'Computer information' means information in electronic form which is obtained from or through the use of a computer or which is in a form capable of being processed by a computer."[703] This term includes a copy of the information, associated documentation, or packaging.[704] This Act applies to "contracts to develop, modify, or create software and other computer information, such as a computer database."[705] This Act also applies to transactions to distribute or to grant a right to use a computer program[706] or to obtain by electronic means access to information.[707]

The Drafting Committee made significant modifications to the previous Article 2B drafts by reducing the scope of the Article to "computer information transactions," basically to software and on-line licences and directly related services. The core businesses of movies, sound recording, print publishing and broadcasting are no longer covered.

In the U.C.I.T.A., " '[i]nformation' means data, text, images, sounds, mask works, or computer programs.' "[708] " 'Computer program' means a set of statements or instructions to be used directly or indirectly in a computer to bring about a certain result."[709]

On the other hand, " '[i]nformational content' means information that is intended to be communicated to or perceived by an individual in the ordinary use of the information, or the equivalent

---

[702] *Id.* § 102(a)(11).
[703] *Id.* § 102(a)(10).
[704] *Id.* § 102(a)(10).
[705] *Id.* § 103 cmt 2a.
[706] *Id.* § 103 cmt 2b.
[707] *Id.* § 102(a)(1), § 102 cmt. 1, § 103 cmt. 2c.
[708] *Id.* § 102(35).
[709] *Id.* § 102(12); *see also* Copyright Act, 17 U.S.C. §101 (2001) ("A 'computer program' is a set of statements or instructions to be used directly or indirectly in a computer in order to bring about a certain result.")

of that information."[710] "Informational content" refers to output that communicates to a human being, such as human-readable content of electronic database, whereas "[c]omputer program" refers to the functional and operating aspects of a digital system such as a search program of an electronic database.[711] The difference between the two concerns is whether the issue addresses operations (program) or communicated content (informational content). [712] This distinction is important in determining liability, risk and performance obligation.

"'Published informational content' means informational content prepared for or made available to recipients generally, or to a class of recipients, in substantially the same form."[713] This type of information is "most closely associated with free expression," and includes the material of newspapers, books, or motion pictures, which are outside the scope of the Act, intended to communicate to a human being and created for, or distributed to, a group of recipients as a whole in generally the same form.[714] The term does not include content tailored to meet a specific recipient's needs and information provided in a special relationship of reliance, where "special relationship of reliance refers to transactions in which the provider knows that a particular licensee plans to rely on particular data provided by the licensor and that the licensee expects the licensor to tailor the information to the client's specific business or personal needs."[715]

[b] Three Different Legal Traditions

Section 402 provides for express warranties, created by an affirmation of fact or promise made by the licensor to its licensee in

---

[710] U.C.I.T.A. § 102(37).
[711] *Id.* § 102 cmt. 10
[712] *Id.* § 102 cmt. 33.
[713] *Id.* § 102(52).
[714] *Id.* § 102 cmt 46.
[715] *Id.*

any manner, such as advertising, which relates to the information and becomes part of the basis of the bargain. A sample, model, or demonstration of a final product may also create an express warranty.[716]

Section 403(a) provides the implied warranty similar to Article 2, that a computer program is merchantable, fit for the ordinary purpose for which such computer programs are used. For the cases where a merchant in a special relationship of reliance provides informational content or services to collect, compile, process or transmit, informational content, section 404(a) provides for implied warranties similar to the common law duty under service contracts, to exercise reasonable care. Section 405(b) provides that such implied warranty is not applicable to transactions for the aesthetics, market appeal, or subjective quality of informational content or published informational content.

The merchantability warranty provided in section 403(a) and the warranty in section 404(a) for the accuracy of data may both apply to the same transaction. The merchantability warranty applies to the program and its functions, and section 404(a) applies to the informational content and data.[717]

Section 405(a)(1) provides for the implied warranty for fitness for a particular purpose in cases where a licensor has reason to know any particular purpose for which the information is required. However, if a licensor was to be paid for the amount of her or his time or effort regardless of the fitness of the resulting information, there is an implied warranty that the information will not fail to achieve the licensee's particular purpose as a result of the licensor's lack of reasonable care.

---

[716] *Id.* § 402(a)(3); *see infra* § 3.03 Express Terms or Warranties [4] The U.C.I.T.A.
[717] *Id.* § 403 cmt. 2.

[8] Classification of Contracts with Respect to Information in Electronic Form

By taking examples of traditional subject matters, I have shown that many of the factors in determining the classification are not determinative, therefore, classification may leave more scope for flexibility and the courts may be able to arrive at conclusions which seem most appropriate to do justice. This trend may be amplified in classifying transactions involving information in electronic form because of the complex nature of transactions.

Contracts for information in electronic form involve complicated obligations and such obligations cannot adequately be defined by classifications such as contracts for goods or contracts for services.

Many of the transactions with respect to human-readable information in electronic form, can be classified as sales of goods or supply of services. For that category of information made available to the public in substantially the same format, which are neither classified as sale of goods nor as supply of services, the same discussions as to whether the tort liability exists with respect to such subject matters may be applicable to the discussions with respect to contract, just as in cases of human-information in traditional form. Essentially, a duty with respect to the accuracy of the content of the information is imposed only if a special relationship exists.[718]

However, some notable distinctions exist between information in electronic form and in traditional form, which may affect liabilities for information in electronic form. Such distinction is discussed in Chapter 2.[719]

---

[718] *See supra* § 2.03 Theories Relevant To Imposing Liability [4] Negligent Misrepresentation; § 3.02 Classification of Contracts [d] Contracts for Information.

[719] *See supra* § 2.03 Theories Relevant To Imposing Liability [4] Negligent Misrepresentation [a] Negligent Misrepresentation and Information in Electronic Form.

With respect to transactions involving computer programs, the standard of performance expected should be determined, taking into account the unique functional nature of computer technology and the reliance on the professional skills involved in exercising such technology.

In considering the nature of computer technology, both English law and United States law seem to have reached the sensible conclusion that many of the transactions involving computer programs may be treated as sale of goods, or the standard of performance in relation to computer programs may be judged by reference to a result- oriented outcome.

However, as provided in English law and as in the comments to the U.C.I.T.A., the dual application of different implied warranty provisions to the same transaction seems more suitable for transactions involving computer programs. As discussed above, it is more practical to focus on the different nature of each element of one transaction as is done in English law, than to treat the entire contract as one object.[720] Compared to United States courts, English courts have been more equipped for taking into account the unique nature of transactions involving computer programs by treating the different nature of each element of one transaction. Nevertheless, it may be more preferable in England to enact a similar law specifically designed for computer information as has been done in the United States. The enactment of such a law may allow the courts to impose different obligations more clearly.

The U.C.I.T.A. is a valuable attempt, enacted to deal specifically with the issues relating to computer information, by taking into account the unique nature of transactions involving computer information and adopting and reinstating all the basic category of the subject matter of contracts, to ensure that different elements of one transaction are treated differently in terms of the standard of

---

[720] *See supra* § 3.02 Classification of Contracts [5] England [b] Classification and Application of Statute.

performance.

It has adopted the basic structure of sales of goods provisions, including express and implied warranties, and blended the basic structure with common law rules regarding service contracts and rules regarding contracts for informational contents.

In this Act, there will be no need to classify the transactions into the sale of goods, the supply of services, and the supply of information. Multiple applications of the different standards ensure that there will be fewer misapplication problems. Section 403 (a) provides the implied warranty that a computer program is merchantable. A sample, model, or demonstration of a final product may create an express warranty.

However, with regard to the implied warranty for fitness for a particular purpose, the courts are still required to determine which standard of performance is to be applicable to each transaction, the result-oriented, the process-oriented or the informational content standard. Furthermore, the suppliers of computer programs can claim, for instance, to be paid for their amount of time or effort; therefore, there is no implied warranty that the information shall be fit for that purpose, though, there is an implied warranty that the information will not fail to achieve the licensee's particular purpose as a result of the licensor's lack of reasonable effort.[721] The reason for this comes from the complexity of obligations in transactions in relation to computer technology. As stated previously, even though the enactment of the U.C.I.T.A. was a big step toward the clarification of the classification issues, the United States' courts are still faced with, in a more restricted manner, making the determinations as to what type of obligation is appropriate in a given transaction.

---

[721] U.C.I.T.A. § 405(a)(2)(2001).

§ 3.03 Express Terms or Warranties

[1] Express Obligations

It has to be noted first that contractual terms between the parties primarily define the parties, the content and extent of their obligations, and the types of remedies available for breach. In the absence of detailed agreements between the parties or where the application of their contractual terms is not appropriate, then the law will supplement the terms of the contract. Contractual liabilities relating to transactions involving computer programs may differ in accordance with the legal classification of a given transaction as sale of goods, supply of services, or licence.

Statements or promises dealt with in this section are part of the contract itself - not those statements that induce but are not part of a contract. I am using warranty in its wide sense of statement or promise about the goods and services supplied, not in its narrow sense as in section 61(1) of the Sale of Goods Act 1979.[722]

Regarding express warranties, there are two fundamental issues. One issue concerns whether and how the express warranties were created, and the other concerns whether liability for breach of them was excluded or limited.

Statements or representations regarding the subject matter may be part of the contract or expressed outside the contract. Such statements or representations may, or may not, be deemed express terms or warranties. The determination as to whether there is an express warranty requires careful analysis of the nature of the representations or statements and the nature of the relationship between the parties. It has been said that the important

---

[722] Sales of Goods Act 1979(c.54), s.61(1). (" '[W]arranty' means an agreement with reference to goods which are the subject of a contract of sale, but collateral to the main purpose of such a contract, the breach of which gives rise to a claim for damages, but not to a right to reject the goods and treat the contract as repudiated.")

factor is whether what the representor said was intended and was understood as a legally binding promise, and whether the other party reasonably assumed that the representor was to be regarded as undertaking liability.[723] However, there is always a problem in distinguishing a statement which gives rise to obligations from a statement which does not give rise to obligations.

The cases described below show how express obligations were created and disclaimed in relation to transactions concerning computer programs and ancillary services. I do not deal with human-readable information as it is rare to guarantee the accuracy of the content of information. Express obligations tend to be upheld when clear and specific representations regarding suitability were made, and such representations were reasonably relied on. The relative knowledge of the parties also seems to be considered in determining whether express obligations arose.

In this section, as I am dealing with many aspects of the contractual clauses in leading cases, I have to revisit those leading cases in order to consider them from different perspectives.

[2] England
[a] *Type of Express Terms and Remedies*
[i] **Result-Oriented Terms and Process-Oriented Terms**

The contents of express terms incorporated in the contracts are largely categorised as result-oriented terms or process-oriented terms. There are representations referring to the result of the work to be done or referring to how the work is done. In transactions concerning computer programs and ancillary services, such representations regarding technical aspects of the subject matter, when relied upon, tend to be considered as express warranties.

---

[723] Pasley v. Freeman (1789) 3 T.R. 51, 57; J. P. BENJAMIN, SALE OF GOODS §§10-001 - 007 (A.G. Guest ed., 5th ed. 1997).

When an obligation arises by process-oriented terms, for example, when each person assigned to the project would exercise skills appropriate to a competent person, defendants may assert that they have carried out their obligations in accordance with the process-oriented terms. However, the breach of such terms may be upheld when an obligation to procure certain results after a reasonable time fails, or a defendant has not acted in any way to fulfil obligations.[724]

[ii] Collateral Contract

Valid consideration needs to have been given in order to claim compensation for the breach of a promise. However, a party may provide consideration by making another contract. A typical case is where three parties are concerned. A buyer buys sand from a distributor, relying on the statement of the original supplier of the sand that the sand is fit for growing chrysanthemums. There can be, between the buyer and the original supplier, a contract collateral to the main contract.[725] In a collateral contract, presentations and promises can be made outside of the main contract between non-contractual parties.

Mackenzie Patten & Co. v. British Olivetti Ltd.,[726] dealt with a collateral contract. In this case, the statements made by a sales representative employed by the defendants to induce the plaintiffs to enter into a leasing contract with a finance company were held to constitute collateral, contractual warranties, not a mere puff. The plaintiffs were a small law firm with one active lawyer and a receptionist. The lawyer contacted a supplier of office computers, intending to keep proper accounts and a proper diary without hiring an accountant. The plaintiffs requested a bookkeeping computer

---

[724] *See supra* § 3.02 Classification of Contracts [5] England [e] Breach of Express Duties.

[725] *See* Wells v. Buckland Sand and Silica Co. [1965] 2 Q.B. 170.

[726] 11 January 1984 (Q.B.) (unreported) LEXIS; 1 C. L. & P. 92 (1984); 48 M.L.R. 344 (1985).

system with a diarising record function. The defendants reassured the plaintiffs that the equipment was the most suitable in the market for the plaintiffs. The plaintiffs were convinced that the machine was suitable for the purpose and could be operated by a person with no particular skill. A "sales contract" was signed by the plaintiffs and the defendant, but the plaintiffs entered into a leasing agreement with Mercantile Credit to finance the purchase.[727] The court found that there was a collateral contract between the plaintiffs and the defendants; this contained the warranty by the defendant that the machine was suitable for the plaintiffs' needs, and the court found that the defendants were in breach of warranty under this contract. The machine was unsuitable for the plaintiffs' needs as known to the defendants, for operation by the plaintiffs' employees; it did not perform all the functions promised, and the defendants were not in a position to provide the necessary training and help for the plaintiffs. The plaintiffs were awarded damages to compensate for the loss arising from the breach of warranty of the collateral contract. This is a typical case promising suitability for the computer systems supplied. The court protected the reliance of the users, incurred prior to the contract.

[iii] Result-Oriented Terms

In *St. Albans City & District Council v. International Computers Ltd.*,[728] the court held that there was an express contractual obligation to supply the plaintiff with software "that would maintain a reliable database of the names entered onto the community charge register accurately count the names and accurately retrieve and display the figures resulting from the count."[729] The plaintiff was clear about the requirements when it invited tenders. In accordance with the express term, the

---

[727] *See infra* § 3.03 Express Terms or Warranties [2] England [b] Exclusion of Express Terms [ii] Disclaimer (discussing the content of the sale contract.).
[728] [1996] 4 All E.R. 481.
[729] *Id.* at 486; *see* [1995] F.S.R. 686, 697.

system had to be reasonably fit for the plaintiff's purpose of maintaining and retrieving a reliable register. The defendant supplied faulty software, which overstated the total figure for the relevant population of the plaintiff's local community. The plaintiff suffered a loss in the community charge that it ought to have collected. The plaintiff recovered compensation for the community charge, which, because of the defendant's breach, it could not collect.[730]

In this case, the supplier seemed to have guaranteed a result-oriented outcome. Such clear statements may have assured the result that the court recognised this as creating an obligation to achieve a specific result, namely, the fitness of the program for the intended purpose. Moreover, the court stated *obiter* that even in the absence of any express term as to quality or fitness for purpose, or any term to the contrary, a contract for the transfer into a computer of a program intended by both parties to instruct or enable the computer to achieve specified functions is subject to an implied term that the program will be reasonably fit for, i.e. reasonably capable of achieving the intended purpose.[731] Therefore, the suppliers are liable to deliver computer systems which function satisfactorily, provided that the purpose of the computer system is well known to them.

[iv] Process-Oriented Terms

In *Salvage Assoc. (SA) v. Cap Financial Services Ltd. (CAP)*,[732] the court found that there was an express term, with respect to the quality of the staff and the quality of the work, to be executed with competency. SA entered into two contracts with the defendant to implement computerisation of its own system of Head Office Accounting. The first contract was for carrying out analysis of SA's requirements and for specifying how those

---

[730] *St. Albans*, [1996] 4 All E.R. at 494.
[731] *Id.* at 498.
[732] [1995] F.S.R. 654.

requirements were to be achieved, for a fixed price of £ 30,000. The second contract was to develop and provide appropriate computer software to meet SA's requirements for computerisation of its Head Office Accounting System (System), for a fixed price of £ 291,654 excluding VAT.[733]

With regard to the first contract, both parties regarded it as satisfactorily completed. For the second contract, part of the payment, £ 261,388, was made by SA while the system was being developed and implemented. The system was developed and delivered, but its implementation was abandoned due to significant functional problems. SA eventually terminated the second contract with immediate effect; SA abandoned the incomplete system.[734]
SA brought these proceedings for breach of the contracts, in which it claimed repayment of the contractual price and damages for wasted expenditure.[735]

The court determined that there was an express term that each person assigned to the project would exercise skills appropriate to a competent person. The breach of such a term would amount to negligence by failing to exercise reasonable care as defined in section 1(1) (a) and under section 2(2) of the Unfair Contract Terms Act 1977. Such a term cannot be excluded unless it satisfies a requirement of reasonableness[736]

There was a significant lack of knowledge, experience and expertise on the part of those assigned to the project by CAP. The contract was breached as CAP had failed to deliver a usable system and there was no prospect of delivering the usable system within a reasonable time.[737] The plaintiff was able to terminate the contracts as the defendant was in repudiatory breach; however, the

---

[733] *Id.* at 657.
[734] *Id.* at 658-59.
[735] *Id.* at 659.
[736] *Id.* at 662; Unfair Contract Terms Act 1977 (c. 50), s. 2(2) and s. 3.
[737] *Salvage*, [1995] F.S.R. at. 680.

court denied a claim in restitution on the basis of total failure of consideration. Such a claim was nearly impossible in cases of a service contract, and the fact that the final product was defective was not enough to render total failure of consideration.[738]

In this case, there was a process-oriented term; the court found that the defendant lacked the knowledge, experience and expertise needed.[739] However, the court seemed also to impose an obligation to procure certain results after a reasonable time.

In *Eurodynamics Sys. plc.* (ED) *v. General Automation Ltd.* (GA),[740] the express provisions of the franchise agreement imposed an obligation on a computer manufacturer (GA) to support the franchisee's (ED's) own COBOL-based operational software. This is another example of a process-oriented term, namely, to provide "support". Under clause 7(iv) of the franchise agreement, there was an obligation to support COBOL software. The computer manufacturer (GA) became less inclined to offer free support, to which ED was entitled, while continuing to support other customers who were regarded as more valuable. GA refused to provide support for ED, and ED accepted GA's repudiation. As this obligation to support was of critical importance, ED was awarded the loss of the profit it would have made. The loss of profit was calculated on the basis that ED would have made seven sales of their applications packages to the existing GA user-base with a profit of about 95 percent, and compensation for the disruption of ED's business.

This case presents the clearest example of breach of an express warranty. As the defendant offered no support, the court did not even have to determine whether the support rendered was adequate or not. The court seemed to have considered that the supplier was unfair in prioritising other clients for providing

---

[738] *Id.* at 682.
[739] *Id.* at 679.
[740] 6 September 1988 (Q.B.) (unreported).

support services. The franchise agreement, if successful, was supposed to procure certain profit and such profit was foreseeable for the defendants.

[b] Exclusion of Express Terms

[i] Statutes

In England, the Unfair Contract Terms Act 1977 plays an essential role in restricting the effect of the disclaimer clauses. Unlike the Uniform Commercial Code in the United States, the Sale of Goods Act 1979 and the Supply of Goods and Services Act 1982 do not deal with the specific language of disclaimers in detail.

In addition, section 6(2) of the Unfair Terms in Consumer Contracts Regulations 1999, which implemented the Council Directive of April 1993 on Unfair Terms in Consumer Contracts[741] provides that:

> In so far as it is in plain intelligible language, the assessment of fairness of a term shall not relate- (a) to the definition of the main subject matter of the contract, or (b) to the adequacy of the price or remuneration, as against the goods or services supplied in exchange.

Section 6(1) provides that the unfairness of a contractual term shall be assessed, in the light of all the circumstances attending the conclusion of the contract. Section 7(2) provides that "If there is doubt about the meaning of a written term, the interpretation which is most favourable to the consumer shall prevail."

The Unfair Contract Terms Act 1977 provides that, as between contracting parties where one of them deals as consumer or on the other's written standard terms of business, the contract term must satisfy the requirement of reasonableness when excluding or restricting any liability in respect of the breach.[742] In the case

---

[741] The Council Directive (EEC) 93/13 on Unfair Terms in Consumer Contracts.
[742] Unfair Contract Terms Act 1977 (c. 50), s. 3.

of other loss or damage, a person cannot exclude liability for negligence without satisfying the requirement of reasonableness.[743] Liability for death or personal injury resulting from negligence cannot be excluded.

[ii] Disclaimer

In this section, I will focus on the defendants' attempts to disclaim express terms by using specific language disclaiming obligations or limiting obligations within the scope of written agreements.

Express terms are hard to disclaim, especially in cases where the obligation arose from a result-oriented term to achieve a specific result, for instance, the fitness of the program for the intended purpose.

It has to be noted that suppliers may resort to the following alternative ways to restrict the remedies available to users, rather than trying literally to disclaim an express obligation itself; there are largely four methods for excluding or limiting the available remedies aimed at: 1) obligations incurred; 2) cure to which the victim is entitled; 3) damage for which compensation is payable; and 4) money payable on breach. These methods will be discussed in § 3.06 Limitation or Exclusion of Remedies.

In *Mackenzie Patten & Co. v. British Olivetti Ltd.*,[744] the contract between the parties excluded all the supplier's liability, except for the negligent causing of death or injury, and contained an integration clause that the agreement was in lieu of and to the exclusion of all other liabilities, obligations, warranties and conditions.

In accordance with the Unfair Contract Terms Act 1977, the defendants may exclude or restrict their liability here only in so

---

[743] Unfair Contract Terms Act 1977 (c. 50), s. 2.
[744] 11 January, 1984 (unreported); 1 C. L. & P. 92 (1984); 48 M.L.R. 344 (1985); *see supra* § 3.03 Express Terms or Warranties [2] England [a] Type of Express Terms and Remedies [ii] Collateral Contract.

far as the contract term relied upon satisfies the requirement of reasonableness. The court found that, in light of the nature of the breach and the circumstances in which it occurred, it was not fair or reasonable to allow the supplier to place reliance on a contract, excluding or limiting liability for a breach of contract.

[iii] Integration Clauses

In England, the traditional rule provided that parol evidence could not be admitted to add to, vary or contradict a deed or other written instrument.[745] However, the modern interpretation has been adopted by the Law Commission, which stated that there is no rule of law precluding the admissibility of evidence solely because a document exists which looks like a whole contract.[746] In England, discussion concerning whether a particular integration clause is valid in disclaiming express or implied obligations or excluding or limiting remedies is scarce, since the substance of such disclaimer or the exclusion or limitation would be likely to be determined in the light of the reasonableness test under Unfair Contract Terms Act 1977 and under the Unfair Terms in Consumer Contracts Regulations 1999.[747]

[3] United States
[a] *Types of Express Warranties and Remedies*
[i] Statutes

U.C.C. section 2-313[748] provides that express warranties may be created by any affirmation of fact or promise, or description concerning goods, which becomes part of the bargain. Therefore, the express warranty does not have to be contained in the written agreement between the parties. Representations

---

[745] *See* Jacobs v. Batavia and General Plantations Trust [1924] 1 Ch. 287, 295.
[746] Law Commission, *Law of Contract: The Parol Evidence Rule* (Law Com. No. 154, 1986).
[747] S.I. 1999, No. 2083.
[748] 1998 Official Text.

concerning essential functions or required specifications often tend to be regarded as express warranties, as such representations are considered the basis of the bargain. A mere-puff is considered not to create an obligation under an express warranty.[749]

An express warranty can be made orally or in writing and such warranty can be in an agreement or in advertising brochures. Suppliers of computers frequently set up showrooms to demonstrate their products and prepare well-presented promotional materials. Representations or promises made in advertising material regarding the specification of the equipment may become an express warranty under certain limited circumstances, i.e. if these specifications are important aspects of the transactions and were relied on by the users. The cases discussed below illustrate the circumstances where the suppliers gave such specific representations and promised a result-oriented outcome.

[ii] Express Warranties and Advertising or Demonstration -Result-Oriented Terms

In *Cricket Alley Corp. v. Data Terminal Systems, Inc.*,[750] the plaintiff Cricket Alley Corporation sued the defendant Data Terminal Systems, Inc. (DTS) for breach of express warranty. The plaintiff purchased computerised cash registers, which were intended to communicate with a Wang computer installed in its general office, to transfer inventory records. The president of the plaintiff company, who was not an expert in this field, visited the DTS showroom and asked whether the DTS's cash register equipment would work with the Wang computers and was answered affirmatively. DTS advertised that its products could communicate with Wang computers; there was a display showing the Wang and DTS cash registers communicating in the showroom. A DTS employee also stated that such communication was a fact. The manual published by DTS reinforced this representation as to

---

[749] U.C.C. §2-313(2) (1998).
[750] 732 P.2d 719 (Kan. 1987).

DTS equipment's capacity.[751]

After the purchase, the DTS equipment developed many problems, including bugs. It was not possible for the DTS equipment to communicate with the Wang computer. The defendant asserted that the DTS cash register could occasionally communicate. The court stated that "undependable communication is, in some ways, worse than no communication at all"[752] and affirmed the District Court's jury award of $78,781.79 in damages for breach of express warranty, which contained the costs attributable to the failure of DTS equipment to perform properly. The plaintiff was awarded consequential damages consisting of increased labour costs attributable to the failure of the DTS cash registers to communicate with the Wang computer.[753]

In this case, the court imposed a result-oriented outcome in terms of communication. The importance of the functions regarding communication and the statement by a DTS employee that such communication was a "fact" probably helped to support the plaintiff's assertion.

Likewise, in *Fargo Machine & Tool Co. v. Kearney & Trecker Corp.*,[754] the court considered that the representations in the seller's catalogue, such as the machine's "absolute repetitive accuracy" and "small-lot production automation by sequential production of up to thirty tools for separate steps without an operator intervening" were of particular importance to Fargo and became express warranties.[755]

Representations in brochures concerning an essential technical aspect of the system would be likely to be relied upon. The plaintiffs should be allowed to rely upon such technical representations.

---

[751] *Id.* at 722.
[752] *Id.* at 723.
[753] *Id.* at 726.
[754] 428 F. Supp. 364 (E.D. Mich. 1977).
[755] *Id.* at 371.

[iii] Express Warranties Concerning Important Functions -Result-Oriented Terms

In *USM Corp. v. Arthur D. Little Systems, Inc.*,[756] the supplier of a "turn-key" system expressly warranted that, at the time of delivery, the system would be free of defects in design and in substantial accordance with the functional specifications. Acceptable response time was one of the important functions specified in the agreement. Response time was described as "directly related to, and primarily determined by, the number of disk accesses that must be accomplished to satisfy the requirements of the command given by the operator."[757] Even though the defendants continually made assurances that the response time would be in an acceptable range, the actual response time was substantially in excess of the acceptable time; therefore, the express warranty was considered breached.[758]

The court took into account the fact that such representations were the "essence of the bargain." The plaintiff was advised by the defendant that the specific problems regarding response time could be solved, and the court allowed the plaintiff to rely upon the defendant's capability of solving the problem.[759]

[b] Exclusion of Express Warranties
[i] Statutes

Once an express warranty is attached, it is hard to disclaim the warranty. U.C.C. section 2-316[760] provides that "Words or conduct relevant to the creation of an express warranty and words or conduct tending to negate or limit warranty shall be construed wherever reasonable as consistent with each other." Since express warranties are considered as incorporating the "essence of the

---

[756] 546 N.E.2d 888 (Mass. App. Ct. 1989).
[757] *Id.* at 890-91.
[758] *Id.* at 891 n.5.
[759] *Id.* at 896.
[760] 1998 Official Text.

bargain", they are hard to disclaim. In some jurisdictions, clauses disclaiming the express warranty are considered contradictory unless there is a clear agreement between the parties to the contrary.[761] A number of cases discussed below show that specific express representations regarding essential functions of the computer systems would not be likely to be disclaimed.

Therefore, as discussed before, more effective ways to restrict the remedies available to the users are mainly the following; restricting the 1) obligations incurred; 2) cure to which the victim is entitled; 3) damage for which compensation is payable; and 4) money payable on breach.[762]

[ii] Inconsistent Disclaimer

In *USM Corp. v. Arthur D. Little Systems, Inc.*[763] discussed above, as the actual response time was substantially in excess of acceptable time, the express warranty was considered breached.[764] Therefore, an "inconsistent" disclaimer clause negating all the express or implied warranties except for the "defects in design" and that the system would be "in substantial accordance with the functional specifications" at the time of delivery was found inoperative, in terms of express warranties.[765]

Likewise, under New York law, the highly particularised language of express warranty prevails over a general disclaimer of warranty liability.[766] This is illustrated in *Consolidated Data Terminals v. Applied Digital Data Systems, Inc.*,[767] Applied Digital

---

[761] *See* Teknekron Customer Info. Solutions, Inc. v. Watkins Motor Lines, 1994 WL 11726 (N.D. Cal. 1994).

[762] *See infra* § 3.06 Limitation or Exclusion of Remedies.

[763] 546 N.E.2d 888 (Mass. App. Ct. 1989); *see supra* § 3.03 Express Terms or Warranties [3] United States [a] Types of Express Warranties and Remedies[iii] Express Warranties Concerning Important Functions -Result-Oriented Terms.

[764] *USM Corp.*, 546 N.E.2d at 895.

[765] *Id.*

[766] *See* N.Y. U.C.C. § 2-316(1) (2001).

[767] 708 F.2d 385 (9th Cir. 1983).

Data Systems (ADDS), a manufacturer of computer equipment, and Consolidated Data Terminals (CDT), a distributor, entered into a written distributorship agreement. Under the agreement, CDT became a non-exclusive sales outlet for ADDS terminals.

ADDS manufactured computer equipment, including cathode-ray computer terminals and stated in the promotional literature that specified terminals, would operate at the high speed of 19.200 baud and were "inherently reliable."[768] In fact, these terminals were not capable of attaining such a speed and were full of design errors. CDT received complaints and returns from their customers.

The court held that the statements regarding the specifications constituted an express warranty because CDT relied on the specifications when ordering the terminals.[769] The warranty disclaimer clause, which stated that "there is no warranty express or implied other than a ninety-day guarantee covering materials and workmanship", was found invalid. The court stated that such a disclaimer did not override the highly particularised warranty created by the specifications as, under New York law, specific warranty language prevails over a general disclaimer of warranty liability.[770]

[iii] Integration Clauses
[A] Examination of all the Documents

An integration clause is a useful tool for limiting the scope of agreements to the statements or promises made in a particular writing, capable of invalidating representations or warranties made outside the writings. However, despite the existence of integration clauses, the court may always find that the writing was not intended as a complete and exclusive statement of the terms of the agreement. A writing may be explained or supplemented by course of dealing or usage of trade, by course of performance, and

---

[768] *Id.* at 388.
[769] *Id.* at 391.
[770] *Id.*

Civil Liability for Defects in Information in Electronic Form

by evidence of consistent additional terms, unless the court finds the writing to have been also intended as a complete and exclusive statement of the terms of the agreement.[771]

In determining whether a writing was intended by the parties as a final expression of their agreement, courts consider various factors relating to the transaction, which will be discussed below.

In *Sierra Diesel Injection Service, Inc. v. Burroughs Corp.*,[772] in deciding on the effect of the merger clause, the court considered the intent and the sophistication of the parties, the type of the contract, other writings involved, other representations made, and the evidence of the defendant's conduct to live up to the representations made.[773]

Sierra Diesel Injection Services, Inc. (Sierra) purchased from Burroughs Corporation (Burroughs) a B-80 computer, consisting of hardware and software to speed up Sierra's invoicing and accounting. Prior to purchase, Burroughs' sales staff sent a letter to Sierra to the effect that the machine could put the inventory, receivables, and invoicing under complete control. Sierra and Burroughs entered into contracts for a sale of hardware and software as well as for maintenance services. The B-80 computer did not perform as expected. To remedy the problem, Sierra

---

[771] U.C.C. § 2-202(1998)("Terms with respect to which the confirmatory memoranda of the parties agree or which are otherwise set forth in a writing intended by the parties as a final expression of their agreement with respect to such terms as are included therein may not be contradicted by evidence of any prior agreement or of a contemporaneous oral agreement but may be explained or supplemented
(a) by course of dealing or usage of trade (Section 1-205) or by course of performance (Section 2-208); and
(b) by evidence of consistent additional terms unless the court finds the writing to have been intended also as a complete exclusive statement of the terms of the agreement.").
[772] Sierra Diesel Injection Serv., Inc., v. Burroughs Corp., 874 F. 2d 653 (9th Cir. 1989), *amended by* 890 F. 2d 108 (9th Cir. 1989).
[773] *Id.* at 656-57.

purchased another computer, a B-91, by recommendation of the seller, which also failed to perform. Sierra consulted an independent computer consultant who concluded that these computers would never achieve the functions for which they had been purchased.

There was a gap in knowledge between the parties, and the contract was a pre-printed form drawn up by a sophisticated seller and presented to the buyer without any real negotiations. The owner of Sierra, Mr. Cathey, was an unsophisticated businessman, without any knowledge of computers or contract terms, whereas Burroughs was knowledgeable and knew the purpose of the purchase. Furthermore, there were several writings; a contract for the sale of the hardware, a contract for the sale of the software, a contract for a lease to finance the transaction, and a contract for service and maintenance. However, the transaction was on its face a lease, and a contract for service and maintenance. No one writing was independent. It was not possible to understand the basic structure of the agreement without reference to all the writings. Therefore, it was justified for Mr. Cathey to look beyond the contract to determine its contents.[774] There was evidence that the defendant intended to live up to the representations made in the letter, which were not part of the contract, and knew Mr. Cathey's expectations as to the scope and terms of their agreement. The warranty disclaimer clauses in the form contracts were not effective to waive the express warranties stated in the letter assuring the quality of the B-80 computer.[775]

Likewise, in *L. H. Heath & Son v. AT & T Information Systems*,[776] the Master Agreement, the allegedly integrated writing, was found not to reveal the basic transaction without reference to the other documents. However, in this case, there was no indication that the plaintiff lacked sophistication in business transactions.

---

[774] *Id.* at 657.
[775] *Id.*
[776] 9 F.3d 561 (7th Cir. 1993).

L.H. Heath & Son (Heath), a manufacturer of chocolate products, sought to upgrade and enhance its computer and telecommunications capabilities and decided to adopt AT & T Information Systems' (AT & T's) Recommendation and Proposal, which expressly indicated that the parties intended that AT&T provide a fully integrated, custom-tailored information, meeting all of Heath's stated objectives. The parties signed the Master Agreement, which, while it contained a merger clause, did not identify any prices, products, services, software applications or configurations. In addition, Heath signed the Computer Systems Amendments for the supplemental equipment purchased subsequently.

The Court of Appeals found that the Master Agreement and the Computer System Amendments did not reflect the complete and exclusive agreement between the parties.[777] The warranty disclaimer contained in the Master Agreement its amendments were found inconsistent with the express warranty, and was thus inoperative. The Master Agreement and its amendments, the allegedly integrated writing, did not reveal the basic transaction without reference to the other documents.[778] Therefore, transactions involving many documents, instead of a single document describing the whole transaction could be interpreted as a whole.[779]

In the two cases discussed above, the courts examined all the documents with respect to any transactions that might be contradictory to the integration clauses. The *Sierra* court also emphasised the gap in expertise between the parties.

[B] Application of Parol Evidence Rule

The application of the parol evidence rule may exclude the evidence of any prior agreement or contemporaneous oral agreement. *Jaskey Finance & Leasing* (Jaskey) *v. Display Data*

---

[777] *Id.* at 569.
[778] *Id.* at 570.
[779] *Id.*

Corp. (Display Data),[780] held that a disclaimer clause along with an integration clause were sufficient to preclude either express or implied warranties of fitness.[781] Jaskey purchased a 32 K computer from Display Data. There were two contracts between the parties. One was for the sale of equipment, programming and installation services, and the other for maintenance of the computer system. The first contract provided, apart from the names of the parties and the price of the goods, that: 1) the seller warrants that it will provide maintenance service in accordance with a separate maintenance contract; 2) the seller will make reasonable efforts to remedy any errors for a period of one year after the delivery; 3) the seller excludes any other express or implied warranties not provided in the contract; 4) the seller excludes from the buyer's remedies loss of profits or other economic loss including special and consequential damages arising out of the breach; and, 5) the contract contains the entire agreement between the parties. The latter contract also provided that the seller excludes any other express or implied warranties not provided in the contract.[782]

The plaintiff alleged that Display Data expressly warranted that the computer and programs constituted a "turn-key" system, which required the plaintiff to perform only routine maintenance and was particularly suitable for the business, even though the contract did not contain any of those alleged representations. The plaintiffs also received the advertising materials, which contained such representations. However, the court stated that Maryland's parol evidence rule excluded the evidence of any prior agreement or contemporaneous oral agreement when the parties intended the written contract to be a final expression of their agreement.[783] The contract could not be supplemented when the parties intended

---

[780] 564 F. Supp. 160 (E.D.Pa. 1983).
[781] *Id.* at 163.
[782] *Id.* at 162.
[783] *Id.* at 164.

the contract to be the complete and exclusive statement of their agreement.[784] The court determined that the language disclaiming the express warranties and the implied warranties of fitness for a particular purpose was conspicuous and sufficient to disclaim those warranties.[785] The court referred to the bargaining power of both parties and stated that there was no suggestion that the plaintiffs were unaware of the significance of the disclaimer and integration clauses. Therefore, the plaintiffs could not base warranty claims on language not present in the contract.[786]

Several factors may have been important in the determination of the *Jaskey* court: 1) bargaining power of the parties; 2) disclaimer clauses for exclusion of warranties; 3) integration clause; and, 4) drafting techniques to separate the issues of maintenance and repair from the main agreement. However, in transactions involving high technology, particularly, "turn-key" systems, customers without specific knowledge of the technology tend to rely on the representations in advertising materials. The U.C.I.T.A. takes a sensible approach in providing that advertising materials, which become part of the basis of the bargain, create express warranties.[787] "[T]he disclaimer or modification is inoperative to the extent that this construction is unreasonable," though such disclaimer or modification is subject to sections with regard to parole or extrinsic evidence.[788]

However, if advertising is highly specific, then the court may be justified in disregarding the disclaimer as in *Consolidated Data Terminals v. Applied Digital Data Systems, Inc.*[789] The promotional materials relating to the supply of computer technology tend to be

---

[784] *Id.*
[785] *Id.*
[786] *Id.*
[787] U.C.I.T.A. § 402 (2001).
[788] *Id.* § 406.
[789] 708 F.2d 385 (9th Cir. 1983).

more specific than in the cases of products such as cosmetic creams. Therefore, such materials and the disparities between suppliers and customers may create reasonable reliance for achieving of a specific, intended purpose. Furthermore, if there was a supply of a "turn-key" computer, as in *Jaskey Finance & Leasing v. Display Data Corp.*,[790] such circumstances could have been considered more favourable for the users in terms of the respective knowledge of the supplier and the user, and the reliance by the user.

[4] The U.C.I.T.A.

The U.C.I.T.A. has adopted the basic structure of the sales of goods' provisions with some amendments. Section 402 provides that an express warranty is created by a licensor by

> An affirmation of fact or promise made by the licensor to its licensee, including by advertising, which relates to the information and becomes part of the basis of the bargain creates an express warranty that the information to be furnished under the agreement will conform to the affirmation or promise.[791]

Any description of the information that is made part of the bargain may also create "an express warranty that the information will conform to the description."[792] A sample, model, or demonstration of a final product which is made part of the basis of the bargain may also create

> [A]n express warranty that the performance of the information will reasonably conform to the performance of the sample, model, or demonstration, taking into

---

[790] 564 F. Supp. 160 (E.D.Pa. 1983).
[791] U.C.I.T.A. § 402(a)(1) (2001).
[792] *Id.* § 402(a)(2).

account differences that would appear to a reasonable person in the position of the licensee between the sample, model, or demonstration and the information as it will be used.[793]

Express warranty based on advertising was first introduced in the 15 April 1998 draft,[794] and the scope of express warranty law in Article 2 has been expanded by this provision.[795] A warranty arises only if the advertising statement becomes part of the bargain. Although the comments state that a warranty does not arise from "mere puffing", the comments recognise the fact that the closer the statement is related to describing the technical specifications, the more likely it is to be an express warranty when made part of the bargain.[796] Section 402 (a)(3) provides that express warranties may be created by demonstrations and models; however, the comments are careful to limit the scope of application in stating that "in mercantile experience, the mere exhibition of a "sample", a "model" or a "demonstration" does not of itself show whether it is intended to "suggest" or to "be" the character of the subject-matter of the contract." The comments also state that "what is being demonstrated on a small scale or tested on a beta model is not necessarily representative of actual performance or of the eventual product."[797]

---

[793] *Id.* § 402(a)(3).

[794] *See* § 2B-403 [Alternative A](1998 March Draft)(One of the alternative sections of the March 1998 draft treated the physical medium and the computer program separately. It provided that the the physical medium is to be merchantable and the computer program is to perform in substantial conformance with any promise or affirmations of fact contained in the documentation provided by the licensor.)

[795] U.C.I.T.A. § 402 cmt. 3.

[796] *Id.* § 402 cmts. 3- 4.

[797] *Id.* § 402 cmt. 5; *see also* NMP Corp. v. Parametric Tech. Corp., 958 F.Supp. 1536 (S.D. Okla. 1997).

Cases concerning demonstrations such as *Fargo Machine & Tool Co. v. Kearney & & Trecker Corp.*[798] or *Cricket Alley Corp. v. Data Terminal Systems, Inc.*[799] support the principle of this provision regarding the creation of express warranties. Representations concerning specific, or essential functions tend to be relied on by the customers. However, as the suppliers may always claim that circumstances of demonstration are different from the actual circumstances, the actual performance should not deviate greatly from such demonstration, disparate from the basic description.

Furthermore, section 406(a) provides that:

> Words or conduct relevant to the creation of an express warranty and words or conduct tending to disclaim or modify an express warranty must be construed wherever reasonable as consistent with each other. Subject to Section 301 with regard to parol or extrinsic evidence, the disclaimer or modification is inoperative to the extent that such construction is unreasonable.

Therefore, express warranties can be disclaimed as long as consistent with words or conduct relevant to the creation of an express warranty. Furthermore, evidence of any previous agreement or of a contemporaneous oral agreement which contradicts the terms of a record intended as a final expression of the agreement may not be introduced in accordance with section 301.

[5] Comparison

In both jurisdictions, result-oriented promises for suitability or performance tend to be considered to create express obligations.

English courts consider that computer programmers, like

---

[798] 428 F. Supp. 364 (E.D. Mich. 1977).
[799] 732 P.2d 719 (Kan. 1987).

dentists, are expected to exercise expertise and special skills to achieve specified functions, even without express terms. The Unfair Contract Terms Act 1977 plays an essential role in restricting the effect of disclaimer clauses. The reasonableness test allows the courts to examine all relevant circumstances including the adoption of standardised contracts, allocation of risks of the transactions, reasonableness of the upper limit of the damages or availability of insurance.

In the United States, representations or promises made within or outside of the contract regarding specifications or functions of the equipment may become an express warranty, especially if these specifications are important aspects of the transactions and were relied on by the users. Warranties in highly particularised language may be hard to disclaim. This was confirmed in the U.C.I.T.A., which provides that advertising and demonstrations can become express warranties. However, it has to be noted that a number of courts hold that a disclaimer clause along with an integration clause may be sufficient to preclude express warranties. Furthermore, the parol evidence rule may exclude the evidence of any prior agreement or contemporaneous oral agreement when the parties intended the written contract to be a final expression of their agreement.

§ 3.04 Implied Terms or Warranties

[1] England
[a] Statutory Control Over Implied Terms
Statutory control over implied terms is discussed in § 3.02 Classification of Contracts [d] Implied Obligation.
[b] Implied Terms: Contract for the Supply of Services
Section 13 of the Supply of Goods and Services Act 1982 provides that "In a contract for the supply of a service, where the supplier is acting in the course of a business, there is an implied term that the supplier will carry out the service with reasonable

care and skill." In *Salvage Assoc. v. Cap Financial Services Ltd.,*[800] the court found that there was an implied term pursuant to section 13 of the Supply of Goods and Services Act 1982 in accordance with the terms of the first and the second contracts.[801]

[c] Implied Terms: From Merchantable Quality to Satisfactory Quality

In *Eurodynamics Sys. plc.*(ED) *v. General Automation Ltd.,*[802] the court found that the implied terms of merchantability and fitness for purposes had been established. However, it was acceptable to supply computer programmes that contain errors and bugs, as the suppliers correct errors and bugs in accordance with their support obligation. The court examined several bugs, such as incompatible print instructions and incompatible VDT. Some of the malfunctions could be corrected easily while others remained uncorrected. The court admitted that it was perfectly true, as ED argued, that even errors which were capable of easy solution constituted blemishes in the system until corrected. Nevertheless, the court determined that ED had not established a breach of implied warranties of fitness for purpose or merchantability.

This result might now be different as a result of amendments made to the Sale of Goods Act 1979 and the Supply of Goods and Services Act 1982. Section 14(2) of the Sale of Goods Act 1979, as amended in 1994, and section 4(2) of the Supply of Goods and Services Act 1982, as amended in 1994 now require that the goods be of satisfactory quality.

Prior to such amendments that took place in 1994, the Law

---

[800] [1995] F.S.R.654; *see supra* § 3.03 Express Terms or Warranties [2] England [a] Type of Express Terms and Remedies [iv] Process-Oriented Terms.
[801] *Salvage,* [1995] F. S. R. at 667.
[802] 6 September 1988 (Q.B.) (unreported); *see supra* § 3.03 Express Terms or Warranties [2] England [a] Type of Express Terms and Remedies [iv] Process-Oriented Terms.
[803] Law Commission, *Sale and Supply of Goods* (Law Com. No.160, 1987).

Commission[803] made recommendations on the implied term as to quality. It was argued that the word "merchantable" was not suitable for consumer transactions, did not cover minor defects and defects of appearance, and did not expressly say that goods must be reasonably durable. The recommendation stated that the basic principle would simply provide that the goods supplied under the contract must be of good quality or sound quality. Therefore, the court would be likely to consider the goods unsatisfactory if the system did not work, even though computer suppliers would be likely to be given a reasonable time to cure the bugs or defects.[804]

Section 14 (2A) of the Sale of Goods Act 1979 as amended in 1994 provides that goods are of satisfactory quality if they meet the standard that a reasonable person would regard as satisfactory, taking account of any description of the goods, the price if relevant, and all other relevant circumstances. Section 14(2B) provides the following considerations in determining the quality of goods: fitness for all the purposes for which goods of the kind in question are commonly supplied; appearance and finish; freedom from minor defects; safety; and, durability.

Whether rejection of the goods is possible may depend on the status of buyers. Sections 15(A) and 30(2A) of the Sale of Goods Act 1979, as amended in 1994, provide that where a buyer takes goods in the course of business and would otherwise have the right to reject the goods for breach of the implied terms as to description, satisfactory quality or fitness for purpose, she or he is now deprived of that right to reject the goods for breach "so slight that it would be unreasonable for her or him to reject them."

[d] *Implied Terms: Fitness for Intended Purpose*

In *Saphena Computing Ltd. v. Allied Collection Agencies Ltd.*,[805] the supplier of the computer system sued the purchasers

---

[804] *Id.* at 3.
[805] [1995] F.S.R. 616; *see supra* § 3.02 Classification of Contracts [5] England [b] Classification and Application of Statute.

for the price of the software and the purchasers counterclaimed for, amongst other things, the party's failure to supply software reasonably fit for the purposes for which it was required. There were two contracts between the parties; both had already been terminated by mutual assent, even though there were some faults to be corrected.[806]

The recorder held that there was an implied term as to the fitness for such purposes as had been notified to the suppliers. However, as software is not necessarily a commodity which is handed over or delivered once and for all at one time, it would not necessarily be a breach of contract to deliver software in the first instance with a defect in it. The court found that the reasonable time allowed for the suppliers to correct and modify the program to fit it for its intended purpose had not expired.[807]

In this case, the court emphasised that the suppliers of software should be given reasonable time, after the time of the delivery, to fulfil their obligations to complete their performance.

[e] Exclusion of Implied Terms

[i] Statutes

The implied term as to the seller's undertaking as to title cannot be excluded or limited.[808] There are separate rules regarding the exclusion of implied terms depending on whether or not the transaction is for consumer sale.

For consumer transactions for the sale of goods, the implied undertakings as to conformity of goods with description or sample or as to their quality of fitness for a purpose cannot be excluded.[809]

If the transaction is not with a consumer, the exclusion of such implied terms is subject to the reasonableness test.[810] Section

---

[806] *Saphena*, [1995] F.S.R. at 650.
[807] *Id.* at 652-53.
[808] The Unfair Contract Terms Act 1977 (c. 50), s. 6(1).
[809] *Id.* s. 6(2).
[810] *Id.* s. 2.

55(1) of the Sale of Goods Act 1979 provides that subject to the Unfair Contract Terms Act 1977, an implied obligation can be negatived or varied by express agreement. Section 55(2) provides that an express term does not negative an implied term unless inconsistent with it. Similarly, section 16(1) of the Supply of Goods and Services Act 1982 provides that where a duty or liability would arise under a contract for supply of a service, it may be negatived or varied by express agreement. Section 16(2) provides that any express term does not negative a implied term unless inconsistent with it.

For transactions involving the supply of services, exclusion of implied terms as to reasonable care and skill[811] is subject to the test of reasonableness.[812]

With respect to the reasonableness test, the Unfair Contract Terms Act 1977 section 11 provides that contract terms must be fair and reasonable at the time the contract was made. Schedule 2 provides "Guidelines for Application of Reasonableness Test." The factors relevant to the determination are as follows; the strength of the bargaining position of the parties; whether the customer received an inducement to agree the term; availability of entering into other similar contracts; customer's knowledge of the term; exclusion or restriction of relevant liability if some condition is not compiled with; and, whether goods were specially ordered.

[ii] Inconsistent Terms

In the *Salvage* case, the implied warranties to exercise reasonable skill and care were found not to have been disclaimed. The contract successfully disclaimed implied terms as to merchantability or fitness for purpose, but not the implied term as to reasonable care and skill. Furthermore, such a term was not inconsistent with the express terms in the contract to carry out the service with reasonable care and skill, as provided by section 16(2)

---

[811] Supply of Goods and Services Act 1982 (c. 29), s. 13.
[812] Unfair Contract Terms Act 1997, ss. 2 and 3.

of the Supply of Goods and Services Act 1982. Therefore, there was no need to determine whether the disclaimer was reasonable or not. Ordinarily, the exclusion of such a term as to take reasonable care or exercise reasonable skill must satisfy the requirement of reasonableness under sections 1(1)(a) and 2(2) of the Unfair Contract Terms Act 1977.

[f] Contract to Transfer Information

For contracts for information, see discussion above in § 3.02 Classification of Contracts [1] Classification of Contracts [d] Contracts for Information.

[2] United States

[a] Implied Warranties of Merchantability

U.C.C. § 2-314[813] provides for an implied warranty of merchantability in cases where the seller is a merchant with respect to goods of that kind. The standards for determining merchantability, amongst other things, are as follows: (1) pass without objection in the trade under the contractual description; (2) are fit for the ordinary purposes for which such goods are used; (3) run, within the variations permitted by the agreement, of even kind, quality and quantity within each unit and among all units involved; (4) are adequately contained, packaged, and labelled as the agreement may require; and, (5) conform to the promises or affirmations of fact, made on the container or label if any.

In *Neilson Business Equipment Center, Inc. v. Monteleone*[814] the court determined that there was an implied warranty that the computer system be "merchantable." The computer system should have been capable of passing without objection in the trade under the contractual description, and be fit for the ordinary

---

[813] Official Text 1998.
[814] 524 A.2d 1172 (Del. 1987); *see supra* § 3.02 Classification of Contracts [6] United States [b] Predominant Test, Contract for the Sale of Goods [i] Turn-Key Computer System.

purpose for which it was intended. The court found that such criteria were not satisfied as the computer system did not meet Monteleone's expressed record and bookkeeping needs, contrary to the representation made by Neilson's sales representatives. The plaintiff established all the elements for proving a breach of warranty of merchantability.

[b] Implied Warranty of Fitness for Particular Purpose

U.C.C. section 2-315 provides that the implied warranty for fitness for particular purpose can be attached if, 1) the seller at the time of contracting has reason to know any particular purpose for which the goods are required and, 2) the buyer is relying on the seller's skill or judgement to select or furnish suitable goods.

In transactions involving computer technology, this type of warranty may be attached for customised computer systems or software. In the *Neilson* case, the court found that there was an implied warranty of merchantability and an implied warranty of fitness for a particular purpose.[815] Neilson knew that Monteleone needed a computer system to meet specific information processing needs; he was responsible for selecting the proper equipment and also agreed to customise the software so that the computer system would be compatible with Monteleone's manual record. The court stated that "[t]here could hardly be a clearer case where a buyer relied on the professional expertise of the seller than that presented here."[816]

In the *Neilson* case, as in *St. Albans City & District Council v. International Computers Ltd.*[817] and *Saphena Computing Council v. International Computers Ltd.,*[818] the professional skill of the computer suppliers was relied upon and such circumstances helped

---

[815] *Neilson*, 524 A.2d at 1175.
[816] *Id.* at 1176.
[817] [1996] 4 All E.R. 481.
[818] [1995] F.S.R. 616.

to support the user's claims regarding implied obligations for fitness for intended purpose.

[c] Exclusion of Implied Warranties
[i] Statutes

U.C.C. §2-316 provides that, to exclude or modify the implied warranty of merchantability, the language must mention merchantability and, in case of a writing, the language must be conspicuous. To exclude or modify any implied warranty of fitness, the exclusion must be conspicuous and in writing. It is sufficient, in excluding all implied warranties of fitness, to state, for example, "There are no warranties which extend beyond the description on the face hereof." It must be noted that, as stated above in relation to express warranty, the court may examine, in addition, the validity of integration clauses or unconscionability in determining whether implied warranties can be disclaimed in particular circumstances.[819]

[ii] Sufficient Language in Disclaiming Implied Warranty

In *Jaskey Finance and Leasing v. Display Data Corp.*,[820] discussed above, the court found, in accordance with Maryland law, that the language to exclude all implied warranties of fitness is sufficient if it states "There are no warranties which extend beyond the description on the face hereof."[821] The disclaimer of the implied warranty of fitness also has to be conspicuous. A clause has to be conspicuous enough for a reasonable person to notice,

---

[819] *See supra* § 3.03 Express Terms or Warranties [3] United States [b] Exclusion of Express Warranties [iii] Integration Clauses.

[820] 564 F. Supp. 160 (E.D. P.A. 1983); *see supra* § 3.03 Express Terms or Warranties [3] United States [b] Exclusion of Express Warranties [iii] Integration Clauses [B] Application of Parol Evidence Rule.

[821] MD. CODE ANN., [Com.Law] § 2-316(2).

and in a larger or contrasting typeface or colour.[822] The disclaimers were found to be conspicuous as they were printed in larger and in contrasting type. The fact that the disclaimer was written on the reverse side of the contract did not weaken the effect of the disclaimer.[823] The language to disclaim the express warranties and the implied warranty of fitness were considered sufficient, even though the disclaimer for the implied warranty did not specifically mention the implied warranty of fitness.[824]

The court referred to the bargaining power of both parties and stated that there was no suggestion that the plaintiffs were unaware of the significance of the disclaimer and integration clauses.[825] The clause that stated that the seller would make reasonable efforts to remedy any errors for a period of one year after the delivery would also count in favour of the supplier. On the other hand, the language disclaiming implied merchantability was not sufficient, though conspicuous, because it failed to mention the word "merchantability".[826]

Likewise, in *AMF, Inc. v. Computer Automation, Inc.*,[827] the court referred to the bargaining positions of the parties. The court stated that both parties were commercially sophisticated businesses, thus "it strains credulity to hold that a business like AMF was not, or should not have been, aware of the language disclaiming implied warranties."[828]

In the United States, so long as the statutory requir-ements in terms of language are fulfilled, courts would be likely to

---

[822] *Id.* § 1-201(10).
[823] *Jaskey*, 564 F. Supp. at 164-65.
[824] *Id.* at 163, 165.
[825] *Id.* at 164.
[826] MD. CODE ANN., [Com. Law] § 2-316(2).
[827] 573 F. Supp. 924 (S.D. Ohio 1983).
[828] *Id.* at 930.

validate the disclaimer clauses, especially in cases where the parties with equal bargaining power enter into an agreement with full knowledge of the transactions.

[iii] Conspicuousness of the Warranty Exclusion

In *Sierra Diesel Injection Service, Inc., v. Burroughs Corp.,*[829] in determining whether a disclaimer was conspicuous, the court considered not only the format of the clauses, including the type size, but also whether a reasonable person in the buyer's position would not have been surprised to find the warranty disclaimer in the contract. As the plaintiff did not notice the warranty disclaimer clauses on the back and lacked sophistication, it would have required more than a collection of standardised form contracts to notify a reasonable person in the plaintiff's position to notice that there was no warranty of merchantability.[830]

In *Eaton Corp. v. Magnavox Co.* (Magnavox),[831] the court held that Magnavox's attempt to disclaim implied warranties failed because the language did not mention "merchantability" and was not conspicuous.[832] The contract clause merely stated there was a warranty against defects in workmanship and material for a limited time and that there was no responsibility for consequential damages.

The adequacy of the format in disclaimers including the type size, difference in bargaining positions, the disparities in expertise of the parties and the availability of alternative remedies would be likely to be important factors in explaining the diversity of the holdings regarding the validity of the disclaimer clause for implied

---

[829] 874 F. 2d 653 (9th Cir. 1989), *amended by* 890 F. 2d 108 (9th Cir. 1989)., *see supra* § 3.03 Express Terms or Warranties [3] United States [b] Exclusion of Express Warranties [iii] Integration Clause.

[830] *See Sierra Diesel,* at 659.

[831] 581 F. Supp 1514 (E.D. Mich.1984).

[832] *Id.* at 1533.

warranties. The expertise here includes an understanding of the legal terms as well as the understanding of the specific technology involved in the transaction.

[iv] Integration Clauses, Unconscionability

The validity of disclaimers may be affected by the presence of integration clauses. As discussed above,[833] an integration clause is a useful tool for limiting the scope of agreements to the statements or promises made in a particular writing; however, the court may always find that the writing was not intended as a complete and exclusive statement.

The courts may refuse to enforce contracts or contractual clauses deemed "unconscionable" to prevent oppression and unfair surprise. This topic is discussed in § 3.07 Construction and Statutory Controls on Contractual Terms [3] Reasonableness Test and Unconscionability [b] Unconscionability.

[d] Contract for Information

For contracts for information, see discussion above in § 3.02 Classification of Contracts [1] Classification of Contracts [d] Contracts for Information.

[3] The U.C.I.T.A.

[a] Implied Warranties

Section 403 of the U.C.I.T.A. provides that:

(a) Unless the warranty is disclaimed or modified, a licensor that is a merchant with respect to computer programs of the kind warrants:
(1) to the end user that the computer program is fit for the ordinary purposes for which such computer programs are used;..

---

[833] *See supra* § 3.03 Express Terms or Warranties [3] United States [iii] Integration Clauses.

This section is applicable if the program itself is the subject matter of the agreement. As stated above, comment 2 to section 403 states that this merchantability warranty and the warranty in section 404(a) for the accuracy of data may both apply to the same transaction. Section 403 applies to the program and its functions, and the other applies to the accuracy of data.

Comment 3a to section 403 of the U.C.I.T.A., states that:

> To be fit for ordinary purposes does not require that the program be the best or most fit for that use or that it be fit for all possible uses. To an extent greater than for goods, computer programs are often adapted and employed in unlimited or inventive ways or ways that go well beyond the uses for which they were distributed.

Comment 3a also states that, "[m]erchantability does not require a perfect program, but that the subject matter be generally within the average standards applicable in commerce for programs having the particular type of use." As it is virtually impossible to produce software of complexity that contains no errors and presence of "bugs" is commonly expected, the important issue is "whether, the program still comes within the middle belt of quality in the applicable trade or industry, i.e., whether it is reasonably fit for the ordinary purposes for which such programs are used in accordance with average levels of quality and reasonable standards of program capability."

For some cases where the suppliers are merely providing services to provide informational content, section 404(a) would be applicable. This section provides that:

> Unless the warranty is disclaimed or modified, a merchant that, in a special relationship of reliance with a licensee, collects, compiles, processes, provides, or transmits informational content warrants to that licensee that there is no inaccuracy in the informational content caused by

the merchant's failure to perform with reasonable care.

This warranty does not arise with respect to published informational content or to a person who acts as a conduit or provides no more than editorial services in collecting, compiling, distributing, processing, providing, or transmitting informational content that under the circumstances can be identified as that of a third person.

The U.C.I.T.A. adopted in part the tortious standard in determining the existence of the special relationship by citing Restatement (Second) of Torts section 552 (1976), which imposes liability upon information suppliers who supply false information for the guidance of others who justifiably rely on the information.[834] However, this standard is somewhat unclear as applied to cases. The courts may find "guidance" and a justifiable reliance; however, the bargaining principle[835] or liability in an indeterminate amount for an indeterminate time to an indeterminate class[836] may prevent the imposition of liability.

Comment 3a to section 404 states that:

---

[834] *See supra* note 239.

[835] *See* A.T. Kearney, Inc., v. IBM Corp., 73 F.3d 238 (9th Cir. 1995); AccuSystems, Inc. v. Honeywell info. Sys., Inc., 580 F.Supp. 474 (S.D.N.Y. 1984); J.R. Wolfson, *Electronic Mass Information Providers and Section 552 of The Restatement (Second) of Torts, The First Amendment Casts A Long Shadow,* 29 RUTGERS L.J. 67, 69-70 (1997)("If one were to assume that Section 552 is an accurate restatement of the law of negligent misrepresentation as applied to mass information providers, one would likely conclude that mass information providers such as Dun & Bradstreet, or Dow Jones would constantly be liable for the tort of negligent misrepresentation. In fact, Section 552 is not an accurate statement of the law of negligent misrepresentation for mass information providers, and mass distributors of information have almost never been held liable for inaccurate information, even where such information was justifiably and foreseeably relied upon in economic transactions. Most often, the courts simply refuse to impose liability under Section 552.").

[836] *See* Ultramares Corp. v. Touche, 174 N.E. 441, 444 (N.Y. 1931).

The special element of reliance comes from the relationship itself, a relationship characterized by the provider's knowledge that the particular licensee plans to rely on the data in its own business and expects that the provider will tailor the information to its needs. The obligation arises only with respect to persons who possess unique or specialized expertise and who are in a special position of confidence and trust with the licensee such that reliance on the inaccurate information is justified and the party has a duty to act with care.
The relationship also requires that the provider make the information available as part of its own business of providing such information. The licensor must be in the business of providing that type of information. This adopts the rationale of cases holding that information provided as part of a differently focused commercial relationship, such as the sale or lease of goods, does not create protected expectations about accuracy except as might be created under express warranty law...A fundamental aspect of a special reliance relationship is that the information provider is specifically aware of, and personally tailors information to the needs of the licensee.

Section 404 may effectively relieve the liability of the suppliers who are considered sellers, and those who are in a "special relationship" with the clients for providing inaccurate informational content; as long as the suppliers can prove that there was no failure to exercise reasonable care in their performance. This provision may make it easier for a highly specialised and costly database provider to assert that there was no failure to exercise reasonable care, thus escaping liability for providing inaccurate information.

Comment 3b to section 404 states that information distributed to the public is not within the scope of this provision for the fear that creating greater liability risk in contract would place an undue burden on the free flow of information, as discussed above[837] in *Daniel v. Dow Jones & Co., Inc.*[838] Therefore, there is no implied warranty for published informational content on an Internet web site that lists information about local restaurants or services that provide data about current stock or monetary exchange prices, distributed in general or by subscription services.[839] Published informational content is, by definition, made available to the public as a whole or to a range of subscribers on a standardised, not a personally tailored basis.[840]

This warranty relating to the duty to exercise reasonable care for the accuracy of the content under 404(a) can be disclaimed, and is not subject to the preclusion in section 113 (a)(1), which provides:

> Obligations of good faith, diligence, reasonableness, and care imposed by this [Act] may not be disclaimed by agreement, but the parties by agreement may determine the standards by which the performance of the obligation is to be measured if the standards are not manifestly unreasonable.

However, section 113(a)(2) provides:

> The limitations on enforceability imposed by unconscionability under Section 111 and fundamental public policy under Section 105(b) may not be varied by agreement.

---

[837] *See supra* § 2.03 Theories Relevant To Imposing Liability [4] Negligent Misrepresentation [c] United States [ii] Economic Loss [D] Content of Information in Electronic Form.

[838] 520 N.Y.S.2d 334 (Civ. Ct. 1987); *see supra* § 3.02 Classification of Contracts [d] Contracts for Information.

[839] U.C.I.T.A. § 405 cmt 3b (2001).

[840] *Id.* § 102(52).

Section 405 provides for the implied warranty for system integration. This section illustrates three different standards of performance required for different types of transactions.

(a) Unless the warranty is disclaimed or modified, if a licensor at the time of contracting has reason to know any particular purpose for which the computer information is required and that the licensee is relying on the licensor's skill or judgment to select, develop, or furnish suitable information, the following rules apply:
(1) Except as otherwise provided in paragraph (2), there is an implied warranty that the information is fit for that purpose.
(2) If from all the circumstances it appears that the licensor was to be paid for the amount of its time or effort regardless of the fitness of the resulting information, the warranty under paragraph (1) is that the information will not fail to achieve the licensee's particular purpose as a result of the licensor's lack of reasonable effort.
(b) There is no warranty under subsection (a) with regard to:
(1) the aesthetics, appeal, suitability to taste, or subjective quality of informational content; or
(2) published informational content, but there may be a warranty with regard to the licensor's selection among published informational content from different providers if the selection is made by an individual acting as or on behalf of the licensor.
(c) If an agreement requires a licensor to provide or select a system consisting of computer programs and goods, and the licensor has reason to know that the licensee is relying on the skill or judgment of the licensor to

select the components of the system, there is an implied warranty that the components provided or selected will function together as a system.

(d) The warranty under this section is not subject to the preclusion in Section 113(a)(1) on disclaiming diligence, reasonableness, or care.

Section 405 corresponds to the section concerning an implied warranty for fitness for particular purpose in Article 2. The U.C.I.T.A. section 405 adopts three different standards in (a)(1) and (c), (a)(2), and (b): (a)(1) and (c) apply the result-oriented standard that information is fit for the purpose, or that the components provided or selected will function together as a system. This is analogous to the sale of goods standard. (a)(2) applies the process-oriented standard to exercise reasonable effort, as in the cases of supply of services. There is no warranty under (b) for the aesthetics, appeal, suitability to taste, or subjective quality of informational content; or published informational content.[841]

In order to apply those provisions, courts still need to make determinations as to whether the performance is judged in reference to the result-oriented standard, the process-oriented standard or the informational content standard, even though there is no need to classify and label the contracts as the sale of goods, the supply of services, and the supply of information.

The principle of the (a)(1) and (c) provision is the same as in the English cases of *St. Albans City & District Council v. International Computers Ltd.*[842] and *Saphena Computing Ltd. v. Allied Collection Agencies Ltd.,*[843] where contracts to deliver computer programs were judged in reference to the result-oriented standard in accordance with the Sale of Goods Act 1979 and the

---

[841] *Id.* § 405 cmts.
[842] [1996] 4 All E.R. 481.
[843] [1995] F.S.R. 616.

Supply of Goods and Services Act 1982.

[b] Disclaimer or Modification of Warranty

Section 406 provides for disclaimer or modification of warranty. Section 406(a) provides that "Words or conduct relevant to the creation of an express warranty and words or conduct tending to disclaim or modify an express warranty must be construed wherever reasonable as consistent with each other." To disclaim or modify the implied warranty under section 403, that the computer program is fit for the ordinary purposes, language must mention "merchantability" or "quality" or use words of similar import and, if in a record, must be conspicuous.[844]

As in Article 2, disclaiming an implied warranty is not difficult under U.C.I.T.A., so long as the language and the format used are appropriate. To disclaim or modify the implied warranty arising under section 404, that there is no inaccuracy in the informational content caused by the merchant's failure to perform with reasonable care, language in a record must mention "accuracy" or use words of similar import.[845] Language to disclaim or modify the implied warranty arising under Section 405 must be in a record and be conspicuous. The language such as "[t]here is no warranty that this information, our efforts, or the system will fulfil any of your particular purposes or needs," is sufficient for the purpose.[846] Section 406(b)(3) provides that

> Language in a record is sufficient to disclaim all implied warranties if it individually disclaims each implied warranty or, except for the warranty in Section 401, if it is conspicuous and states "Except for express warranties stated in this contract, if any, this 'information' 'computer program' is provided with all faults, and the entire risk as

---

[844] U.C.I.T.A. § 406(b)(1)(A) (2001).
[845] *Id.* § 406(b)(1)(B).
[846] *Id.* § 406(b)(2).

to satisfactory quality, performance, accuracy, and effort is with the user", or words of similar import.

All implied warranties except for the warranty under Section 401, concerning non interference and non infringement from the third party, may be disclaimed by expressions like "as is" or "with all faults" or other language,[847] unless a disclaimer of obligation concerning good faith, dili-gence, reasonableness, and care imposed by the U.C.I.T.A. is not manifestly unreasonable, or contrary to the doctrine of unconscionability, preempted by federal law, or violates a fundamental public policy.[848]

[4] Comparison

In England, the courts tend to impose result-oriented terms with respect to transactions involving computer programs. As in *St. Albans City & District Council v. International Computers Ltd.*[849] and *Saphena Computing Ltd. v. Allied Collection Agencies Ltd.*,[850] a contract for the transfer of software to achieve a specific, known purpose should be subject to an implied term that the program would be reasonably fit for the intended purpose. The Unfair Contract Terms Act 1977 plays an essential role in determining the validity of any terms restricting or excluding the express or implied terms. The Unfair Contract Terms Act 1977 imposes an absolute prohibition of disclaimers for certain implied terms, and a reasonableness test. Therefore, the use of particular language disclaiming the express or implied terms or the insertion of the integration clauses may not be as effective as are the particular restrictions or limitations considered in the light of the reasonableness test, despite the existence of the particular language

---

[847] *Id.* § 406(c).
[848] *Id.* § 105, § 111, §113.
[849] [1996] 4 All E.R. 481
[850] [1995] F.S.R. 616.

in disclaiming different contract terms.

In the United States, when considering disclaimer clauses, the courts tend to consider the effectiveness of each method of disclaimer in accordance with individual provisions of the U.C.C. The technical requirements imposed by the U.C.C., such as the use of specific language, and the format for disclaiming warranties are essential. If the requirements are fulfilled, such contract terms would be likely to be valid. The existence of integration clauses, parol and extrinsic evidence rules, a doctrine of unconscionability or a fundamental public policy may also have an effect on the validity of the disclaimer.

§ 3.05 Remedies and Standard of Performance

Transactions involving computer technology often involve customisation of the computer system, which requires analysis of the current system and customisation of the system to the client's needs. As stated in *Saphena Computing Ltd. v. Allied Collection Agencies Ltd.*, software is not necessarily a commodity which is handed over or delivered once and for all at one time.[851] It may have to be tested and modified as necessary. It would not necessarily be a breach of contract to deliver software in the first instance with a defect in it.[852] Therefore, it was not reasonable to expect a perfect system on the first delivery.

Section 11(3) of the Sale of Goods Act 1979 provides that a breach of warranty gives rise to a claim for damages, but not to a right to reject the goods and treat the contract as repudiated. However, section 11(3) also provides that whether a stipulation in a contract is a condition or a warranty depends in each case on the construction of the contract. The dichotomy between condition and warranty seems to have become more flexible in modern

---

[851] *Id.* at 652
[852] *Id.*

applications.[853] As discussed previously, sections 15(A) and 30 (2A) provide that, in cases where the buyer does not deal as a consumer, the breach is not to be treated as a breach of condition, but possibly as a breach of warranty, if the breach is so slight that it would be unreasonable for him or her to reject it. Therefore, the categorisation may change in accordance with the type of transaction, whether the transaction involves consumers or not.

In the United States, despite the perfect tender rule provided in U.C.C. section 2-601,[854] minor nonconformity is not an adequate basis for rejection.[855] Therefore, minor bugs could not amount to an adequate reason to reject the performance even if the transaction were considered a sale of goods.

Both in England and in the United States, even if transactions involving software are construed as sales of goods, the suppliers are not expected to tender "perfect software" which will function immediately. Section 403(a) of the U.C.I.T.A. confirmed this by providing that a merchant licensor of a computer program warrants to the end user that the computer program is fit for the ordinary purposes for which such computer programs are used. The comments state that merchantability does not require the best or most fit program for that use or that the program be fit for all possible uses, and that the focus is on the ordinary purposes for which such programs are used.[856] The U.C.I.T.A. adopted the approach taken by the U.C.C. section 2-314,[857] with regard to the concept in terms of "fair average," i.e., goods that centre around the middle of a belt of quality.

---

[853] *See* Hong Kong Fir Shipping Co. Ltd. v. Kawasaki Kisen Kaisha Ltd. [1962] 2 Q.B. 26,70 (regarding intermediate or innominate terms).

[854] 1998 Official Text.

[855] *See* D.P. Technology Corp. v. Sherwood Tool, Inc., 751 F. Supp. 1038, 1044 (D. Conn. 1990); Alden Press Inc. v. Block & Co., 527 N.E.2d 489, 493 (Ill. App. Ct. 1988).

[856] U.C.I.T.A. § 403 cmt. 3a (2001).

[857] 1998 Official Text.

Furthermore, the level of the standard of performance is affected by the validity of contract terms disclaiming express and implied obligations, especially implied obligations, as it is hard to disclaim express obligations. Therefore, even if a contract is categorised as a sale of goods, a result-oriented outcome of "perfect tender" or "satisfactory quality" may not be required as a standard of performance.

§ 3.06 Limitation or Exclusion of Remedies

[1] Different Methods of Limiting or Excluding Remedies

There are various ways to limit the available remedies. None of the methods seems to be one hundred percent effective. As discussed previously, there are largely four methods for limiting or excluding the available remedies aimed at: 1) obligations incurred; 2) the cure to which the victim is entitled; 3) damage for which compensation is payable; and, 4) money payable on breach. All the methods described above may be combined in a single contract.

As discussed previously, when determining whether contract terms limiting or excluding remedies are valid, the English courts seem to place emphasis on the overall "reasonableness" of the contract clauses, taking into account all the circumstances of the transactions, including the bargaining position of the parties. Many of the English cases examine the reasonableness of the limitation of the stated amount of the damages in the contract clauses.

On the contrary, in the United States, U.C.C. provisions provide several different rules for various methods of limiting or excluding remedies, when determining whether such contract terms are valid. The similar concept to the English reasonableness test which effects the validity of the contract clauses is the doctrine of unconscionability, which will be discussed later.[858]

---

[858] See *infra* § 3.07 Construction and Statutory Controls on Contractual Terms [3] Reasonableness Test and Unconscionability.

[a] England

[i] Restricting Obligations Incurred, Damage for which Compensation is Payable

As discussed above in *Mackenzie Patten & Co. v. British Olivetti Ltd.,*[859] the contract between the parties excluded all the supplier's liability except for the negligent causing of death or injury and contained an integration clause that the agreement was in lieu of and to the exclusion of all other liabilities, obligations, warranties and conditions. In accordance with the "reasonable test" in section 11 of the Unfair Contract Terms Act 1977, the exclusion or limitation was not valid.

[ii] Restricting the Cure to Which the Victim is Entitled, Damage for which Compensation is Payable, and Money Payable on Breach

In *Salvage Assoc. (SA) v. Cap Financial Services Ltd.* (CAP),[860] both contracts contained provisions restricting express or implied terms that CAP take reasonable care to exercise reasonable skill, and CAP's total liability was limited to £250,000 in respect of physical damage to or loss of tangible property, and in any other case, the lesser of £25,000 or 100 percent of all sums received under the agreement by CAP from the customer (i.e. money back).

The court considered whether these contract terms were reasonable. Both contracts were written and produced in advance, but were freely negotiable and SA could have selected other software houses in competition with CAP.[861] The court decided that the second contract was individually negotiated between parties of equal bargaining power. Therefore, the first contract must satisfy

---

[859] 11 January 1984 (Q.B.) (unreported) LEXIS; 1 C. L. & P. 92 (1984); 48 M.L.R. 344 (1985).
[860] [1995] F.S.R.654; *see supra* § 3.03 Express Terms or Warranties [2] England [a] Type of Express Terms and Remedies [iv] Process-Oriented Terms.
[861] [1995] F.S.R. 654, 676.

section 2(2) and section 3, whereas the second contract must satisfy section 2(2). Section 2(2) provides that "a person cannot exclude or restrict his liability for negligence except in so far as the term or notice satisfies the requirement of reasonableness." The expression "negligence" is also extended to include breach of contract.[862]

The court stated that the limitation of the liability to £25,000 did not satisfy the requirement of reasonableness under the Unfair Contract Term Act 1977.[863] Although the court found that the terms of the contract were considered, negotiated and agreed by the parties as suitable for the transaction of the second contract for the computerisation of its Head Office Accounting System, the court considered factors beyond the appearance of the bargain between the parties. The court considered the following factors: 1) there was no evidence to justify the figure or to show how it had been calculated; 2) inadequacy of £25,000 as the upper limit; and, 3) the defendant made a decision to apply a new limit of £1,000,000. In addition, the court considered that: 1) there was never any suggestion that there was any risk of failure; 2) it was not possible for the plaintiff to obtain insurance against such loss at a realistic premium; and, 3) the defendant had resources, and insurance cover was available against the losses.[864] Even though, both contracts were freely negotiated, the court had examined different factors such as the amendments by CAP to their own policy regarding the limitation of damages or insurance coverage. The court may have considered that it was unfair for the plaintiffs if they were not able to recover at least the price of the contract. This could be one of the reasons for invalidating the limitation on the amount of the damages. The courts may be willing to validate the contract clauses limiting the amount of the damages based on the contractual price.

---

[862] *Id.* at 673.
[863] *See* ss. 2(2) and 3.
[864] [1995] F.S.R.654, 676-77.

However, such circumstances were not necessarily foreseeable or predictable by either party. The court could have balanced the private autonomy and the reasonableness of the contractual clause in clearer and more explicit ways.

In *St. Albans City & District Council v. International Computers Ltd.*,[865] in the contract between the parties, there was a disclaimer that the defendant's liability would not exceed the price or charge payable for the item of equipment, program or service in respect of which the liability arose, or £ 100,000 (whichever was the lesser).[866]

The court applied section 3 of the Unfair Contract Terms Act 1977 and considered resources, insurance, bargaining position, inducement, and knowledge of the term. Determining factors were: 1) the parties were of unequal bargaining power; 2) the defendant failed to justify the figure of £ 100,000, which was small, both in relation to the potential risk and the actual loss; 3) the defendant was insured; and, 4) the practical consequences.[867]

Suppliers of computer systems often attempt to limit their liabilities to a stated amount. Unless this stated amount is reasonable and justified, it is hard to enforce such a limitation in England. Compensation for the amount of the contractual price may be considered reasonable by some courts. The language specifically limiting the kind of obligations or the cure to which the victim is entitled may be more effective to restrict the remedies when considered reasonable in curing the defects. Damages are ordinarily awarded on the basis of the losses foreseeable when the contract is made.[868] This rule produces asymmetry; on making the contract the customers know their maximum exposure to damages,

---

[865] [1996] 4 All E.R. 481; *see supra* § 3.03 Express Terms or Warranties [2] England [a] Type of Express Terms and Remedies [iii] Result-Oriented Terms.
[866] *St. Albans*, [1996] 4 All E.R. at 486.
[867] *St. Albans*, [1995] F.S.R. at 711.
[868] *See* Hedley v. Baxendale (1854) 9 Exch. 341.

i.e. price plus interest, but, while suppliers can foresee the type of loss to the customer, the amount may exceed any profit the suppliers hope to make. Therefore, there is a danger that the suppliers may be held liable for consequences which, at the time of the contract, are foreseeable in kind, but not in quantity. This may occur especially when transactions involve individualised and sophisticated systems rather than mass-produced systems.

In *Victoria Laundry (Windsor) Ltd. v. Newman,*[869] the aggrieved party was entitled to recover loss reasonably foreseeable at the time of the contract. In this case, whether the loss was reasonably foreseeable depended on the state of the defendant's knowledge. The party in breach will be liable only for loss of profits ordinarily resulting from such a breach, unless he or she possesses knowledge of special circumstances outside the "ordinary course of things"[870] Under the *Victoria Laundry* case, it was implied that there is no difference between "reasonable foreseeability" for recovery in contract and in tort.

However, *Heron II (Koufos v. C.Czarnikow Ltd.),*[871] imposed a degree of probability, higher than "reasonably foreseeable loss," described as "very substantial" probability, to satisfy the test of remoteness in contract, as compared to the test in tort.[872] Therefore, "the court has to consider whether the consequences were of such a kind that a reasonable man, at the time of making the contract, would contemplate them as being of a very substantial degree of probability."[873] As such, the remoteness test in contract is narrower than that in tort. Lord Reid stated that:

---

[869] [1949] 2 K.B. 528 (C.A.).
[870] *Id.* at 539; G. TREITEL, THE LAW OF CONTRACT 898-902 (10th ed. 1999).
[871] [1969] 1 A.C. 350 (H.L.(E.)).
[872] *Id.* at 388 (H.L.(E.)).
[873] H. Parsons (Livestock) Ltd. v. Uttley Ingham & Co. Ltd. [1978] Q.B. 791, 801 (C.A.) (L.Denning).

In contract, if one party wishes to protect himself against a risk which to the other party would appear unusual, he can direct the other party's attention to it before the contract is made, and I need not stop to consider in what circumstances the other party will then be held to have accepted responsibility in that event. But in tort there is no opportunity for the injured party to protect himself in that way, and the tortfeasor cannot reasonably complain if he has to pay for some very unusual but nevertheless foreseeable damage which results from his wrongdoing.[874]

In this case, the shipowner was held liable for the loss suffered by the charterers by reason of the fall in the market even though he did not know what the charterers intended to do with the sugar, but he knew there was a market and should have realised that at least it was not unlikely that the sugar would be sold in the market at market price on arrival.[875] The shipowner "must have contemplated that if the market went the other way he would be causing loss" and "it would not be reasonable to exonerate him merely because in advance the measure of the loss could not be calculated."[876] Therefore, the defendants may be held liable for the *incalculable* risks which may not be *specifically* known.

The court considered, both in *Salvage Assoc. v. Cap Financial Services Ltd.* [877] and in *St. Albans City & District Council v. International Computers Ltd.,*[878] factors such as availability of insurance. However, existence of insurance coverage could be a factor which may not be known to the other party. The court may

---

[874] [1969] 1 A.C. 350, 387 (H.L.(E.)).
[875] *Id.* at 382.
[876] *Id.* at 404-05.
[877] [1995] F.S.R.654.
[878] [1996] 4 All E.R. 481.

find it easier to validate the contractual clauses limiting liability to the amount based on a contractual price. It may also be useful for the suppliers to refer to factors justifying the limitation such as the coverage of insurance.

It may be noted that, with respect to physical damage to property, it is easier to justify recovery in circumstances broader than in cases of economic loss. In *H. Parsons (Livestock) Ltd. v. Uttley Ingham & Co. Ltd.*,[879] Lord Denning argued that the remoteness test with respect to physical damage was the same in contract and in tort.[880] He stated that, in such cases, "the defaulting party is liable for any loss or expense which he ought reasonably to have foreseen at the time of the breach as a possible consequence, even if it was only a slight possibility."[881] Therefore, the makers of the hoppers were liable for the death of the pigs, as "They ought reasonably to have foreseen that, if the mouldy pignuts were fed to the pigs, there was a possibility that they might become ill," but were not liable for the loss of profits, even though the possibility of illness was described as "Not a serious possibility. Nor a real danger. But still a slight possibility."[882]

On the contrary, Scarman L.JJ. stated that the same principles should be applicable for both financial and physical damage and physical injury must have been a serious possibility for the purpose of remoteness.[883] His opinion was supported by Orr L.JJ.[884]

If the use of defective computer programs results in property damage, the suppliers may be held liable for the loss reasonably foreseen at the time of the breach as a possible consequence, even for a slight possibility, according to the opinion of Lord Denning.

---

[879] [1978] Q.B. 791(C.A.).
[880] *Id.* at 804.
[881] *Id.* at 803.
[882] *Id.* at 804.
[883] *Id.* at 813.
[884] *Id.* at 805.

[iii] Consequential Damages

Suppliers of computer technology often attempt to limit the consequential damages. In English law, the phrase "consequential loss" did not include the loss flowing directly and naturally from a breach under *British Sugar plc. v. Nei Power Projects Ltd.*[885] Therefore, such losses cannot be excluded by a contractual term excluding consequential loss. The contract between the plaintiffs and defendants was for the design, supply, delivery, testing and commissioning of electrical equipment by the defendants. The defendants' liability for consequential loss was limited to the value of the contract. The contractual price was about £106,585. The plaintiffs alleged that the equipment was poorly designed and badly installed, which resulted in breakdowns in the power supply, and they claimed damages of over £5 million due mainly to increased production costs and loss of profits due to the said breakdowns. The court determined that the word "consequential" does not cover any loss which directly and naturally results in the ordinary course of events from late delivery.

Therefore, according to this holding, the phrase "consequential loss" is not treated in the same way in the United States as it is in England. Consequential damages in England may not include loss of profits; this can be considered direct loss, which directly and naturally results from the breach.

[b] United States
[i] The Cure to which the Victim is Entitled

U.C.C. section 2-719(2)[886] provides that where circumstances cause an exclusive or limited remedy to fail in its essential purpose, a plaintiff may pursue all the remedies available under the Act. U.C.C. section 2-719 (3) provides that the consequential damages may be limited or excluded unless the limitation or exclusion

---

[885] British Sugar plc. v. Nei Power Projects Ltd., Court of Appeal, 8 October 1997, 87 Build L.R 42, 14 Const. LJ 365.
[886] 1998 Official Text.

is unconscionable. It should be noted that the U.C.I.T.A. also provides in section 803(b) that if performance of an exclusive or limited remedy causes the remedy to fail of its essential purpose, the aggrieved party may pursue other remedies under the U.C.I.T.A. Section 803(d) provides that "Consequential damages and incidental damages may be excluded or limited by agreement unless the exclusion or limitation is unconscionable."

In *Fargo Machine & Tool Co.* (Fargo) *v. Kearney & Trecker Corp.* (Kearney),[887] the defendant had effectively limited the buyer's remedy to repair or replacement of defective parts and excluded consequential damages. However, as the repairs were not effective to cure the defects completely, a limited remedy failed in its essential purpose.[888] The court decided that such exclusion of the consequential damages was not valid, even though not unconscionable,[889] as there were two breaches of the contract; failure to deliver conforming goods to the express warranty and failure to correct such non-conformity.[890] Therefore, the limitation of the buyer's remedy was inoperative.[891] The court awarded damages to Fargo, including expenditures to make the goods conform to warranty and lost profits. The court found in favour of Kearney for the remaining balance due on the purchase price. Therefore, the plaintiff was put into a position as if the contract had been performed satisfactorily.[892]

Likewise, in *Consolidated Data Terminals* (CDT) *v. Applied*

---

[887] 428 F. Supp. 364 (E.D. Mich. 1977); *see supra* § 3.03 Express Terms or Warranties [3] United States [a] Types of Express Warranties and Remedies [ii] Express Warranties and Advertising or Demonstration -Result-Oriented Terms.
[888] *Fargo Machine*, 428 F. Supp. at 381; *see* U.C.C. § 2-719(2) (1998).
[889] *Fargo Machine*, 428 F. Supp. at 381; *see* U.C.C. § 2-719(3) (1998).
[890] *Fargo Machine*, 428 F. Supp. at 382.
[891] *Id.*
[892] *Id.* at 383-84.

Civil Liability for Defects in Information in Electronic Form

Digital Data Systems, Inc.,[893] the contract between the parties contained terms that the buyer's remedies were restricted to repair of the defective equipment; as CDT would be left with no effective remedy with such limitations, they were considered not valid.[894]

On the other hand, in *Colonial Life Insurance Co. v. Electronic Data Systems, Corp.*,[895] the court stated that, in transactions between sophisticated business parties, represented and advised by attorneys, even when a limited remedy fails of its essential purpose, consequential or incidental damages may be excluded unless limitation or exclusion is unconscionable.[896] The bargaining position and the sophistication of the parties were important factors in determining the validity of the disclaimer.

The courts also look favourably on evidence showing an effective system to maintain and repair subsequent to delivery. In *Jaskey Finance & Leasing v. Display Data Corp.*,[897] it was held that a disclaimer clause along with an integration clause were sufficient to preclude express warranty under Maryland law.[898] In this case, there was a separate maintenance contract and the seller was obliged to make a reasonable effort to remedy any error for a period of one year after the delivery. The court determined that the language disclaiming the express warranties and the implied warranties of fitness for a particular purpose were conspicuous and sufficient to disclaim those warranties.[899] Furthermore, the court stated that there was no suggestion that the plaintiffs were unaware

---

[893] 708 F.2d 385 (9th Cir. 1983); *see supra* § 3.03 Express Terms or Warranties [3] United States [b] Exclusion of Express Warranties [ii] Inconsistent Disclaimer.
[894] N.Y. U.C.C. § 2-719(2).
[895] 817 F. Supp. 235 (D.N.H. 1993).
[896] *Id.* at 241-42.
[897] 564 F.Supp. 160 (E.D.Pa. 1983); *see supra* § 3.03 Express Terms or Warranties [3] United States [b] Exclusion of Express Warranties [iii] Integration Clauses.
[898] *Jaskey*, 564 F. Supp. at 163.
[899] *Id.* at 163-64.

of the significance of the disclaimer and integration clauses.[900]

[ii] The Damage for which Compensation is Payable

In *Fargo Machine & Tool Co. Kearney & Trecker Corp.*,[901] the defendant was not successful in excluding consequential damages; as the repairs were not effective to cure the defects completely, a limited remedy failed in its essential purpose.

In *Consolidated Data Terminals* (CDT) *v. Applied Digital Data Systems, Inc.* (ADD),[902] the contract contained a term which excluded the recovery of certain consequential damages "in connection with the use or the inability to use its products or goods."[903] The court determined that the consequential damages suffered by CDT consisted of loss of customer goodwill and the expenses incurred to recapture that goodwill. Therefore, the damages did not arise "in connection with the use or the inability to use its products or goods" and the loss of customer goodwill should be a recoverable loss. The court construed the disclaimer very narrowly.[904]

The consequential damages were incurred due to the wholesale failure of ADDS Regent terminals to operate properly and to conform to specifications. The court affirmed the district court's decision to award $15,000 to cover additional costs and lost profits because of numerous service calls incurred by the problems with the terminals, but reversed the additional awards for the loss of profit.[905]

On the other hand, in *Colonial Life Insurance Co. Electronic Data Systems, Corp.*,[906] the court stated that, in transactions

---

[900] *Id.* at 164.
[901] 428 F. Supp. 364 (E.D. Mich. 1977).
[902] 708 F.2d 385 (9th Cir. 1983).
[903] *Id.* at 391.
[904] *Id.* at 392-93.
[905] *Id.* at 393.
[906] 817 F. Supp. 235 (D.N.H. 1993).

between sophisticated business parties, even when a limited remedy fails of its essential purpose, consequential or incidental damages may be excluded unless limitation or exclusion is unconscionable.

[2] Comparison

In England, the reasonableness test is essential to evaluate all the methods for limiting remedies. When suppliers of the computer systems attempt to limit their liabilities to a stated amount, unless such stated amount is reasonable and justified, it is hard to enforce such a limitation. In examining the validity of monetary damages, the courts consider different factors including the distribution of losses among the parties or the insurance coverage. The suppliers have to justify the reasonableness of the restriction of the monetary damages, taking into account whether the users could cover the losses or not. Compensation in the amount of the contractual price may be considered reasonable by some courts. However, this may produce asymmetry; on making the contract the customers know their maximum exposure to damages, on the contrary, the suppliers can foresee the type of loss to the customers but in an amount which may exceed any profit the suppliers hope to make.

In the United States, U.C.C. Article 2 and the U.C.I.T.A. provide detailed rules regarding different methods of limitation or exclusion of remedies. However, courts will rarely examine the appropriateness of any precise specification of liquidated damages. Contractual clauses excluding or modifying warranties are essentially valid unless contrary to provisions requiring the use of specific language or format under the U.C.C. section 2-316 and the U.C.I.T.A. section 406. Under the U.C.C. section 2-719 and the U.C.I.T.A. section 803, if an exclusive or limited remedy fails in its essential purpose, or if the limitation or exclusion of consequential damages is unconscionable, the court may find contractual clauses limiting or excluding remedies invalid. However, in some courts, even when a limited remedy fails of its essential purpose, consequential or incidental damages may be excluded unless limitation or exclusion is unconscionable. A number of courts may look closely into the seriousness of the breach, including the condition of the delivered subject matters, effectiveness of the remedy to repair, and bargaining position or sophistication of the parties to examine whether to justify such limitation or exclusion.

§ 3.07 Construction and Statutory Controls on Contractual Terms

[1] England

English courts traditionally adopted a strict approach to construction of disclaimer clauses. The warranty disclaimer clauses need to cover exactly the liability which it is sought to disclaim; for instance, disclaimer clauses for implied conditions and warranties are not effective in excluding express terms[907] and the disclaimer clauses for breach of implied warranty are not effective in excluding liability for breach of condition,[908] including those so classified by the Sale of Goods Act 1979.

However, such a strict approach may no longer be necessary as the Unfair Contract Terms Act 1977 imposes a reasonableness test for determining the validity of the contractual clauses excluding or limiting the liability.[909] Traditionally, strict construction was directly connected to the enforcement of such clauses in the contract. However, it should be noted that, even then, conspicuous and clear language disclaiming all liabilities was not adequate to disclaim all the liabilities concerned; courts have to question

---

[907] *See* Andrews Bros. Ltd. v. Singer & Co. Ltd. [1934] 1 K.B. 17.
[908] *See* Baldry v. Marshall [1925] 1 K.B. 260.
[909] *See* Salvage Assoc. v. Cap Fin. Servs. Ltd. [1995] F.S.R. 654; St. Albans City & Dist. Council v. Int'l Computers Ltd. [1995] F.S.R. 686 (Q.B.D.), [1996] 4 All E.R. 481; *see supra* § 3.03 Express Terms or Warranties [2] England [b] Exclusion of Express Terms.

the enforcement of such clauses.[910] At present, imposition of the reasonableness test may prevent the enforcement of these clauses, the enforcement of which may create unfair results.

If there is ambiguity in the language used, such ambiguity should be resolved against the party proffering the written documents. This *"contra proferentem"* rule is particularly useful in balancing the conflicting interests involving standard form contracts.[911] The rule has been incorporated in the United States' Restatement (Second) of Contracts section 211 (1979), which provides that standardised take it or leave it form contracts are construed against the drafter; they are subject to the general obligation of good faith and of not imposing unconscionable terms upon a party.

[2] United States

Restatement (Second) of Contracts section 203 (1979) provides for standards of preference in interpretation: an interpretation which gives a reasonable, lawful, and effective meaning to all the terms is preferred to an interpretation which leaves a part unreasonable, unlawful, or of no effect; express terms are given greater weight than course of performance, course of dealing, and usage of trade; specific terms and exact terms are given greater weight than general language; separately negotiated or added terms are given greater weight than standardised terms or other terms not separately negotiated. U.C.I.T.A. section 302 provides for similar construction.

As described above, in the United States, the U.C.C. Article 2 and the U.C.I.T.A. provide detailed rules regarding different methods in limitation or exclusion of remedies. U.C.C. Article 2, section 316 and U.C.I.T.A. section 406 provide for excluding or modifying warranties. U.C.C. Article 2, section 719 and the

---

[910] *See* Lee & Son Ltd. v. Ry. Executive [1949] 2 All E.R. 581. (Denning J.).
[911] *See Id.*

U.C.I.T.A. section 803 provide for invalid clauses limiting or excluding remedies. In addition, U.C.C. Article 2, section 202 and the U.C.I.T.A. section 301 provide rules for parol or extrinsic evidence, and exceptions to those rules, that contractual terms can be supplemented by course of performance, course of dealing, or usage of trade, and evidence of consistent additional terms despite the presence of an integration clause. U.C.C. Article 2 section 302 and the U.C.I.T.A. section 111 provide that the courts may refuse to enforce unconscionable contracts or clauses to avoid unconscionable results.[912]

[3] Reasonableness Test and Unconscionability
    [a] Reasonableness Test

As discussed above,[913] the Unfair Contract Terms Act 1977 actively controls the exclusion or limitation of liability and imposes a reasonableness test, having considerable impact even on the construction of the contract.[914] I will not discuss the intervention of equity by reason of undue influence or unconscionable bargains since English cases discussed above have applied the Unfair Contract Terms Act 1977 rather than those principles.

Section 11(2) and Schedule 2 of the Unfair Contract Terms Act 1977 provide guidelines for the circumstances to be taken into account. These are 1) the strength of the bargaining position of the parties; 2) whether the customer received any inducement to agree to the term; 3) whether the customer knew or ought reasonably to have known of the existence and extent of the term; 4) where the term excludes or restricts any relevant liability if some condition

---

[912] See infra § 3.07 Construction and Statutory Controls on Contractual Terms [4] Standard Form Contracts and Consumers.
[913] See supra § 3.03 Express Terms or Warranties [b] Exclusion of Express Terms [i] Statutes and in § 3.04 Implied Terms or Warranties [1] England [a] Statutory Control Over Implied Terms.
[914] See Photo Prod. v. Securicor Transp. [1980] A.C. 827, 843 (L. Wiberforce).

is not complied with, whether it was reasonable at the time of the contract to expect that compliance with that condition would be practicable; and, 5) whether the goods were manufactured, processed, or adapted to the special order of the customer.

If a contractual term seeks to restrict liability to a specified sum of money, Section 11(4) requires reference to 1) the resources which the defendant would expect to be available to him for the purpose of meeting the liability should it arise; and, 2) how far it was open to him to cover himself by insurance.

The court considered, both in *Salvage Association v. Cap Financial Services Ltd.*[915] and in *St. Albans City & District Council v. International Computers Ltd.,*[916] among other factors, the justification of the amount of damages in terms of the defendant's resources and insurance coverage.[917]

However, simple comparison of insurance coverage may cause problems in some cases, though insurance coverage may be an indication of the parties' bargaining power. The court may impose liability on those who are insured, rather than on those who are not, raising the insurance premium for the insured party in the future. Insurance companies would surely be keen to insulate themselves from paying for suppliers' extravagant promises. It may become extremely hard for suppliers to obtain insurance for breach of promise or contract.

The English approach, which articulates the criteria of determining "reasonableness," seems helpful in examining the respective positions of the parties, provided the courts balance this examination with respect for the private autonomy of the parties.

[b] Unconscionability

The doctrine of unconscionability may affect the validity of

---

[915] [1995] F.S.R. 654.
[916] [1995] F.S.R. 686, [1996] 4 All E.R. 481.
[917] *See supra*, § 3.03 Express Terms or Warranties [2] England [b] Exclusion of Express Terms.

the whole or a part of a contract. U.C.C. section 2-302(1) provides that "If the court as a matter of law finds the contract or any clause of the contract to have been unconscionable at the time it was made the court may refuse to enforce the contract, or it may enforce the remainder of the contract without the unconscionable clause, or it may so limit the application of any unconscionable clause as to avoid any unconscionable result."

U.C.C. section 2-302 official comment provides that:

> The basic test is whether, in the light of the general commercial background and the commercial needs of the particular trade or case, the clauses involved are so one-sided as to be unconscionable under the circumstances existing at the time of the making of the contract...The principle is one of the prevention of oppression and unfair surprise... and not of disturbance of allocation of risks because of superior bargaining power.

The examples given in the official comment seem to deal with the effect of specific disclaimer clauses, such as the case where a clause limiting time for complaints was held inapplicable to latent defects which could be discovered only by microscopic analysis.[918] The doctrine of unconscionability may be useful when there is a gap in expertise between the parties.

In *Sierra Diesel Injection Service, Inc., v. Burroughs Corp.*,[919] discussed above, in determining whether a disclaimer was conspicuous, the court adapted the unconscionability principle. The court first stated that exclusion of warranties is generally

---

[918] *See* Kansas City Wholesale Grocery Co. v. Weber Packing Corp., 73 P.2d 1272 (Utah 1937).

[919] 874 F. 2d 653 (9th Cir. 1989), *amended by* 890 F. 2d 108 (9th Cir 1989); *see supra* § 3.04 Implied Terms or Warranties [2] United States [c] Exclusion of Implied Warranties [iii] Conspicuousness of the Warranty Exclusion.

disfavoured and the form contract in the case was to be construed against the drafter,[920] and such warranty exclusions are subject to the general obligation of good faith and do not impose unconscionable terms upon a party. With respect to the examination of conspicuousness, the court would consider whether a reasonable person against whom it is to operate ought to have noticed the warranty disclaimer, and that a reasonable person in the buyer's position would not have been surprised to find such a disclaimer in the contract. The court considered the lack of the sophistication of the plaintiff in justifying that disclaimers were not conspicuous.

The bargaining power between the parties is not taken into consideration in examination of the unconscionability. In *Teknekron Customer Information Solutions, Inc. v. Watkins Motor Lines,*[921] the United States' District Court of California stated that there were "factual issues as to whether a contractual party was 'surprised' by the disclaimer, a procedural component of unconscionability, and factual issues as to whether the agreement entered into by the parties deprived one of the contracting parties of meaningful choice, the substantive component of unconscionability."[922]

In this case, the supplier was a small computer technology company, which employed between 18 and 30 people and the company's annual sales averaged approximately from $3 million to $4 million, while the licensee was a large national interstate trucking carrier company, which employed over 4000 people and the company's annual sales exceeded $320 million. The plaintiff Teknekron Customer Information Solutions, Inc. (Teknekron), sued defendant Watkins Motor Lines, Inc. (Watkins), seeking payment under a "Development Agreement" to implement an Integrated Shipping Information [Computer] System (ISIS) and "Maintenance Agreement" for ISIS system's hardware and software. Watkins

---

[920] *See* RESTATEMENT (SECOND) OF CONTRACTS § 211 cmt. c (1979).
[921] 1994 WL 11726 (N.D Cal. Jan. 5, 1994).
[922] *Id.* at *5.

counterclaimed that Teknekron breached express and implied warranties.

The court determined that Watkins was entitled to present evidence that enforcing Teknekron's purported disclaimer of implied warranties would be unconscionable, even if the disclaimer of the implied warranty was in writing, conspicuous and larger than the surrounding text. Thus, Teknekron's motion to dismiss Watkins' counterclaim for breach of implied warranty was denied.[923] Therefore, the existence of the evidence regarding unconscionability was important, and the respective bargaining position (scale of the entities) of the parties was irrelevant in this case.

It is important that the contractual terms are literally conspicuous enough to be noticed, using the proper language provided by the statute. The court may consider, in addition, any disparity between the parties with respect to legal expertise or technological expertise; and whether the parties who are signing the contract are fully aware of the content of the contractual terms, or fully aware of the nature of the subject matter supplied with their scope of knowledge. The comparison of bargaining power is not considered under the doctrine of unconscionability; parties with superior bargaining power fare better in the United States than in England because of the more literal approach to construction inhibits the implication of warranties parties.

[4] Standard Form Contracts and Consumers
  [a] Necessity of Statutory Control over Standard Form Contract and Consumer Contracts

Control over standard form contracts and consumer contracts may be necessary as the parties to such contracts have no choice in determining contractual clauses. England and the United States have different provisions in their attempts to ensure that such contracts are not unfairly drafted.

---

[923] *Id.*

[b] England
[i] Unfair Contract Terms Act 1977

The Unfair Contract Terms Act 1977 provides provisions applicable to consumers and standard term contracts. As discussed above, even though the parties involved are not consumers, such parties may benefit from the fact that the contract imposes standardised terms.

Section 12 of the Unfair Contract Terms Act 1977 provides that:

> (1) A party to contract 'deals as consumer' in relation to another party if -
> (a) he neither makes the contract in the course of a business nor holds himself out as doing so; and
> (b) the other party does make the contract in the course of a business; and
> (c) in the case of a contract governed by the law of sale of goods or hire-purchase, or by section 7 of this Act, the goods passing under or in pursuance of the contract are of a type ordinarily supplied for private use or consumption.

Section 6(2) of the Unfair Contract Terms Act 1977 provides that liability for breach of the obligations arising from Sections 13, 14 and 15 of the Sale of Goods Act 1979 cannot be excluded or restricted as against a person dealing as a consumer. Therefore, the seller's implied undertakings as to conformity of goods with description or a sample, or as to their quality of fitness for a particular purpose cannot be excluded or restricted. It is a criminal offence to exclude contractual terms which can not be excluded in the Unfair Contract Terms Act 1977.[924]

---

[924] Consumer Transactions (Restrictions in Statements) Orders (S.I. 1976 No. 1813 and S.I. 1978 No. 127).

This is significantly different from the United States' treatment of mass-market transactions. U.C.C. and the Magnuson-Moss Act provide that such warranties can be disclaimed in consumer transactions under certain conditions.[925] Section 3 of the Unfair Contract Terms Act 1977 provides that where one of the contracting parties deals as a consumer or on the other's written standard terms of business, the exclusion of the liability must satisfy the requirement of reasonableness.[926] Under this test, as discussed above, factors such as the strength of the bargaining position of the parties, whether the customer received an inducement to agree to the terms, the customer's knowledge of the term, and whether the goods were specially ordered by the customer, would be taken into account. Therefore, even if both parties were acting in the course of a business, the court would still consider whether or not one party was dealing on written standard terms supplied by another party, or whether there was an opportunity to negotiate the terms.

Furthermore, in England, the scope of business activities is construed narrowly. For instance, in accordance with the holding of *R & B. Customs Brokers Co. Ltd. v. United Dominions Trust Ltd.*,[927] as long as people are not in the business of buying particular goods, even companies are considered consumers.

In *St. Albans City & District v. International Computers Ltd.*, even though Section 14 of the 1977 Act defines business as embracing the activities of a local authority, the court determined that the plaintiff dealt on the defendants' written standard terms. The court considered resources, insurance bargaining position, inducement, and knowledge of the term. This means that even if the users are business entities, they may benefit from the suppliers' use of standard form contracts.

---

[925] U.C.C. § 2-316 (1998), Magnuson-Moss Act, 15 U.S.C. § 2308 (1997).
[926] s. 3; *see* Section 11 and Schedule 2 for the reasonableness test.
[927] [1988] 1 W.L.R. 321.

[ii] The Unfair Terms in Consumer Contracts Regulations 1999

The Council Directive on Unfair Terms in Consumer Contracts[928] was implemented as the Unfair Terms in Consumer Contracts Regulations 1999.[929] Section 8(1) provides that "An unfair term in a contract concluded with a consumer by a seller or supplier shall not be binding on the consumer." Therefore, unlike the Unfair Contract Terms Act 1977, the Unfair Terms in Consumer Contracts Regulations 1999 deals with all the contractual terms concluded with a consumer by a seller or supplier.

Section 6(1) of the Unfair Terms in Consumer Contracts Regulations 1999 provides that:

> [T]he unfairness of a contractual term shall be assessed, taking into account the nature of the goods or services for which the contract was concluded and by referring, at the time of conclusion of the contract, to all the circumstances attending the conclusion of the contract and to all the other terms of the contract or of another contract on which it is dependent.

Section 6(2) provides that "In so far as it is in plain intelligible language, the assessment of fairness of a term shall not relate- (a) to the definition of the main subject matter of the contract; or (b) to the adequacy of the price or remuneration, as against the goods or services supplied in exchange."

Section 6 of the previous 1994 Regulations[930] provided that "A seller or supplier shall ensure that any written term of a contract is expressed in plain intelligible language, and if there is doubt about the meaning of a written term, the interpretation most favourable

---

[928] Council Directive (EEC) 93/13 on Unfair Terms in Consumer Contracts.
[929] S.I. 1999/2083.
[930] Unfair Terms in Consumer Contracts Regulations 1994, S.I. 1994/3159.

to the consumer shall prevail" Compared to section 6 of the 1994 Regulations, the 1999 Regulations restrict the scope of section 6(2) to the circumstances listed in (a) and (b). This may mean that even if in plain intelligible language, the assessment of fairness of a term restricting or excluding sellers' or suppliers' obligations may be examined. The Unfair Terms in Consumer Contracts Regulations 1999, as compared to the 1994 Regulations, seem to place more emphasis on all the circumstances of the contract and place less emphasis on the presentation of the terms.

Section 5(1) of the Unfair Terms in Consumer Contracts Regulations 1999 provides that " A contractual term which has not been individually negotiated shall be regarded as unfair if, contrary to the requirement of good faith, it causes a significant imbalance in the parties' rights and obligations arising under the contract, to the detriment of the consumer." Furthermore, section 5(2) provides that "A term shall always be regarded as not having been individually negotiated where it has been drafted in advance and the consumer has therefore not been able to influence the substance of the term."

"Consumer" means any natural person who, in contracts covered by these Regulations, is acting for purposes which are outside his trade, business or profession.[931]

Therefore, companies cannot be consumers under the Unfair Terms in Consumer Contracts Regulations 1999. Under the Unfair Contract Terms Act 1977, a person is a consumer if he or she neither makes the contract in the course of a business nor holds himself or herself out as doing so. As long as the purchasers' business is not computer-related, most of the transactions involving computers may be considered consumer transactions under the

---

[931] Unfair Terms in Consumer Contracts Regulations 1999. S.I. 1999/2083, s. 3(1); Council Directive (EEC) 93/13 on Unfair Terms in Consumer Contracts, art.2 (b).

Unfair Contract Terms Act 1977.[932] On the contrary, in the Unfair Terms in Consumer Contracts Regulations 1999, under the same, circumstances, purchasers may not be considered consumers, as long as the purpose is within the scope of purchaser's business.

Section 4(3) and schedule 2 of the 1994 Regulations provided that, in assessment of good faith, the court would take into consideration the strength of the bargaining positions of the parties, whether the consumer had an inducement to agree to the term, whether the goods or services were specially ordered, and the extent to which the seller or supplier has dealt fairly and equitably with the consumer. In assessing good faith, the 1994 Regulations imposed similar considerations to the guidelines for the reasonableness test under the Unfair Contract Terms Act schedule 2. These provisions were deleted in the Unfair Terms in Consumer Contracts Regulations 1999.

Section 5(5) and schedule 2 of the previous Unfair Terms in Consumer Contracts Regulations 1994 provide possible lists of the terms which may be considered unfair. These terms include terms excluding or limiting the legal liability of a seller in the event of the death of a consumer or personal injury, or inappropriately excluding or limiting the legal rights of the consumer in the event of total or partial non-performance or inadequate performance.

The Unfair Contract Terms Act 1977 covers a wider range of parties and a wider scope of matters to be examined under the reasonable test than do the Unfair Terms in Consumer Contracts Regulations 1999.

[c] United States

The approach taken in United States is significantly different from the approach taken in England.

In the United States, the exclusion of warranties is generally disfavoured and the form contract is construed against the drafter, as

---

[932] *See* C.TAPPER, COMPUTER LAW 204 (1989).

discussed in *Sierra Diesel Injection Service v. Burroughs Corp.*,[933] however, there are no strict statutory restrictions comparable to those in England.[934]

The Magnuson-Moss Act provides restrictions on disclaimers or modifications for consumer products, where a consumer product is defined in section 2301(1) as "any tangible personal property which is distributed in commerce and which is normally used for personal, family, or household purposes". Section 2308 restricts disclaimers or modifications by limiting the supplier's power to disclaim implied warranties when a written warranty is given.[935] The Act also provides for minimum standards for warranties concerning consumer products.[936]

---

[933] *See supra* § 3.03 Express Terms or Warranties[3] United States [b] Exclusion of Express Warranties [iii] Integration Clauses.

[934] RESTATEMENT (SECOND) OF CONTRACTS § 211 (1979).

[935] 15 U.S.C. § 2308 (1997) ((a) Restrictions on disclaimers or modifications
No supplier may disclaim or modify (except as provided in subsection (b) of this section) any implied warranty to a consumer with respect to such consumer product if (1) such supplier makes any written warranty to the consumer with respect to such consumer product, or (2) at the time of sale, or within 90 days thereafter, such supplier enters into a service contract with the consumer which applies to such consumer product.
(b) Limitation on duration
For purposes of this chapter (other than section 2304(a)(2) of this title), implied warranties may be limited in duration to the duration of a written warranty of reasonable duration, if such limitation is conscionable and is set forth in clear and unmistakable language and prominently displayed on the face of the warranty.
(c) Effectiveness of disclaimers, modifications, or limitations
A disclaimer, modification, or limitation made in violation of this section shall be ineffective for purposes of this chapter and State law)

[936] 15 U.S.C. § 2304 (1997) (Federal Minimum Standards for Warranties
(a) Remedies under written warranty; duration of implied warranty; exclusion or limitation on consequential damages for breach of written or implied warranty; election of refund or replacement
In order for a warrantor warranting a consumer product by means of a written

[d] Shrink-Wrap Licences

Producers of software often adopt standard form contracts such as shrink-wrap licences to be distributed together with the software. The contractual position of shrink-wrap licence is significant considering the volume of the transactions involving individual consumers. A typical shrink-wrap licence sets forth the terms of the licence on the outside of the packaging which are deemed to be accepted if the package is opened.[937] Shrink-wrap licences ordinarily include limitation of permissible use, limitation of warranty, limitation of liability or choice of governing law.[938] Such shrink-wrap licences purport to protect the intellectual property of the proprietors by establishing a contractual relationship

---

warranty to meet the Federal minimum standards for warranty--

(1) such warrantor must as a minimum remedy such consumer product within a reasonable time and without charge, in the case of a defect, malfunction, or failure to conform with such written warranty;

(2) notwithstanding section 2308(b) of this title, such warrantor may not impose any limitation on the duration of any implied warranty on the product;

(3) such warrantor may not exclude or limit consequential damages for breach of any written or implied warranty on such product, unless such exclusion or limitation conspicuously appears on the face of the warranty; and

(4) if the product (or a component part thereof) contains a defect or malfunction after a reasonable number of attempts by the warrantor to remedy defects or malfunctions in such product, such warrantor must permit the consumer to elect either a refund for, or replacement without charge of, such product or part (as the case may be). The Commission may by rule specify for purposes of this paragraph, what constitutes a reasonable number of attempts to remedy particular kinds of defects or malfunctions under different circumstances. If the warrantor replaces a component part of a consumer product, such replacement shall include installing the part in the product without charge.").

[937] *See* G.Smith, *Software Contracts in* COMPUTER LAW, 57 (C. Reed ed., 3d ed. 1996).

[938] *See* D. L. Hayes, *Shrinkwrap License Agreements: New Light On a Vexing Problem,* 9 THE COMPUTER LAWYER 1-2 (Sept. 1992).

with the customer to achieve the goals stated above.[939] In many cases, the party who receives the contract neither signs nor reviews the contract. Therefore, issues arise as to whether the terms of the standard form contract actually become part of the contract between the parties.[940]

With regard to warranty disclaimers of shrink-wrap licences, in England, section 3 and section 6(2) of the Unfair Contract Terms Act 1977 are applicable to consumer transactions as stated above. Therefore, there is a strict statutory control on contractual terms.

In the United States, enforceability of warranty disclaimer clauses was litigated in *Step-Saver Data Systems, Inc. v. Wyse Technology*,[941] and *Arizona Retail Systems, Inc. v. Software Ink, Inc.*[942] In both cases, the main issue was whether the contractual terms on the licences became part of the contract pursuant to U.C.C. section 2-209, which requires assent to proposed modifications; both courts concluded that the assent must be express and could not be inferred merely from a party's conduct in continuing with the agreement more[943].

In *Step-Saver Data Systems, Inc. v. Wyse Technology,* the court determined, by applying U.C.C Article 2, that shrink-wrap licence clauses disclaiming warranties were not enforceable in accordance with section 2-209, in cases where sufficiently definite contractual terms had been agreed upon between the parties apart

---

[939] *See* Hayes, *supra* note 938 9, at 1.

[940] *See* P. Klinger & R. Burnett, DRAFTING AND NEGOTIATING COMPUTER CONTRACTS 68 (1994), (Suggesting the return of the registration card which is often included for the user to sign, may create an enforceable contract. One argument for its contractual validity is that the shrink-wrap licence may be regarded as a trade custom.); Smith, *supra* note 937 at 71-74.

[941] 939 F.2d 91 (3d Cir.1991).

[942] 831 F. Supp.759 (D. Ariz. 1993).

[943] *Step-Saver*, 939 F.2d at 98-99; *see also Arizona*, 831 F. supp. at 764.

from the shrink-wrap licence.[944]

However, the court seems to be in favour of the method of assent by opening a package. In *ProCD, Inc. v. Zeidenberg*,[945] the court found that a contract was formed when a buyer accepted by performing the acts the vendor proposed to treat as acceptance in the shrink-wrap licence. The court also upheld general enforcement of shrink-wrap licences unless their terms violate a rule of positive law or, are unconscionable.[946] In this event, shrink-wrap licences which contained clauses to limit the use of the application program and database to non-commercial purposes were found to be valid as they were considered not to interfere with federal laws.[947]

In the United States and in England, all terms in the shrink-wrap licences would be likely to be found enforceable if all the terms were clearly visible and accepted by the users before the purchase. A unilateral variation of the terms of the licence agreement subsequent to the purchase by telephone, fax or mail is not permitted.[948] In both the United States and England, an attempt by the suppliers to vary contractual terms or introduce new contractual terms subsequent to the purchase may fail in the light of contractual principles. However, under the U.C.I.T.A., to be discussed in the next section, terms proposed after a party commences performance may be effective if the party had reason to know that terms would be proposed, and assents to the terms.

---

[944] *Step-Saver*, 939 F.2d at 105; *see also Arizona*, 831 F. Supp. at 764 (holding that the plaintiff accepted the defendant's offer on the defendant's terms when the envelope was opened).
[945] 86 F.3d 1447 (7th Cir. 1996).
[946] *Id.* at 1449.
[947] *Id.* at 1455.
[948] *See* Thornton v. Shose Lane Parking Ltd. [1971] 2 Q.B. 163, 169; TAPPER, *supra* note 422, at 283, 287; C. Gringras, *The Validity of Shrink-Wrap Licences*, 4 INT'L J.L. & TECH. 77, 85(1996).

[e] The U.C.I.T.A.
[i] Consumer Contracts

Contrary to English law, the U.C.I.T.A. does not provide detailed provisions for consumer contracts. " 'Consumer' means an individual who is a licensee of information or informational rights that the individual at the time of contracting intended to be used primarily for personal, family, or household purposes." The term does not include an individual who is a licensee primarily for professional or commercial purposes.[949] In the U.C.I.T.A., contrary to the Unfair Contract Terms Act 1977, the definition of "consumer" excludes any individuals who buy software with standardised, un-negotiated terms to be used for work at the office, as the comments state that "[t]he definition distinguishes profit making, professional, or business use, from non-business or family use. Only when the contract is primarily for the latter is there a consumer contract."[950]

Section 803(d) of the U.C.I.T.A. provides that exclusion or limitation of consequential damages for personal injury in a consumer contract for a computer program that is subject to the act and is contained in consumer goods is *prima facie* unconscionable, but exclusion or limitation of damages for a commercial loss is not unconscionable. Therefore, there are no provisions, comparable to the English, with respect to exclusion or limitation of damages for consumer contracts.

[ii] Mass-Market Transactions

"Mass-market transaction" under U.C.I.T.A. means:

(A) a consumer contract; or (B) any other transaction with an end-user licensee if: (i) the transaction is for information or informational rights directed to the gene-

---

[949] U.C.I.T.A. § 102(15) (2001).
[950] *Id.* § 102 cmt. 13.

ral public as a whole, including consumers, under substantially the same terms for the same information; (ii) the licensee acquires the information or informational rights in a retail transaction under terms and in a quantity consistent with an ordinary transaction in a retail market; and (iii) the transaction is not: (I) a contract for redistribution or for public performance or public display of a copyrighted work; (II) a transaction in which the information is customized or otherwise specially prepared by the licensor for the licensee, other than minor customization using a capability of the information intended for that purpose; (III) a site license; or (IV) an access contract.[951]

The phrase "terms and in a quantity consistent with an ordinary transaction" is not clear, and needs to be clarified in the future.

Section 208 provides for a general rule when a party adopts terms of a record[952] as terms of a contract. Section 208(1) provides that "A party adopts the terms of a record, including a standard form, as the terms of the contract if the party agrees to the record, such as by manifesting assent."[953] If the terms of the record are proposed after a party commences performance, the terms are effective "if the parties had reason to know that their agreement would be represented in whole or part by a later record to be agreed on and there would not be an opportunity to review the record or a copy of it before performance or use begins" and if the parties assent to the terms when proposed.

---

[951] *Id.* § 102(45).

[952] *Id.* § 102(55) ("Record" means information that is inscribed on a tangible medium or that is stored in an electronic or other medium and is retrievable in perceivable form.).

[953] *Id.* § 208(1).

These sections promote the idea that terms of contracts will follow or be developed after performance begins.[954] The comments state that under section 208(3), there is no requirement for the party to read, understand or separately assent to each term, thus rejecting the rule of Restatement (Second) of Contracts section 211(3) (1979), which suggests that a term of a standard form which is not unconscionable or induced by fraud may nevertheless be invalidated because a court later holds that a party could not have expected it to be in the standard form.[955]

For mass-market licenses, section 209(a) provides that:

A party adopts the terms of a mass-market license for purposes of Section 208 only if the party agrees to the license, such as by manifesting assent, before or during the party's initial performance or use of or access to the information. A term is not part of the license if:(1) the term is unconscionable or is unenforceable under Section 105(a) or (b); or (2) subject to Section 301, the term conflicts with a term to which the parties to the license have expressly agreed.[956]

---

[954] *Id.* § 208 cmt. 3.
[955] *Id.* § 208 cmt. 7.
[956] *Id.* § 105 ("Relation to Federal Law; Fundamental Public Policy; Transactions Subject to other State Law
(a) A provision of this [Act] which is preempted by federal law is unenforceable to the extent of the preemption.
(b) If a term of a contract violates a fundamental public policy, the court may refuse to enforce the contract, enforce the remainder of the contract without the impermissible term, or limit the application of the impermissible term so as to avoid a result contrary to public policy, in each case to the extent that the interest in enforcement is clearly outweighed by a public policy against enforcement of the term.).

Section 209 (b) provides that "if a mass-market license or a copy of the license is not available in a manner permitting an opportunity to review by the licensee before the licensee becomes obligated to pay and the licensee does not agree," to the license after having an opportunity to review, the licensee is entitled to a return under section 112, and in addition, the licensee may obtain "reimbursement of any reasonable expenses incurred in complying with the licensor's instructions for returning or destroying the computer information or, in the absence of instructions, expenses incurred for return postage or similar reasonable expense in returning the computer information,"[957] and "compensation for any reasonable and foreseeable costs of restoring the licensee's information processing system to reverse changes in the system caused by the installation"[958] under certain circumstances. .[959]

With respect to the difference between mass-market licences and other licences, section 209 comment 2a states:

> If the terms of the record are proposed after a party commences performance, the terms are effective only if the party had reason to know that terms would be proposed and assents to the terms when proposed. For mass-market licenses, however, even if reason to know exists at the outset, the terms must be made available no later than the initial use of the information and the person has a statutory right to a return if it refuses the license.

This means that the terms do not have to be available to be seen when a customer purchase a mass-market computer program as long as the customer has reason to know that the terms will

---

[957] *Id.* § 209(b)(1).
[958] *Id.* § 209(b)(2).
[959] *Id.* § 209(b)(2)(A), (B), (C).

follow. The terms do not need to be printed on the box to be seen but can be printed outside the packaging where the diskettes are wrapped. Licensors are able to restrict much of the warranties as well as transfer rights to eliminate a second-hand market.

These provisions are primarily drafted to validate the terms in mass-market licences, in return for a refund. With these provisions, customers have to agree with the terms even before trying the products. Since computer programs cannot be seen or experienced unless they are loaded in the machines, they require different treatment from ordinary products. There should be no reason why computer programs cannot be tested before purchase. There have been criticisms from the consumer's point of view regarding the provision for validating all mass-market licensing agreements. A motion was raised to consider a proposed draft provision of pending revisions at the NCCUSL (National Conference of Commissioners on Uniform State Laws) annual meeting, attempting to give more protection for consumers, for instance, in cases where the consumer had no knowledge of terms, or such terms vary unreasonably from applicable industry standards.[960] However, the Reporters were satisfied, with the revisions to section 111, that if a contract or a

---

[960] U.C.C. § 2B-403 cmt. (August 1, 1998 proposed draft) (2-105 Unconscionability.

[(b) In a consumer contract [contract between an individual and a merchant], non-negotiable [non-negotiated] terms in a record which the [consumer][individual] has authenticated or to which it has agreed by conduct are unconscionable if:
(1) the consumer [individual] had no knowledge of them; and
(2) the term
   (A) varies unreasonably from applicable industry standards or commercial practices;
   (B) substantially conflicts with one or more negotiated terms in the agre-ement;
   (C) substantially conflicts with an essential purpose of the contract.
This subsection does not apply to a term disclaiming or modifying an implied warranty in accordance with another section of this article.]").

term is found unconscionable at the time it was made, the court may refuse to enforce the contract, or it may enforce the remainder of the contract without the unconscionable term, or it may so limit the application of the application of the unconscionable term so as to avoid an unconscionable result, and with the addition of a provision that a mass-market licence cannot revoke the previously agreed terms.[961]

The comments to section 111 state that a bargain is not unconscionable merely because of the unequal bargaining position, nor because the inequality in the allocation of risks.[962] However, it has been averred that such general provision is not helpful for individual consumers, who have to bear the burden and the cost of litigation in order to challenge such terms.[963]

The United States' approach taken by the U.C.I.T.A. emphasises the freedom of contract between the parties and places emphasis on the commercial practicality of the contract; however, right to return and unconscionability may not be adequate to protect the interest of parties who sign the contract under the U.C.I.T.A.

[f] Comparison

In England, the Unfair Contract Terms Act 1977 and in some cases the Unfair Terms in Consumer Contracts Regulations 1999 actively control the exclusion or limitation of liability by imposing a reasonable standard, whereas in the United States, the U.C.I.T.A. gives greater weight to commercial practice and supplier's interest to enforce clauses in shrink-wrap licences. The Unfair Contract Terms Act 1977 imposes strict controls upon to consumer or standard form contracts. The reasonableness test is applicable to evaluate the appropriateness of the exclusion or limitation of liabilities. As a result, suppliers in the United States may disclaim

---

[961] U.C.I.T.A. § 209(a)(1)-(2). (2001).
[962] *Id.* § 111 cmt. 2.
[963] *See* K. Meymuka, *Unfair !* (1999), *at* http:/www.computerworld.com/home.

or restrict their obligations which may not be disclaimed or restricted in England.

§ 3.08 Contractual Liability on Information in Electronic Form

England and the United States attempt to deal with liability for information in electronic form within the pre-existing legal framework. The pre-existing legal framework has been working sufficiently under English law where two elements of the contract, the sale of goods and the supply of services, can be dealt by different principles of law. Whereas in the United States, the classification of the contract created uncertainty as to the standard of performance with respect to computer programs. This is going to be changed in transactions in which the U.C.I.T.A. is applicable. However, there is no reason why English law should not adopt the unique law specifically designed to deal with issues relating to the standard of performance to clarify existing law.

With respect to express obligations, in transactions involving computer programs, there are many cases where representations were made as to the suitability of the systems. If there is a gap in expertise and bargaining power between suppliers and customers, it is reasonable for the customers to rely on such statements.

In England, any contractual terms disclaiming express obligations is restricted by the reasonableness test in the Unfair Contract Terms Act 1977.

In the United States, express obligations created by advertising or demonstration regarding the capacity of the system or representations regarding functions are hard to disclaim, as the express warranty and the disclaimer shall be construed as consistent with each other. However, even with advertising materials with respect to suitability, the parol evidence rule may exclude the evidence of any prior agreement or contemporaneous oral agreement when the parties intended the written contract to be a final expression of their agreement.

The U.C.I.T.A. also provides expressly that demonstrations and representations can create express warranties, and that disclaimer of such warranties is subject to the rule with regard to parol or extrinsic evidence.

If computer programs are classified as goods, default rules, such as the Sale of Goods Act 1979, the Supply of Goods and Services Act 1982, the U.C.C. Article 2 and the U.C.I.T.A. provide for implied obligations as to the quality of the computer programs. However, the actual obligations attached depend on availabilies in disclaiming such implied obligations.

In England, the Unfair Contract Terms Act 1977 and in some cases the Unfair Terms in Consumer Contracts Regulations 1999 play an essential role in determining the validity of any terms restricting or excluding the express or implied terms. There are provisions for absolute prohibitions to consumer or standard form contracts. The reasonableness tests are applicable to evaluate the appropriateness of the exclusion or limitation of liabilities. Therefore, the use of particular language disclaiming express or implied terms, or the insertion of the integration clauses may not be as effective to disclaim or restrict the remedies as in the United States.

In the United States, if a contractual term fulfils the requirements imposed by the U.C.C. provisions, such as the use of specific language and the format for disclaiming warranties, such a term would be likely to be considered valid. The existence of integration clauses, parol and extrinsic evidence rules and a doctrine of unconscionability or a fundamental public policy may trigger deeper analysis of the validity of contractual terms by courts to examine factors such as intent, sophistication of the parties and other documents involved.

Comparison of English and United States law between the reasonableness test and the doctrine of unconscionability test reveals the different approach toward statutory control over contractual terms. The United States' law promotes efficiency in commercial transactions and tends to restrict the analysis of contractual terms to the understanding by the parties of the contractual terms, and to the expertise of the parties to assess the quality of articles to be transferred. English courts examine, in addition, the bargaining power, and appropriateness of the damages or the ability of the parties to insure themselves.

Comparison with respect to the strict statutory control over consumer or standard form contracts also shows that English law is more willing directly to control the contractual terms. In the United States, the emphasis is on whether the consumers are well aware of the meaning of the contractual terms by clear and noticeable language in appropriate format. Restatement of Contract (Second) section 211 (1979) provides that:

> (1) where a party to an agreement signs or otherwise manifests assent to a writing and has reason to believe that like writings are regularly used to embody terms of agreements of the same type, he adopts the writing as an integrated agreement with respect to the terms included in the writing.
> (2) Such a writing is interpreted wherever reasonable as treating alike all those similarly situated, without regard to their knowledge or understanding of the standard terms of the writing.
> (3) Where the other party has reason to believe that the party manifesting such assent would not do so if he knew that the writing contained a particular term, the term is not part of the agreement

The section emphasises the efficiency of standardisation of agreements in mass-production and stability in commercial distribution. Assent to unknown terms is allowed, even though the party who assents to the terms does not read or understand them. However, standard terms may be superseded by separately negotiated or added terms under section 203. They are construed against the draftsman under section 206, subjected to the overriding obligation of good faith under section 205, and subjected to the power of the court to refuse to enforce an unconscionable contract or term under section 208. In addition, contracts or terms against public policy may be invalidated.[964] However, such restrictions are not so direct as in English law.

The U.CI.T.A. takes this further and attempts to validate the contractual terms imposed by shrink-wrap agreements, making it easier for suppliers to impose their contractual terms disclaiming all the express or implied warranties or restricting remedies available. Under English law, part of such contractual terms may not be allowed to be disclaimed or restricted. Under the U.C.I.T.A., Restatement of Contract (Second) section 211(3) (1979) is dispensed for such purposes. Such a trend in the United States' law needs to be re-examined in the light of consumer protection. The enactment of law in England specifically designed to deal with information in electronic form may be helpful in reconsidering such a trend in the era of global transactions.

---

[964] RESTATEMENT (SECOND) OF CONTRACTS § 178 *et seq.* (1979).

Chapter 4　Conclusion

§ 4.01 Civil Liability for Information in Electronic Form

[1] Transactions Involving Information in Electronic Form

Law with respect to transactions involving information in electronic form has been created based on previously established principles of law such as law regarding information in traditional form, sale of goods or supply of services. The main objective of this book was to evaluate the application of present law to transactions in information in electronic form, and to consider appropriate ways to regulate such transactions.

Comparative studies of law in England and in the United States offered various solutions to the specific issues discussed in this book, and I have attempted to speculate on what may be the ideal approach to solving those specific issues.

It is not easy to make general statements with respect to the characteristics of information in electronic form. However, there are some characteristics which are repeatedly revealed in cases which are worth noting.

Expertise involved in creating such information, disparities in expertise between suppliers and customers, and customers' reliance on the expertise are some of the essential features characterising many such transactions. Computer programs are intended to perform specific tasks: the suppliers are offering expertise in computer technology, and the customers are relying on such expertise. The level of performance expected differs according to the type of transactions, such as transactions to supply bespoke software or mass-market software. Certain types of specialised on-line databases are assumed to be relatively accurate, and kept up to date. In transactions where information in electronic form is to be used actively, the value of representations, including representation of special skills or representations with respect to specifications, function or instructions is elevated, and therefore induces greater reliance. Analysis of the values of such representations is significant in terms of its effects on liability issues.

Chapter 4

The legal issues surrounding information in electronic form typify the way in which distinctions such as those between information in electronic and in traditional form, contractual and tort liabilities, economic and physical losses, act and statement, products and information, and sale of goods and supply of services are undermined, as such information may cause economic and physical losses; and supply of such information contains elements of act and statement, products and information, and sale of goods and supply of services.

Considering the unique nature of transactions involving information in electronic form, it may be more appropriate to create a law specifically designed for such transactions. In drafting such a law, one of the most important concerns may be balancing commercial efficiency or stability with protection of consumers, based on an understanding of the basic characteristics of transactions with respect to information in electronic form.

Contractual and tortious liabilities with respect to information in electronic form should be considered by taking into account distinctive characteristics of such transactions, particularly, expertise involved in creating such information, disparities in expertise between suppliers and customers, and customers' reliance on the expertise and representations made regarding standards of performance, along with special consideration for the consumer and standard form contracts.

Recent development of English law has addressed the issues of overlapping obligations (a duty of care) under the law of both tort and contract, with respect to transactions involving statements or services (or acts) rendered based on special or specific skills. In such transactions, the required standard of performance becomes similar with respect to the suppliers' duty of care.[965] Such obligations are less affected by the existence or non-existence of contracts than other obligations. Furthermore, the

---

[965] *See* Henderson v. Merrett Syndicates Ltd. (H.L. (E.)) [1995] 2 A.C. 145, 180.

313

characteristics of obligations involved in certain transactions for human-readable information in electronic form, widely distributed in substantially the same format, may be determined in reference to the tort theory with respect to a special relationship.[966] As such, the enactment of law specifically designed for transactions involving information in electronic form is required to adopt both theories of contract and tort.

With respect to contract law, English law attempts to balance commercial efficiency or stability with protection of consumers by statutory restrictions on contractual terms, including restrictions aimed at consumer or standard form transactions. Such statutory restrictions make it unnecessary to resort to tortious remedies when contractual remedies are available. The enactment of law in England reflecting this tendency would encourage discussion as to the appropriate ways to regulate such transactions in the light of international commerce.

[2] Tort Law Relating to Liability for Injury Caused by Information In Traditional Form and in Electronic Form
 [a] *Economic Loss and Special Relationship*

One of the important issues in this chapter dealt with circumstances where the court allows tortious claims for recovery of economic loss independent of the contract in transactions involving computer programs or human-readable information on the Internet or in an on-line database.

With regard to the supply of computer programs and other ancillary services, plaintiffs are often induced into transactions by representations from suppliers.

The relationship between suppliers and customers may, or may not, involve a direct contractual relationship. The customers may lease the subject matter from the third party.

In England, if there is a contract between the parties, the

---

[966] *See* U.C.I.T.A. § 404 (2001).

plaintiffs may be able to obtain sufficient remedies without invoking claims based on fraud because of the strict statutory control over contractual terms provided by the Misrepresentation Act 1967, the Unfair Contract Terms Act 1977, and the Unfair Terms in Consumer Contracts Regulations 1999. Therefore, remedies under the tort of deceit or negligent misrepresentation would be likely to be sought only for those cases where there is no contract between the parties. In English law, a special relationship, required to obtain the remedies under the tort of deceit or negligent misrepresentation, would be likely to be created based on special knowledge or skill, assumption of responsibilities coupled with concomitant reliance, following *Henderson v. Merrett Syndicates Ltd.*[967] Purchasers or users of computer systems may be entitled to rely on the expertise of the computer consultants. The fact that the loss was caused by negligent statements or negligent acts is not essential in those cases involving special skills. As such, professional liability is not restricted to being imposed on specific professionals, as special skill or knowledge is one of the essential factors in allowing recovery.

Whereas in the United States, in order to set aside the restrictions in contractual terms, plaintiffs may be required to bring a cause of action based on fraud in inducement. In those cases, courts would be likely to allow such claims by referring to disparities in expertise between the parties. The cause of action based on negligent misrepresentation may not be allowed unless there is special relationship between the parties. Many courts do not recognise the special relationship for causes of action based on negligent misrepresentation between the parties with respect to the purchase, referral and recommendation of computer systems. Between the parties to a contract, negligent misrepresentation claims can be regarded as ways to avoid the application of contractual terms. This is based on the idea that computer progra-

---

[967] [1995] 2 A.C. 145, 194.

mmers or suppliers are not providing a "professional" service. The relationship between a computer supplier and a customer is often considered as a "buyer-seller relationship." A minority of courts recognises the existence of a special relationship between the parties, based on the special skills of computer suppliers or consultants. In the majority of courts in the United States, claims based on professional liability may be possible only for recognised professions. However, in the United States, some courts tend to distinguish between negligent acts and negligent statements when determining whether recovery is allowed. Some courts allow recovery based on negligent misrepresentation for professionals provided for in Restatement (Second) of Torts section 552 (1976), rather than on general negligence.

Therefore, in both England and the United States, with regard to negligent acts or negligent misstatements, "special relationships" between the parties are required as the prerequisites for the imposition of liability for economic loss. Despite the existence of the contrary holdings of cases in the United States, the general law against the recovery of economic loss should not be applicable in transactions involving computer programs because of the specific nature of such transactions. The programs are meant to perform certain functions and may produce some output or physical acts. In most of these transactions, there exists reliance on special skill in the supply of computer programs.

Compared to the cases involving traditional subject matter, it is more likely that in transactions involving computer programs, there is some disparity of expertise between the parties. In those cases where tortious liability under fraud or negligent misrepresentation is imposed, courts are willing to find that plaintiffs' reliance is justified because of a disparity of expertise and impose a duty on suppliers to perform in accordance with the representations with respect to the computer's specifications or functions. When determining liability, courts should consider the fact that representations regarding functions, capabilities or specifications of computer programs would be likely to be relied upon by customers because of the disparity of expertise between the parties, and those regarding present capabilities of the computer system can often be interpreted as representations about the future performance of the systems as installed for users so that unsophisticated users may simply assume that the system will work.

With regard to liability for not using computer technology, not using readily available and customarily used computer technology in industry would be likely to be considered negligent. Such duties tend to be elevated in cases where physical injury is involved. However, what is customary in industry may be difficult to determine in the context of fast-developing computer technology.

Courts have restricted compensation for economic loss caused by negligent statements fearing the creation of a liability in an indeterminate amount for an indeterminate time to an indeterminate class. However, compensation may be available in circumstances where representors, with special skills, know or should know the purpose for which a report is prepared; for example, if the representors know the identifiable group of people to whom the report is to be shown, and the likelihood of their reliance upon it.

With respect to transactions involving information in electronic form, reliance upon outputs may cause damage. The purpose for which the information is offered and the range of recoverable plaintiffs are two of the important issues in allowing recovery.

The users of such outputs may be the parties who had acquired the computer programs from the manufacturer. In such cases, the court may first examine the contractual terms between the parties.

If there is no such contract, the court may consider the specificity of the computer programs. If the computer programs are custom-made for the users, it would be likely that the purpose is specific, and an identifiable group of people involved. If the computer programs are widely distributed for a general purpose such as calculation, no specific purpose is known to the manufacturer. There may also be a problem in identifying a specific group of plaintiffs who would rely on the outputs.

The users of such outputs may not be the parties who acquired the computer programs from the manufacturer. In such cases, it is rare to find contracts between the manufacturers and the users of information. For instance, outputs of computer programs in an investment bank containing data for investment advice to clients may be relied on by the investors. If clients incur losses, a court would inquire, as a condition for liability, as to how specific the purpose of information was, and whether the manufacturer knew their clients' intentions, i.e. who the bankers or their clients intend the information to benefit. It would be considered favourable to finding liability that the manufacturers knew that the investment bank was intending to target a specific group of people, for instance, a group working in a particular company.

[b] Products Liability

With respect to products liability law, both in England and in the United States, even though the computer program itself is not considered a "product," some courts have recognised that computer programs and instructions may be considered "products."

In both jurisdictions, articles which incorporate computer programs are considered products. However, this analysis may pose difficulties because the party liable for supplying a defective computer program may not be held responsible under strict products liability law. From the original purpose of drafting the products liability law, computer programs themselves, especially mass-market ones, may be considered products.

As implied in the English case of *St. Albans City & District Council v. International Computers Ltd.,* and held in the United State's case of *Aetna Casualty & Surety Co. v. Jeppesen & Co.,* instru-ctions or any information which will be actively used and would be likely to cause damage, may be considered products. The fact of mass-production may also be considered favourable to the applicability of strict liability. It may be wiser for the courts to recognise that some types of information, either in traditional form or in electronic form, have the characteristics to induce actively acts and, therefore, should be considered in the same way as products, for the purpose of the strict products liability law.

[c] Chain of Distribution

In tort, the involvement of different parties in the chain of complex distribution affects liability. With respect to strict products liability, the designers' or computer programmers' obligation is limited to exercising reasonable skills. However, the court should reconsider the applicability of strict products liability law to certain types of information which are mass-distributed or to be actively used. The liability of intermediaries such as publishers, online providers, distributors or sellers differs in accordance with their roles in distribution. They are not generally expected to monitor the content of the information unless expressly assuming such responsibility. However, liability may be imposed in accordance with the level of the involvement of the parties.

[d] Concurrent Liability

Both in England and in the United States, the concurrent liability of professionals has been upheld. In England, the court takes a flexible approach in determining the scope of the kind of professions in cases where special skills are exercised as in *Henderson v. Merrett Syndicates Ltd.,*[968] whereas in the United States, such claims are difficult unless the nature of their services exercised is within the recognised professions.

Under English law, computer consultants are generally held to possess special skills and are expected to be competent in the field of their skills, and concurrent liability is allowed where there is an assumption of duties with special skills, and such skills are relied upon. In the United States, such a special duty is not widely recognised.

---

[968] *See Supra* § 2.03 Theories Relevant To Imposing Liability [3] Negligence [b] England [vi] Transactions Involving Special Skills and [vii] Professional Liability of Computer Programmers.

[3] Contract Law Relating to Liability for Injury Caused by Information in Electronic Form

[a] Special Law for Information in Electronic Form

English law may adopt new law specifically designed to deal with issues relating to standard of performance, so as to clarify existing law in the light of international transactions. The special issues presented by information in electronic form can be better dealt with the special law. In enacting the new law, stability, commercial efficiency, protection of consumers who lack expertise, and bargaining power may be the important factors to be considered.

With respect to transactions involving computer programs, the standard of performance expected should be determined, taking into account the unique functional nature of computer technology, and the degree of reliance on the professional skills of those developing and applying such technology.

In considering the nature of computer technology, both English law and United States' law seem to have reached the sensible conclusion that many of the transactions involving computer programs may be treated as sale of goods, and the standard of performance in relation to computer programs may be judged by reference to a result- oriented outcome.

However, as provided in English law, and according to the comments to the U.C.I.T.A., the dual application of different implied warranty provisions to the same transaction seems more suitable for transactions involving computer programs. It is more practical to focus on the different nature of each element of one transaction as in English law, than to treat the entire contract as one object. Compared to the United States' courts, English courts have been better equipped for taking into account the unique nature of transactions involving computer programs by treating the different nature of each element of one transaction. Nevertheless, it may be preferable for England to enact a similar law specifically designed for computer information as has been done in the United States.

Contracts for information in electronic form involve complicated obligations, and such obligations cannot adequately be defined by classifications such as contracts for goods or contracts for services. For those categories of information made available to the public in substantially the same format, which are neither classified as sale of goods or supply of services, the same discussions as to whether the tortious liability exists with respect to such subject matters may be applicable to the discussions with respect to contract, just as in cases of human-information in traditional form. Essentially, a duty with respect to the accuracy of the content of the information is imposed only if a special relationship exists.[969] However, there are some notable distinctions between information in electronic form and traditional form for the courts to consider. For instance, a certain type of information, that is highly specialised, such as information on new drugs for doctors in an online-database may be relied upon, and may cause direct damage.

[b] Liabilities for Representations

In transactions involving computer programs, there are many cases of transactions involving custom-made computer programs where representations were made as to the suitability of the systems. As there is a gap in expertise, and bargaining power between suppliers and customers, it is reasonable for the customers to rely on such statements The court should not allow the suppliers to disclaim express representations regarding specifications or functions with respect to computer programs. English courts consider that computer programmers, like dentists, are expected to exercise expertise and special skills to achieve functions specified by the parties even without express terms. The reasonableness test in the Unfair Contract Terms Act 1977 plays an essential

---

[969] *See supra* Chapter 2 The Law of Tort Relating to Liability for Injury Caused by Information in Traditional and in Electronic Form; *supra* § 3.02 Classification of Contracts [d] Contracts for Information.

role in restricting the effect of the disclaimer clauses for express obligations.

In the United States, express obligations created by advertising or demonstration regarding the capacity of the system or representations regarding functions are hard to disclaim, as the express warranty and the disclaimer shall be construed as consistent with each other. This was confirmed in the U.C.I.T.A., which provides that advertising and demonstrations can become express warranties. However, even with advertising materials with respect to suitability, the parol evidence rule may exclude the evidence of any prior agreement or contemporaneous oral agreement when the parties intended the written contract to be a final expression of their agreement. The U.C.I.T.A. also expressly provides that demonstrations and representations can create express warranties, and disclaimer of such warranties is subject to the rule with regard to parol or extrinsic evidence.

[c] Implied Obligations

If computer programs are classified as goods, default rules in the Sale of Goods Act 1979, the Supply of Goods and Services Act 1982, the Unfair Contract Terms Act 1977, the U.C.C. Article 2 and the U.C.I.T.A.[970] provide for implied obligations as to the quality of the computer programs. However, the actual obligations attached depend on the rules for disclaiming such implied obligations.

In England, the *St. Albans* case held *obiter* that even in the absence of any express term as to quality or fitness for purpose, or any term to the contrary, a contract for the transfer into a computer of a program intended by both parties to instruct or enable the computer to achieve specified functions is subject to an implied term that the program will be reasonably fit for the intended purpose.

The Unfair Contract Terms Act 1977, and the newly enacted Unfair Terms in Consumer Contracts Regulations 1999, play an

---

[970] Adopted in Virginia and Maryland.

essential role in determining the validity of any terms restricting or excluding the express or implied terms. The Unfair Contract Terms Act 1977 imposes absolute prohibition of disclaimers for certain implied terms, for instance, as to the quality of fitness and the reasonableness test. Therefore, the use of particular language disclaiming the express or implied terms, or the insertion of the integration clauses, may not be as effective to disclaim or restrict the remedies as in the United States. Section 4(3) and schedule 2 of the Unfair Terms in Consumer Contracts Regulations 1994, which had similar provisions with respect to designating unfair terms, have been deleted in the Unfair Terms in Consumer Contracts Regulations 1999. The effect of such deletion is yet to be determined. However, the Unfair Contract Terms Act 1977 will impose a reasonableness test in many cases.

In the United States, when considering the validity of disclaimer clauses, the courts tend to consider the effectiveness of each method of disclaimer in accordance with the provisions of the U.C.C. The technical requirements imposed by the U.C.C., such as the use of specific language and the format in disclaiming warranties, are essential in disclaimers. If such requirements are fulfilled, such contractual terms would be likely to be considered valid. However, the existence of integration clauses, parol and extrinsic evidence rules, and a doctrine of unconscionability or a fundamental public policy may trigger deeper analysis of the validity of contractual terms. Courts may examine factors such as intent of the parties, sophistication of the parties, and other documents involved.

[d] Limiting or Excluding Remedies

In England, the reasonableness test under the Unfair Contract Terms Act 1977 is also essential in evaluating all of the methods in limiting remedies including express or implied obligations. The suppliers have to justify the reasonableness of the restriction of the monetary damages, taking into account whether the users could cover the losses or not. In examining the validity of monetary damages, the courts consider different factors including the distribution of losses among the parties, or insurance coverage. However, this may produce asymmetry; on making the contract the customers know their maximum exposure to damages, but the suppliers can foresee only the type of loss to the customer, which may far exceed any profit the suppliers hope to make. In most cases, compensation in the amount of the contractual price may be considered adequate and reasonable.

In the United States, the U.C.C. Article 2 and the U.C.I.T.A. provide detailed rules regarding different methods in limitation or exclusion of remedies. Contractual clauses excluding or modifying warranties are essentially valid unless contrary to provisions requiring the use of specific language or format under U.C.C. section 2-316 and U.C.I.T.A. section 406. Under U.C.C. section 2-719 and U.C.I.T.A. section 803, if an exclusive or limited remedy fails in its essential purpose, or if the limitation or exclusion of consequential damages is unconscionable, the court may find contractual clauses limiting or excluding remedies invalid. However, in some courts, even when a limited remedy fails in its essential purpose, consequential or incidental damages may be excluded unless limitation or exclusion is unconscionable. To examine whether to justify such limitation or exclusion, a number of courts may look closely into the seriousness of the breach, including the condition of the delivered subject matter, effectiveness of the remedy to repair, and bargaining position or sophistication of the parties.

Comparison of English law and United States' law between the reasonableness test and the doctrine of unconsionability test reveals different approaches toward statutory control over contractual terms. The United States' law promotes efficiency in commercial transactions, and tends to restrict the analysis of contractual terms to the understanding of the parties of the contractual terms and to the expertise of the parties to assess the quality of articles to be transferred. While English courts examine, in addition, factors such as the bargaining power, appropriateness of the damages or the ability of the parties to insure themselves.

Comparison with respect to the strict statutory control over consumer or standard form contracts also shows that English law is more willing directly to control the contractual terms. In the United States, the emphasis is on whether the consumers made aware of the meaning of the contractual terms by clear and noticeable language in appropriate format. The U.C.I.T.A. makes a further attempt to validate the contractual terms imposed by mass-market agreements, making it easier for suppliers to impose their contractual terms disclaiming all express or implied warranties, or restricting remedies available. Some of such contractual terms may not be disclaimed or restricted under English law. Such a trend in the United States' law needs to be re-examined in the light of consumer protection. The enactment of law in England specifically designed to deal with information in electronic form may be helpful in reconsidering such a trend in the era of global transactions.

Table of Cases

ENGLISH CASES

Andrews Bros. Ltd. v. Singer & Co. Ltd. [1934] 1 K.B. 17 285
Andrews v. Hopkinson [1957] 1 Q.B. 229 .... 28, 31
Baldry v. Marshall [1925] 1 K.B. 260 285
Bradford Building Society v. Borders [1941] 2 All E.R. 205, (H.L.) 27
British Sugar plc. v. Nei Power Projects Ltd., Court of Appeal, 8 October 1997, 87 Build L.R 42, 14 Const. LJ 365 280
Candler v. Crane Christmas & Co. [1951] 2 K.B.164 (C.A.) 87, 88, 90, 91, 92
Caparo Industries plc. v. Dickman [1990] 2 A.C. 605 (H.L.(E.)) 12, 87, 95, 177
Clay v. Yates (1856) 1 H. & N. 73 219
De La Bere v. C.A. Pearson, Ltd. [1908] 1 K.B. 280 172
Derry v. Peek (1889) 14 App. Cas. 337 (H.L.(E.)) 27
Dodd and Dodd v. Wilson and McWilliam [1946] 2 All E.R. 691 ... 219
Donoghue v. Stevenson [1932] A.C. 562 (H.L.(Sc.)) 44, 48, 116
Esso Petroleum Co. Ltd. v. Mardon [1976] Q.B. 801 (C.A.) 93
Eurodynamics Sys. plc. v. General Automation Ltd., 6 September 1988 (Q.B.) (unreported) 195, 197, 235, 253
G.H. Myers & Co. v. Brent Cross Service Co. [1934] 1 K.B. 46 .... 190, 202
George Mitchell (Chester hall) Ltd. v. Finney Lock Seeds Ltd. [1983] Q.B. 284 32
Grand Champion Tankers v. Norpipe A/S (The Marion) [1984] A.C. 563 (H.L.(E.)) 56
H. Parsons (Livestock) Ltd. v. Uttley Ingham & Co. Ltd. [1978] Q.B. 791(C.A.) 277, 279

327

Table of Cases

Hedley Byrne & Co. Ltd. v. Heller & Partners Ltd. [1964] A.C. 465
(H.L.(E.)) 28, 51, 52, 88, 89, 90, 92, 94, 162, 174, 177
Hedley v. Baxendale (1854) 9 Exch. 341 276
Henderson v. Henry E. Jenkins & Sons [1970] A.C. 282. (H.L.(E.))
.... 56
Henderson v. Merrett Syndicates Ltd. [1995] 2 A.C. 145 (H.L.(E.))
.... 47, 51, 52, 53, 54, 57, 72, 84, 89, 104, 153, 154, 162, 314, 315, 319
Heron II (Koufos v. C.Czarnikow Ltd.) [1969] 1 A.C. 350 (H.L.(E.))
.... 277
Hong Kong Fir Shipping Co. Ltd. v. Kawasaki Kisen Kaisha Ltd.
[1962] 2 Q.B. 26 272
*Howard Marine and Dredging Co. Ltd. v. A Ogden and Sons
(Excavations) Ltd.* [1978] Q.B. 574 (C.A.) 91
Invercargill City Council v. Hamlin [1996] A.C.624 48
J. Marcel Ltd. v. Tapper [1952] 1 Q.B.D. 15 184
Jacobs v. Batavia and General Plantations Trust [1924] 1 Ch. 287
.... 238
JEB Fastners Ltd. v. Marks, Bloom & Co. [1981] 3 All E.R. 289 ... 95, 100
Junior Books Ltd. v. Veitchi Co. Ltd. [1983] 1 A.C. 520. (H.L.(Sc.))
.... 49, 50, 53, 58, 67, 68
Langridge v. Levy (1837) 2 M. & W. 519 .... 30, 31
Lee & Son Ltd. v. Railway Executive [1949] 2 All E.R. 581 286
Lee v. Griffin (1861) 1B & 272 .... 178, 183, 184
Mackenzie Patten & Co. v. British Olivetti Ltd., 11 January 1984
(Q.B.) (unreported) LEXIS; 1 C. L. & P. 92 (1984); 48 M.L.R. 344
(1985) 31, 33, 112, 231, 237, 274
Micron Computer Sys. Ltd. v. Wang (U.K.) Ltd., 9 May 1990
(Q.B.D)(unreported) 192
Morgan Crucible Co. plc. v. Hill Samuel & Co. Ltd. [1991] Ch. 295
(C.A.) 96
Muirhead v. Industrial Tank Specialities Ltd. [1986] 1 Q.B. 507.
(C.A.) 45
Murphy v. Brentwood D.C. [1991] 1 A.C. 398 (H.L.(E.)) 47, 48, 49

Mutual Life and Citizen's Assurance Co. Ltd. v. Evatt [1971] A.C.
    793 (P.C.) 92, 93
Pasley v. Freeman (1789) 3 T.R. 51 .... 27, 230
Photo Production v. Securicor Transport [1980] A.C. 827 287
Professional Reprographic Services Ltd. v. DPS Typecraft Ltd., 15
    February 1993 CA (unreported) LEXIS 96
R & B. Customs Brokers Co. Ltd. v. United Dominions Trust Ltd.
    [1988] 1 W.L. R. 321 293
Robinson v. Graves [1935] 1 K.B. 579 .... 183, 184
Salvage Association. v. Cap Financial Services Ltd. [1995] F.S.R. 654
    .... 233, 234, 253, 256, 274, 278, 285, 288
Samuels v. Davies [1943], 1 K.B. 526 .... 189, 193, 199
Saphena Computing Ltd. v. Allied Collection Agencies Ltd. [1995]
    F.S.R. 616 .... 190, 193, 198, 220, 254, 255, 258, 268, 270, 271
Slater v. Finning Ltd. [1997] A.C. 473 (H.L.(Sc.)) 168
Spartan Steel & Alloys Ltd. v. Martin & Co. Ltd. [1973] 1 Q.B. 27
    (C.A.) 43, 45
Spring v. Guardian Assurance plc. [1995] 2 A.C. 296, 318 (H.L.(E.))
    93
*St. Albans City & District Council v. International Computers
    Ltd.* [1995] F.S.R. 686 (Q.B.D.), [1996] 4 All E.R. 481 .... 13, 14
    .... 119, 129, 135, 136, 145, 192, 193, 194, 198, 220, 232
    .... 258, 268, 270, 276, 278, 285, 288, 293, 318, 322
Stephenson Blake (Holdings) Ltd. v. Streets Heaver Ltd. Q.B.D.
    (O.R.) H.H.J.Hicks Q.C., March 2, 1994 (unreported)
    .... 59, 85, 155, 162, 198, 199
The Lady Gwendolen [1965] P.294 55
Thornton v. Shoe Lane Parking Ltd. [1971] 2 Q.B. 163 300
Victoria Laundry (Windsor) Ltd. v. Newman [1949] 2 K.B. 528
    (C.A.) 277
Wells v. Buckland Sand and Silica Co. [1965] 2 Q.B. 170 .... 31, 231
White v. Jones [1995] 2 A.C. 207 (H.L.(E.)) 47, 58, 72
Wilkinson v. Downton [1897] 2 Q.B. 57 21

Table of Cases

Young & Marten Ltd. v. McManus Childs Ltd. [1969] 1 A.C. 455 (H.L. (E.)) 219

United States Cases

A.E. Investment Corp. v. Link Builders, Inc., 214 N.W.2d
764 (Wis. 1974) 70
A.T. Kearney, Inc. v. IBM. Corp., 73 F. 3d 239 (9th Cir. 1995) 264
AccuSystems, Inc. v. Honeywell Information Sys., Inc., 580 F.Supp.
474 (S.D.N.Y.1984) 27, 37, 38, 41, 107, 108, 159, 160, 174, 179, 264
Advent Systems, Ltd. v. Unisys Corp., 925 F.2d. 670 (3d Cir. 1991)
.... 213, 215, 217
Aetna Casualty & Surety Co. v. Jeppesen & Co., 642 F.2d *339*
(9th Cir. 1981) 22, 23, 88, 112, 125, 133, 318
Alden Press Inc. v. Block & Co., 527 N.E.2d 489
(Ill. App. Ct. 1988) 272
Alm v. Van Nostrand Reinhold Co., 480 N.E. 2d 1263,
(Ill. App.Ct. 1985) 146
AMF, Inc. v. Computer Automation, Inc., 573 F. Supp. 924
(S.D. Ohio 1983) 260
Anthony Pools, a Div. of Anthony Indus., Inc. v. Sheehan, 455
A.2d 434 (Md. 1983) 201
APLications Inc. v. Hewlett-Packard Co., 501 F. Supp. 129
(S.D.N.Y. 1980) 27, 39
Arizona Retail Systems, Inc. v. Software Ink, Inc., 831 F. Supp.759
(D. Ariz. 1993) 299, 300
Berry v. Commercial Union Ins. Co., 565 So. 2d 487
(La. Ct. App. 1990) 142
Biakanja v. Irving, 320 P.2d 16 (Cal. 1958) 72
Bily v. Arthur Young & Co., 834 P.2d 745, 11 (Cal. 1992)
.... 104, 105, 177
Block v. Block, 135 N.E. 2d 857 (1956) 34
Bowers v. Northern Telecom, Inc., 905 F. Supp. 1004
(N.D. Fla. 1995) 121, 136
Brandenburg v. Ohio, 395 U.S.44 (1969) 98, 135
Braun v. Soldier of Fortune Magazine, Inc., 968 F.2d 1110
(11th Cir. 1992), *cert denied*, 506 U.S.1071 (1993) 99

Table of Cases

Broad Street Bank v. National Bank of Goldsboro, 112 S.E. 11
(N.C. 1922) 74
Cardozo v. True, 342 So. 2d 1053 (Fla. App. 342) 171
Chatlos Sys., Inc. v. National Cash Register Corp., 635 F.2d 1081
(3d Cir. 1980) 215
Citizens State Bank v. Timm, Schmidt & Co., 335 N.W.2d 361
(N.J. 1983) 102
Clements Auto Co. v. Service Bureau Corp., 444 F.2d 169
(8th Cir. 1971) 35, 36, 40, 42
Cloud v. Kit Mfg. Co., 563 P.2d 248, (Alaska 1977) 67
Colonial Life Insurance Co. v. Electronic Data Sys., Corp., 817
F. Supp 235 (D.N.H. 1993) 215, 282, 283
Columbus McKinnon v. China Semiconductor Co., Ltd., 867
F. Supp. 1173 (W.D.N.Y. 1994) 25
Computerized Radiobiological Services Inc. v. Syntax Corp.,
595 F. Supp. 1495 (E.D.N.Y. 1984), *aff'd in part rev'd in part*,
786 F.2d 72 (2d Cir. 1986) 156
Conopco, Inc. v. McCreadie, 826 F.Supp. 855 (D.N.J. 1993), *aff'd* 40
F. 3d 1239 (3rd Cir. 1994) 217
Consolidated Data Terminals v. Applied Digital Data Sys., Inc.,
708 F.2d 385 (9th Cir. 1983). 242, 248, 281, 283
Credit Alliance v. Arthur Andersen & Co., 483 N.E.2d 110
(N.Y. 1985). 100
Cricket Alley Corp. v. Data Terminal Sys., Inc., 732 P.2d 719
(Kan. 1987) 239, 251
Cubby, Inc. v. Compuserve, Inc., 776 F. Supp. 135
(S.D.N.Y. 1991) 110, 147, 151, 171
D.P. Technology Corp. v. Sherwood Tool, Inc., 751 F.Supp. 1038
(D. Conn. 1990) 272
Daniel v. Dow Jones & Co., Inc., 520 N.Y.S.2d 334
(Civ. Ct. 1987) 109, 151, 159, 170, 173, 266
Data Processing Services, Inc. v. L.H. Smith Oil Corp., 492 N.E.
2d 314 (Ind. Ct. App. 1986) 77, 206, 207, 208, 216, 221

Demuth Development Corp. v. Merck & Co., Inc., 432 F. Supp. 990 (E.D.N.Y. 1977) 146
Diversified Graphics, Ltd. v. Groves, 868 F.2d 293 (8th Cir. 1989) 80, 81
Dunn Appraisal Co. v. Honeywell Info. Sys., Inc., 687 F.2d 877 (6th Cir. 1982). 24
East River S.S. Corp. v. Transamerica Delaval, Inc., 476 U.S. 858 (1986) 44, 65, 66, 85, 103, 163
Eaton Corp. v. Magnavox Co. (Magnavox), 581 F. Supp 1514 (E.D. Mich.1984) 261
Fargo Machine & Tool Co. v. Kearney & Trecker Corp., 428 F.Supp. 364 (E.D.Mich. 1977) 240, 251, 281, 283
Fickeisen v. Wheeling Elec. Co., 67 W.Va. 335 (1910) 214
First Equity Corp. of Florida v. Standard & Poor's Corp., 869 F.2d 175 (2d Cir. 1989) 172
Forest v. E.I. Dupont de Nemours' and Company, 791 F.Supp. 1460 (D. Nev. 1992) 125
Gale v. Value Line, Inc., 640 F.Supp. 967 (D.R.I. 1986) 172
Garessy v. Digital Equipment Corp., 980 F. Supp. 640 (E.D.N.Y. 1997) 136
Glovatorium, Inc. v. NCR Corp. 648 F.2d 658 (9th Cir. 1982) 33
Graham v. John R. Watts & Son, 36 S.W.2d 859 (Ky. 1931) 70
Greenman v. Yuba Power Products, Inc., 377 P.2d 897 (Cal. 1962) 64
Gutter v. Dow Jones, Inc., 490 N.E.2d 898 (Ohio 1986) 172
Halstead v. United States, 535 F. Supp. 782 (D.[Conn.]1982) 88, 120, 127, 131, 146, 149
Hanson v. Ford Motor Co., 278 F. 2d 586 (8th Cir. 1960) 36
Henningsen v. Bloomfield Motors, Inc., 161 A.2d 69 (N.J. 1960) 122
Herbert Friedman & Assoc., Inc. v. Lifetime Doors, Inc., 1989 WL 157487 (N.D. Ill. 1990) 210, 211, 212
Herceg v. Hustler Magazine, Inc., 565 F. Supp. 802 (S.D. Tex. 1983). 98, 134, 135

Hosp. Computer Sys., Inc. v. Staten Island Hosp., 788 F. Supp. 1351 (D.N.J. 1992) 72, 79, 80, 83, 156

Huron Tool v. Precision Consulting Services, Inc., 532 N.W.2d 541 (Mich. Ct. App. 1995) 159, 160

In re Estate of Freeman (Lincoln Rochester Trust Co. v. Freeman), 311 N.E.2d 480 (N.Y. 1974) 80

In re Trailer & Plumbing Supplies, 578 A.2d 343 (N.H. 1990) ... 211

Invacare Corp. v. Sperry Corp., 612 F. Supp. 448 (N.D. Ohio 1984) 78

Jaillet v. Cashman, 189 N.Y.S. 743 (Supp. Ct. 1921) 172

Jaskey Finance & Leasing v. Display Data Corp., 564 F. Supp. 160 (E.D.Pa. 1983) 246, 247, 248, 249, 259, 260, 282

JoAnn Homes at Bellmore, Inc. v. Dworetz, 250 N.E.2d 214 (N.Y. 1969) 34, 38

Jones v. J.B. Lippincot Co., 694 F. Supp. 1216 (D.Md. 1988) 146

Jordan v. Whiting Corp., (Mich. Ct. App. 1973), 212 N.W.2d 324, modified [sic] 240 N.W. 2d 468 (Mich. Ct. App. 1976) 137

Kansas City Wholesale Grocery Co. v. Weber Packing Corp., 73 P.2d 1272 (Utah 1937) 289

Kearsarge Computer, Inc. v. Acme Staple Co., 366 A. 2d 467 (N.H. 1976) 200

Kennedy v. Columbia Lumber & Mfg. Co., 384 S.E.2d 730 (S.C. 1989) 158

Keogh v. W.R. Grasle, Inc., 816 P.2d 1343 (Alaska 1991) 141

Klein v. Asgrow Seed Co., 54 Cal Rptr. 609 (Cal. Dist. Ct. App. 1966) 69

K-Mart Corp. v. Midcon Realty Group of Conn., Ltd., 489 F.Supp. 813 (D.Conn. 1980) 130, 132, 149

Kramer v. Lamb-Grays Harbor Co., Inc., 639 P.2d 649 (Or. Ct. App. 1982) 120, 136

L.H. Heath & Son v. AT & T Information Sys., 9 F.3d 561 (7th Cir. 1993) 245, 246

La Rossa v. Scientific Design Co., 402 F.2d 937 (3d Cir. 1968) 122, 123, 130

Langworthy v. Pulitzer Pub. Co., 368 S.W.2d 385 (Mo. 1963) 172
Lerman v. Chuckleberry Publishing, Inc., 521 F.Supp. 228
 (S.D.N.Y. 1981), *rev'd* 745 F.2d 123 (2d Cir. 1994) 147, 171
Lerman v. Flynt Distributing Co., 745 F.2d 123 (2d Cir. 1984),
 cert denied, 471 U.S. 1054, (1985) 147, 150, 171
Lewin v. McCreight, 655 F. Supp. 282 (E.D.Mich. 1987) 146
Lewis v. Timco, Inc., 697 F.2d 1252 (5th Cir. 1983) 120, 136
Littlejohn v. Stanley Structures, Inc., 688 P.2d 1130
 (Colo. Ct. App. 1984) 143
Lohmann v. Pittsburgh Corning Corp., 782 F.2d 1156
 (4th Cir. 1986) 141
Lucas v. Hamm, 364 P.2d 685 (Cal. 1961), *cert. denied*, 368 U.S.
 987 (1962) 72
Lunney v. Prodigy Services Co. 250A. 2d 230
 (N.Y. App. Div. 1999) 110
Macpherson v. Buick Motor Co., 111 N. E. 1050
 (N.Y. 1916) 61
MAI Sys. Corp. v. Peak Computer, Inc., 991 F.2d 511
 (9th Cir. 1993) 222
Micro-Managers, Inc. v. Gregory, 434 N.W. 2d 97
 (Wis. Ct. App. 1988) 209, 217, 220
Milau Assoc., Inc. v. North Avenue Devel. Corp., 368 N.E.2d 1247
 (N.Y. 1977) 168, 201, 216
Neilson Business Equipment Center, Inc. v. Monteleone, 524 A.
 2d 1172 (Del. 1987) 202, 203, 214, 215, 257, 258
NMP Corp. v. Parametric Tech. Corp., 958 F.Supp. 1536
 (S.D. Okla. 1997) 250
Northern Power & Engineering Corp. v. Caterpillar Tractor Co.,
 623 P.2d 324 (Alaska 1981) 62
Pennsylvania Glass Sand Corp. v. Caterpillar Tractor Co., 652
 F.2d. 1165 (3d Cir. 1981) 65
People Exp. Airlines v. Consolidated Rail, 495 A.2d 107, 110
 (N.J. 1985) 60
People v. Barnes, 499 N.Y.S.2d 343 (Sup.Ct. 1986) 76

Table of Cases

Perlmutter v. Beth David Hosp., 123 N.E.2d 792
(N.Y. 1954) 201
Phoenix Technologies, Inc. v. Quotron Systems, Inc., 1997 WL
220285 (E.D.Pa 1997), aff'd, 135 F. 3d 766 (7th Cir. 1997) 39, 41, 107, 159, 174
Pied Piper, Inc. v. Datanational Corp., 901 F.Supp.212
(S.D.W.Va 1995) 25, 108
Plante v. Jacobs, 103 N.W.2d 296 (Wis. 1960) 206
Port City State Bank v. American National Bank, 486 F.2d 196
(10th Cir. 1973) 75
Posey v. Ford Motor Co., 128 So. 2d 149 (Fla. Dist. Ct. App.1961)
.... 69
ProCD, Inc. v. Zeidenberg, 86 F.3d 1447 (7th Cir. 1996) 300
R.W. Murray Co. v. Shatterproof Glass Corp., 697 F.2d 818
(8th Cir. 1983) 156
Randy Knitwear, Inc. v. American Cyanamid Co.,
181 N.E.2d 399 (N.Y. 1962) 69
Raritan River Steel Co. v. Cherry, Bekaert & Holland,
367 S.E.2d 609 (N.C. 1988) 101, 102, 175, 177
Reed v. Bascon, 530 N.E.2d 417 (Ill. 1988). 109
Rio Grande Jewelers v. Data General Corp., 689 P.2d 1269
(N.M. 1984) 156
Ritchie Enterprises v. Honeywell Bull, Inc., 730 F. Supp. 1041
(D.Kan. 1990) 155
RKB Enterprises, Inc. v. Ernst & Young,182 A.D. 2d 971, 582
N.Y.S.2d 814 (App. Div. 1992) 82
Roberts v. Rich Foods, Inc., 654 A.2d 1365 (N.J. 1995)
.... 142
Rockport Pharmacy, Inc. v. Digital Simplistics, Inc., 53 F.3d 195
(8th Cir. 1995) 156, 158
Rosenblum v. Adler, 461 A.2d 138 (N.J. 1983) 102
Rosenstein v. Standard and Poor's Corp., 264 Ill.App.3d 818,
636 N.E.2d 665 (Ill. App. Ct. 1993) 172

RRX Industries, Inc. v. Lab-Con, Inc., 772 F.2d 543
(9th Cir. 1985) 205, 215
Rucker v. Norfolk & Western Ry., Co., 396 N.E.2d
534 (Ill. 1979). 141
R.W. Murray Co. v. Shatterproof Glass Corp., 697 F.2d 818
(8th Cir 1983) 156
Saloomey v. Jeppesen & Co., 707 F.2d 671 (2d Cir. 1983)
.... 88, 130, 131, 148, 149
Sara Lee Corp. v. Homastote Co., 719 F. Supp.417
(D.Md. 1989) 125
Santor v. A & M Karagheusian, Inc., 207 A2d. 305
(N.J. 1965) 62, 63, 64, 66, 67, 69
Schmidt v. Rozier, 98 S.W. 791 (Mo. Ct. App. 1906) 183
Seely v. White Motor Co., 403 P.2d 145 (Cal. 1965)
.... 61, 62, 65, 66, 68, 69, 85
Sexton v. Bell Helmets, Inc., 926 F.2d 331 (4th Cir. 1991) 141
Shultz v. Merriman, 303 F. Supp. 1174, 1177 (D.N.H. 1969),
modified 425 F.2d 228 (1st Cir. 1970) 127
Sierra Diesel Injection Service, Inc., v. Burroughs Corp., 874 F. 2d 653
(9th Cir. 1989), amended by 890 F. 2d 108(9th Cir. 1989) 244, 246, 261, 289, 297
Sommer v. Federal Signal Corp., 593 N.E. 2d 1365 (N.Y. 1992)
.... 156
Sparacino v. Andover Controls Corp., 592 N.E.2d 431,
(Ill. App. Ct. 1992) 24, 25, 136, 138, 144
Stenograph v. Bossard, 46 U.S.P.Q.2d 1936 (D.C. Cir. 1998) 222
Step-Saver Data Systems, Inc. v. Wyse Technology, 939 F.2d 91
(3d Cir. 1991) 299, 300
Stratton Oakmont, Inc. v. Prodigy Service Co., 23 Media L. Rep.
(BNA) 1794, 1995 WL 323710 (N.Y. Sup. Ct. 1995) *renewal denied*,
24 Media L. Rep. (BNA) 1126, 1995 WL 805178 (N.Y. Sup. Ct.
1995). 110, 151, 170
Sun Bank/Miami, N.A. v. First Nat'l Bank, 698 F Supp 1298
(Md.1988) 75

Table of Cases

Swanson v. Domning, 86 N.W. 2d 716 (Minn. 1975) 36
T.J. Hooper, 60 F.2d 737 (2d Cir. 1932) 72, 73, 143
Teknekron Customer Information Solutions, Inc. v. Watkins Motor Lines, 1994 WL 11726 (N.D. Cal. 1994) 242, 290
Torres v. North Am. Van Lines, 658 P.2d 835 (Ariz. Ct. App. 1982) 73
Touche Ross & Co. v. Commercial Union Ins., 514 So.2d 315 (Miss. 1987) 102
Triangle Underwriters, Inc. v. Honeywell, Inc., 457 F. Supp. 765 (E.D.N.Y. 1978), *aff'd. in part, rev'd. in part*, 604 F.2d 737 (2d Cir. 1979) 204, 215
Ultramares Corp. v. Touche, 174 N.E. 441 (N.Y. 1931) 48, 99, 101, 173, 175, 177, 264
United Nuclear Corp. v. Cannon, 564 F. Supp. 581, 591 (D.R.I., 1983) 76
United States v. Microsoft, 253 F.3d 34 (D.C. Dir. 2001), *cert. denied,* 122 S. Ct. 350 (2001) 11
United States Welding, Inc. v. Burroughs Corp., 587 F. Supp. 49 (D. Colo. 1984), rev'd on other grounds, 640 F. Supp. 350 (D. Colo. 1985). 78, 79
USM Corp. v. Arthur D. Little Sys., Inc., 546 N.E.2d 888 (Mass. App. Ct. 1989) 214, 215, 241, 242
Utah Int'l, Inc. v. Caterpillar Tractor Com., 775 P.2d 741 (N.M. Ct. App. 198) 60
Vault Corp. v. McQuaid Software Ltd., 655 F. Supp.750 (E.D.La. 1987) *aff'd*, 847 F.2d 255 (5th Cir. 1988) 187
Walter v. Bauer, 439 N.Y.S.2d 821, (Sup. Ct. 1981) 133, 134
Weirum v. RKO General, Inc., 539 P.2d 36, 123 (Cal. 1975) 98, 135
Wharton Management Group v. Sigma Consultants, Inc., 1990 WL 18360 (Del. Super. Ct. 1990), *aff'd*, 582 A.2d 936 (Del. 1990) 178, 214, 215
Winter v. G.P. Putnam's Sons, 938 F.2d. 1033 (9th Cir.,1991) 120, 128, 129

Wirtz v. A,S. Giometti & Associates, Inc., 399 F.2d 738
 (5th Cir. 1968) 127
Worrell v. Barnes, 484 P.2d 573 (Nev. 1971) 133, 201
Yoder v. Honeywell Inc., 104 F.3d 1215 (10th Cir. 1997) 151

OTHER CASES

Beta Computers (Europe) Ltd. v. Adobe Sys. (Europe) Ltd.,
 [1996] S.L.T. 604 (O.H.) 195, 196
Esanda Finance Corp. Ltd. v. Peat Marwick Hungerfords [1997]
 142 A.L.R. 750 (H.C.) 96
European Commission v. United Kingdom, Case [1997]
 3 C.M.R. 923 140
*Toby Constructions Products Ltd. v. Computer Bar Sales Pty
 Ltd.* [1983] 2 N.S.W.L.R. 48 .... 194, 195
Voli v. Inglewood Shire Council (1963) 110 C.L.R. 74 50

Table of Statutes and Statutory Instruments

ENGLISH STATUTES AND STATUTORY INSTRUMENTS

Civil Evidence Act 1995 (c.38), s.13 8
Consumer Protection Act 1987 (c. 43) 116, 118
Consumer Protection Act 1987 (c. 43), s. 1(1) 140
Consumer Protection Act 1987 (c. 43), s. 1(2) 117, 118
Consumer Protection Act 1987 (c. 43), s. 2(1) 116
Consumer Protection Act 1987 (c. 43), s. 2(2) 116
Consumer Protection Act 1987 (c. 43), s. 3(1) 117
Consumer Protection Act 1987 (c. 43), s. 3(2) 117
Consumer Protection Act 1987 (c. 43), s. 3(2)(a) 117, 119, 124
Consumer Protection Act 1987 (c. 43), s. 4(1)(e) 139, 140
Consumer Protection Act 1987 (c. 43), s. 4(1)(f)(ii) 143
Consumer Protection Act 1987 (c. 43), s. 45(1) 118
Contracts (Rights of Third Parties) Act 1999 (c.31), s. 1 51
Consumer Transactions (Restrictions in Statements) Ordens (S.I. 1976 No. 1813 and S.I. 1978 No127) 292
Copyright, Design and Patent Act (C.D.P.A.) 1988 as amended (c. 48), s. 30 11
Copyright, Design and Patent Act (C.D.P.A.) 1988 as amended (c. 48), s. 31 11
Copyright, Design and Patent Act (C.D.P.A.) 1988 as amended (c. 48), ss. 32-36 11
Copyright, Design and Patent Act (C.D.P.A.) 1988 as amended (c. 48), s. 50A-C 11
Data Protection Act 1998 (c. 29) 9
Date Protection Act 1998 (c. 29), s. 1(1) 9
Defamation Act 1996 (c. 31) 147
Defamation Act 1996 (c. 31), s. 1 147

Table of Statutes and Statutory Instruments

Defamation Act 1996 (c, 31), s. 1(3)(e) 150
Defective Premises Act 1972 (c.35), s. 1 48
Limitation Act 1980 (58), ss. 2-5 178
Limitation Act 1980 (58),s. 11(2) 179
Local Government Finance Act 1992 (c.14), sch. 4 8
Merchant Shipping Act 1894 (c. 60) 56
Merchant Shipping (Liability of Shipowners and Others) Act
   1958 (c. 62) 56
Misrepresentation Act 1967 (c.7) 29, 42, 57, 315
Misrepresentation Act 1967 (c.7), s. 2 32
Misrepresentation Act 1967 (c.7), s. 2(1) 28
Sale of Goods Act (1893), s. 4 178
Sale of Goods Act 1979 (c. 54) 13, 129, 130, 155, 178
   .... 179, 190, 193, 198, 236, 253, 268, 285, 308, 322
Sale of Goods Act 1979 (c. 54), s. 4 178
Sale of Goods Act 1979 (c. 54), s.11(3) 271
Sale of Goods Act 1979 (c. 54), s.13 292
Sale of Goods Act 1979 (c. 54), s.14 .... 130, 168, 292
Sale of Goods Act 1979 (c. 54), s.14(2) 54, 179, 253
Sale of Goods Act 1979 (c. 54), s.14(2A-B) 254
Sale of Goods Act 1979 (c. 54), s.14(3) 54, 168, 179, 220
Sale of Goods Act 1979 (c. 54), s.15(A) 254, 272, 292
Sale of Goods Act 1979 (c. 54), s.30(2A) 254, 272
Sale of Goods Act 1979 (c. 54), s.55(1) 256
Sale of Goods Act 1979 (c. 54), s.55(2) 256
Sale of Goods Act 1979 (c. 54), s.61(1) 229
Supply of Goods and Services Act 1982 .... 155, 169
Supply of Goods and Services Act 1982 (c. 29)
   .... 179, 181, 191, 193, 198, 236, 253, 269, 308, 322
Supply of Goods and Services Act 1982 (c. 29), s. 4(1) 169
Supply of Goods and Services Act 1982 (c. 29), s. 4(2) 179, 253
Supply of Goods and Services Act 1982 (c. 29), s. 4(4) 179, 220
Supply of Goods and Services Act 1982 (c. 29), s. 4(5) 179, 220

Table of Statutes and Statutory Instruments

Supply of Goods and Services Act 1982 (c. 29), s.13 .... 55, 180, 256
Supply of Goods and Services Act 1982 (c. 29), s.14 168
Supply of Goods and Services Act 1982 (c. 29), s.16(1) 256
Supply of Goods and Services Act 1982 (c. 29), s.16(2) 256, 257
Unfair Contract Terms Act 1977 (c. 50) 29, 32, 42, 54, 57
.... 155, 199, 236, 237, 238, 252, 256, 270, 285, 287, 292
.... 294, 295, 296, 301, 306, 307, 308, 315, 322, 323, 324
Unfair Contract Terms Act 1977 (c. 50), s. 1(1)(a) 234, 257
Unfair Contract Terms Act 1977 (c. 50), s. 2 .... 54, 199, 200, 237, 255
Unfair Contract Terms Act 1977 (c. 50), s. 2(2)
.... 54, 234, 257, 275
Unfair Contract Terms Act 1977 (c. 50), s. 3
.... 54, 199, 200, 234, 236, 256, 275, 276, 293, 299
Unfair Contract Terms Act 1977 (c. 50), s. 6(1) 255
Unfair Contract Terms Act 1977 (c. 50), s. 6(2)
.... 255, 292, 299
Unfair Contract Terms Act 1977 (c. 50), s.11 .... 256, 274, 293
Unfair Contract Terms Act 1977 (c. 50), s.11(2) 287
Unfair Contrant Terms Act 1977 (c. 50), s.11(4) 288
Unfair Contract Terms Act 1977 (c. 50), s.12 292
Unfair Contract Terms Act 1977 (c. 50), s.14 293
Unfair Contract Terms Act 1977 (c. 50), sch. 1(c) 199
Unfair Contract Terms Act 1977 (c. 50), sch. 2 .... 256, 287, 296
Unfair Terms in Consumer Contracts Regulations 1994, S.I. 1994/3159, s. 4(3) 296, 323
Unfair Terms in Consumer Contracts Regulations 1994, S.I. 1994/3519, s. 5(5) 296
Unfair Terms in Consumer Contracts Regulations 1994, S.I. 1994/3159, s. 6 .... 294, 295
Unfair Terms in Consumer Contracts Regulations 1994, S.I. 1994/3159, sch. 2 .... 296, 323
Unfair Terms in Consumer Contracts Regulations 1999, S.I. 1999/2083 .... 29, 42, 57, 155, 238, 294, 295, 296, 306, 308, 315, 323

Table of Statutes and Statutory Instruments

Unfair Terms in Consumer Contracts Regulations 1999, S.I.
1999/2083, s. 3(1) 295
Unfair Terms in Consumer Contracts Regulations 1999, S.I.
1999/2083, s. 5(1) 295
Unfair Terms in Consumer Contracts Regulations 1999, S.I.
1999/2083, s. 5(2) 295
Unfair Terms in Consumer Contracts Regulations 1999, S.I.
1999/2083, s. 6(1) 236, 294
Unfair Terms in Consumer Contracts Regulations 1999, S.I.
1999/2083, s. 6(2) 236, 294, 295
Unfair Terms in Consumer Contracts Regulations 1999, S.I.
1999/2083, s. 7(2) 236
Unfair Terms in Consumer Contracts Regulations 1999, S.I.
1999/2083, s. 8(1) 294

UNITED STATES STATUTES

Ariz, Rev, Stat. Ann. § 12.686 (2001) 141
Copyright Act, 17 U.S.C. §101 (2001) 17, 223
Magnuson-Moss Act, 15 U.S.C. § 2301(1) (1997) 297
Magnuson-Moss Act, 15 U.S.C. § 2304 (1997) 297
Magnuson-Moss Act, 15 U.S.C. § 2308 (1997) 293, 297, 298
MD CODE ANN. [Com.Law] § 1-201(10) 260
MD CODE ANN. [Com.Law] § 2-316(2) 259, 260
Mo. Ann. Stat. § 537. 764 (2000) 141
N.Y. U.C.C. § 2-316(1) 242
N.Y. U.C.C. § 2-719(2) 282
RESTATEMENT (SECOND) OF CONTRACTS § 178 (1979) 310
RESTATEMENT (SECOND) OF CONTRACTS § 203 (1979) 286, 310
RESTATEMENT (SECOND) OF CONTRACTS § 205 (1979) 310
RESTATEMENT (SECOND) OF CONTRACTS § 206 (1979) 310
RESTATEMENT (SECOND) OF CONTRACTS § 208 (1979) 310
RESTATEMENT (SECOND) OF CONTRACTS § 211 (1979)
.... 286, 290, 297, 309

Table of Statutes and Statutory Instruments

Restatement (Second) of Contracts § 211(3) (1979) 303, 310
Restatement (Second) of Torts § 299A (1965) 78, 132, 149, 168
Restatement (Second) of Torts § 388 (1965) 124
Restatement (Second) of Torts § 400 (1965) 151
Restatement (Second) of Torts § 402 A (1965)
.... 119, 122, 127, 130, 131, 133
Restatement (Second) of Torts § 525 (1979) 34
Restatement (Second) of Torts § 526 (1979) 34
Restatement (Second) of Torts § 552 (1976)
.... 79, 101, 105, 163, 169, 170, 177, 264, 316
Restatement (Second) of Torts § 581 (1976) 110, 151
Restatement (Second) of Torts § 581 cmt. d. (1976) 147, 171
U.C.C. 62, 171, 181, 202, 210, 211, 220, 236, 271, 273, 293, 308, 322
U.C.C. Art 2A 222
U.C.C. Art. 2 .... 79, 180, 208, 222, 225, 250, 268
.... 269, 284, 286, 299, 308, 324
U.C.C. § 1-205 (1998) 244
U.C.C. § 2-102 (1998) 213
U.C.C. § 2-105(1)(1998) 213
U.C.C. § 2-201 (1998) 178, 185
U.C.C. § 2-202 (1998) 244, 287
U.C.C. § 2-208 (1998) 244
U.C.C. § 2-209 (1998) 299
U.C.C. § 2-302 (1998) 287, 289
U.C.C. § 2-302(1) (1998) 289
U.C.C. § 2-313 (1998) 238
U.C.C. § 2-313(2) (1998) 239
U.C.C. § 2-314 (1998) 168, 180, 257, 272
U.C.C. § 2-315 (1998) 168, 180, 258
U.C.C. § 2-316 (1998) 30, 202, 241, 259, 284, 286, 293, 324
U.C.C. § 2-601 (1998) 272
U.C.C. § 2-719 (1998) 284, 286, 324
U.C.C. § 2-719(2) (1998) 280
U.C.C. § 2-719(3) (1998) 280

Table of Statutes and Statutory Instruments

U.C.C. § 2-725(1) (1998)	179
U.C.C. § 2B-103 cmt. 3 (February 1, 1999 proposed draft)	221
U.C.C. § 2B-403 cmt. (August 1, 1998 proposed draft)	305
U.C.C. 2B (August 1, 1998 proposed draft)	221, 222, 223
U.C.I.T.A. (2001)	4, 167, 169, 218, 221, 222, 223, 227, 228
	248, 249, 252, 262, 264, 269, 270, 272, 284, 286
	300, 301, 306, 307, 308, 310, 320, 322, 324, 325
U.C.I.T.A. § 102 cmt. 1 (2001)	223
U.C.I.T.A. § 102 cmt.10 (2001)	224
U.C.I.T.A. § 102 cmt.13 (2001)	301
U.C.I.T.A. § 102 cmt.33 (2001)	224
U.C.I.T.A. § 102 cmt.46 (2001)	224
U.C.I.T.A. § 102(12) (2001)	223
U.C.I.T.A. § 102(15) (2001)	301
U.C.I.T.A. § 102(35) (2001)	223
U.C.I.T.A. § 102(37) (2001)	224
U.C.I.T.A. § 102(45) (2001)	302
U.C.I.T.A. § 102(51) (2001)	174
U.C.I.T.A. § 102(52) (2001)	224, 266
U.C.I.T.A. § 102(55) (2001)	302
U.C.I.T.A. § 102(a)(1) (2001)	223
U.C.I.T.A. § 102(a)(10) (2001)	223
U.C.I.T.A. § 102(a)(11) (2001)	223
U.C.I.T.A. § 103(a) (2001)	222
U.C.I.T.A. § 103 cmt. (2001)	223
U.C.I.T.A. § 105 (2001)	270, 303
U.C.I.T.A. § 105(a) (2001)	11, 303
U.C.I.T.A. § 105 b (2001)	266, 303
U.C.I.T.A. § 111 (2001)	266, 270, 287, 305
U.C.I.T.A. § 111 cmt. 2 (2001)	306
U.C.I.T.A. § 112 (2001)	304
U.C.I.T.A. § 113 (2001)	270
U.C.I.T.A. § 113(a)(1) (2001)	266, 268
U.C.I.T.A. § 113(a)(2) (2001)	266

Table of Statutes and Statutory Instruments

U.C.I.T.A. § 208 (2001) 302, 303
U.C.I.T.A. § 208 cmt. 3 (2001) 303
U.C.I.T.A. § 208 cmt. 7 (2001) 303
U.C.I.T.A. § 208(1) (2001) 302
U.C.I.T.A. § 208(3) (2001) 303
U.C.I.T.A. § 209(a) (2001) 303
U.C.I.T.A. § 209(a)(1)-(2) (2001) 306
U.C.I.T.A. § 209(b) (2001) 304
U.C.I.T.A. § 209(b) cmt. 2a (2001) 304
U.C.I.T.A. § 301 (2001) 251, 287, 303
U.C.I.T.A. § 302 (2001) 286
U.C.I.T.A. § 401 (2001) 11, 270
U.C.I.T.A. § 402 (2001) 224, 248
U.C.I.T.A. § 402 cmt. 3 (2001) 250
U.C.I.T.A. § 402 cmt. 4 (2001) 250
U.C.I.T.A. § 402 cmt. 5 (2001) 250
U.C.I.T.A. § 402 cmt. 8 (2001) 170
U.C.I.T.A. § 402(a)(1) (2001) 249
U.C.I.T.A. § 402(a)(2) (2001) 249
U.C.I.T.A. § 402(a)(3) (2001) 224, 225, 250
U.C.I.T.A. § 403 (2001) 262, 263, 269
U.C.I.T.A. § 403 cmt. 2 (2001) 168, 225, 263
U.C.I.T.A. § 403 cmt. 3a (2001) 263, 272
U.C.I.T.A. § 403(a) (2001) 225, 228, 272
U.C.I.T.A. § 404 (2001) 265, 269, 314
U.C.I.T.A. § 404 cmt. 3a (2001) 264
U.C.I.T.A. § 404 cmt. 3b (2001) 174, 265
U.C.I.T.A. § 404(a) (2001) 225, 263, 266
U.C.I.T.A. § 405 (2001) 267, 268, 269
U.C.I.T.A. § 405 cmts. (2001) 268
U.C.I.T.A. § 405 cmt. 3b (2001) 266
U.C.I.T.A. § 405(a)(1) (2001) 225, 268
U.C.I.T.A. § 405(a)(2) (2001) 228, 268
U.C.I.T.A. § 405(b) (2001) 225, 268

Table of Statutes and Statutory Instruments

U.C.I.T.A. § 405(c) (2001) 268
U.C.I.T.A. § 406 (2001) 248, 269, 284, 286, 324
U.C.I.T.A. § 406(a) (2001) 251, 269
U.C.I.T.A. § 406(b)(1)(A) (2001) 269
U.C.I.T.A. § 406(b)(1)(B) (2001) 269
U.C.I.T.A. § 406(b)(2) (2001) 269
U.C.I.T.A. § 406(b)(3) (2001) 269
U.C.I.T.A. § 406(c) (2001) 270
U.C.I.T.A. § 803 (2001) 284, 287, 324
U.C.I.T.A. § 803(b) (2001) 281
U.C.I.T.A. § 803(d) (2001) 281, 301

INTERNATIONAL STATUTES

The Council Directive (EEC) 85/374 on Product Liability 116
The Council Directive (EEC) 85/374 on Product Liability, preamble 122, 139
The Council Directive (EEC) 85/374 on Product Liability, art. 1 116
The Council Directive (EEC) 85/374 on Product Liability, art. 2 118
The Council Directive (EEC) 85/374 on Product Liability, art. 3 116
The Council Directive (EEC) 85/374 on Product Liability, art. 6 .... 118, 119
The Council Directive (EEC) 85/374 on Product Liability, art. 7(e) 139, 140
The Council Directive (EEC) 85/374 on Product Liability, art. 7(f) 143
The Council Directive (EEC) 91/250 on Legal Protection of Computer Programs 11
The Council Directive (EEC) 91/250 on Legal Protection of Computer Programs, preamble 11

347

The Council Directive (EEC) 91/250 on Legal Protection of
   Computer Programs, art 6 11
The Council Directive (EEC) 93/13 on Unfair Terms in
   Consumer Contracts 236, 294, 295

Bibliography

[BOOKS]

BENJAMIN, J.P., SALE OF GOODS (5th ed. 1997)

FARNSWORTH, E.A., FARNSWORTH ON CONTRACTS (2d ed. 1990)

HART, H.L.A. & HONORE, T., CAUSATION IN THE LAW (2d ed. 1985)

KLINGER, P. & BURNETT, R., DRAFTING AND NEGOTIATING COMPUTER CONTRACTS (1994)

HAWKLAND, W.D., UNIFORM COMMERCIAL CODE SERIES (1995)

LLOYD, I. J., INFORMATION TECHNOLOGY LAW (2d ed. 1997)

MARKESINIS, B.S. & DEAKIN, S.F., TORT LAW (4th ed. 1998)

NIMMER, R. T., LAW OF COMPUTER TECHNOLOGY (1992)

PROSSER, W.L. AND KEETON, W.P., PROSSER AND KEETON ON TORTS (5th ed. 1984)

REED, C. (ed.), COMPUTER LAW (3d ed. 1996)

ROGERS, W.V. H., WINFIELD & JOLOWICZ ON TORT (15th ed. 1994)

STAPLETON, J., PRODUCT LIABILITY (1994)

TAPPER, C., COMPUTER LAW (4th ed. 1989)

WILLISTON, S., A TREATISE ON THE LAW OF CONTRACTS (3d ed. 1961)

TREITEL, G., THE LAW OF CONTRACT (10th ed. 1999); TREITEL, G. (ed.), CONSENSUS AD IDEM: ESSAYS IN THE LAW OF CONTRACT IN HONOUR OF GUENTER (1996)

[ARTICLES]

Anshel, J.R., *Improving Visual Comfort at a Computer Workstation*'(1999)<http://www.tifaq.com/articles/visual_comfort-jan99-jeffrey_anshel.html>

Reprinted from 34 The RSI Network (1999)

Gaebler, D.B., *Negligence, Economic Loss, and the U.C.C.*, 61 IND. L. J.593(1986)

Gringras, C., *The Validity of Shrink-Wrap Licences*, 4 INTERNATIONAL JOURNAL OF LAW AND INFORMATION TECHNOLOGY 77 (1996)

Bibliography

Hayes, D. L., *Shrinkwrap License Agreements: New Light On a Vexing Problem,* 9 THE COMPUTER LAWYER 1 (Sept. 1992)

Nimmer, R.T., *Breaking Barriers: The Relation Between Contract and Intellectual Property Law* (1998) *at* http://www.2BGuide.com/docs/rncontract-new.html

Meymuka, K., *Unfair !* (1999) *at* http:/www.computerworld.com/home

Montgomery, J.E. and Owen, D.G., *Reflections on the Theory and Administration of Strict Liability for Defective Products,* 27 S.C.L. REV. 803 (1976)

Prosser, W.L., *The Assault Upon the Citadel* (*Strict Liability to the Consumer*), 69 YALE L.J. 1099 (1960)

Reed, C., *Liability,* in COMPUTER LAW 86 (C. Reed ed., 3d ed. 1996)

Smith, G., *Software Contracts* in COMPUTER LAW 57 (C. Reed ed., 3d ed. 1996)

Stapleton, J., *Software, Information and the Concept of Product,* 9 TEL AVIV U. STUDIES IN LAW, 147 (1989); *Duty of Care and Economic Loss: A Wider Agenda,* 107 L.Q.R. 249 (1991); *The Normal Expectancies Measure in Tort Damages,* 113 L.Q.R. 257 (1997)

Tapper, C., *Some Aspects of Contractual Licences for Software* in CONSENSUS AD IDEM: ESSAYS IN THE LAW OF CONTRACT IN HONOUR OF GUENTER 283 (Treitel ed. 1996)

Whittaker, S., *European Product Liability and Intellectual Products,* 105 L.Q.R. 125 (1989)

Wolfson, J.R., *Electronic Mass Information Providers and Section 552 of The Restatement* (*Second*) *of Torts, The First Amendment Casts A Long Shadow,* 29 RUTGERS L.J. 67 (1997)

〈著者略歴〉

川和 功子（かわわ のりこ）
大阪府立大学経済学部助教授
ニューヨーク州弁護士

Civil Liability for Defects in Information in Electronic Form

2002年（平成14年）3月10日	第1版第1刷発行 3103-0101	
著 者	川和 功子	
発行者	今井 貴	
発行所	株式会社信山社	
	〒113-0033 東京都文京区本郷6-2-9-102	
	電話 03 (3818) 1019	
	FAX 03 (3818) 0344	
出版編集	信山社出版株式会社	
販売所	信山社販売株式会社	
	Printed in Japan	

Ⓒ川和功子, 2002. 印刷・製本／エーヴィスシステムズ・大三製本
ISBN4-7972-3103-3 C3332
NDC 324. 551

新刊・既刊

潮見佳男 著
債権総論Ⅱ（第2版） 4,800円
契約各論Ⅰ 4,200円
不法行為法 4,700円

藤原正則 著
不当利得法 4,500円

岡本詔治 著 12,800円
不動産無償利用権の理論と裁判

小栁春一郎 著 12,000円
近代不動産賃貸借法の研究

伊藤 剛 著 9,800円
ラーレンツの類型論

梅本吉彦 著
民事訴訟法 5,800円

東京　信山社　文京
Tel 03+3818+1019　FAX 03+3811+3580